THE AFFECTED TEACHER

At a time when teaching and learning policy too often presents itself in a simplistic input-output language of measurable targets and objectives, *The Affected Teacher* explores the role played by emotionality in how professional life is experienced by school teachers. The book argues that, in the very highly organised and structured social spaces of public institutions, emotionality – or, more precisely, all that is included in the concept of 'affect' – needs to be recognised and validated, rather than ignored or pathologised.

It explores how neoliberal education policy seeks to mould professional subjectivities, relationships and practices; how teachers experience and 'manage' their feelings; and the role that affect plays in guiding either compliance with or resistance to often unpopular policy directives. Drawing on a rich body of original data comprising formal and informal discussions with a range of teachers, the case is argued for psychoanalytically and politically informed individual and group reflexivity, both as a form of professional and personal development and as a way of keeping alive alternative beliefs and understandings regarding the purposes of education.

The Affected Teacher is relevant to practising schoolteachers and to undergraduate and graduate students and academics involved in education related courses such as policy studies, education management and the sociology of education, as well as disciplines related to psychosocial studies and psychoanalysis.

Alex Moore is an Emeritus Professor at UCL Institute of Education. Previously, he taught in inner-city secondary schools for eighteen years, and was Head of the PGCE Secondary and MA in Education Programmes at Goldsmiths University of London. His earlier books include *The Good Teacher: Dominant Discourses in Teacher Education* (2004) and *Understanding the School Curriculum: Theory, Politics and Principles* (2014), both published by Routledge.

THE AFFECTED TEACHER

Psychosocial Perspectives on
Professional Experience and
Policy Resistance

Alex Moore

Routledge
Taylor & Francis Group

LONDON AND NEW YORK

First published 2018
by Routledge
2 Park Square, Milton Park, Abingdon, Oxon OX14 4RN

and by Routledge
711 Third Avenue, New York, NY 10017

Routledge is an imprint of the Taylor & Francis Group, an informa business

British Library Cataloguing-in-Publication Data
A catalogue record for this book is available from the British Library

Library of Congress Cataloging-in-Publication Data
A catalog record has been requested for this book

ISBN: 9781138784017 (hbk)
ISBN: 9781138784024 (pbk)
ISBN: 9781315768397 (ebk)

Typeset in Bembo
by Servis Filmsetting Ltd, Stockport, Cheshire

Printed and bound by CPI Group (UK) Ltd, Croydon, CR0 4YY

ACKNOWLEDGMENTS

Particular thanks, as always, to my wife Anna for her encouragement, love, understanding and advice as I have struggled to translate 200,000 words of notes into something approaching a coherent argument; to Matthew Clarke, for sharing his ideas and for pointing me so perceptively in the direction of new readings; to Stephen and Trinidad Ball and to Chris Edwards for their friendship, encouragement and interest over the years, and for regularly restoring my flagging confidence; to Anna Clarkson and her team at Routledge, as helpful, patient and supportive as ever; and to all those unnamed teachers and headteachers who have allowed me into their lives over the years, given so generously of their time, and helped me to believe that what I was doing was both interesting and worthwhile.

PERMISSIONS

The discussion of professionalism, discourse and affect in the section 'Internalising Performativity' in Chapter 6 is included by kind permission of the *Journal of Education Policy*, in which it originally appeared as part of the paper '"Cruel Optimism": Teacher Attachment to Professionalism in an Era of Performativity' (*Journal of Education Policy* 31(5): 666–677), and of Matthew Clarke, co-author of the original paper. The discussion around the testimonies of Graeme, Bill and Edward in Chapter 6 first appeared in the *Oxford Review of Education* (32(4): 487–503).

CONTENTS

PREFACE

Background and presentation

Purpose and themes

There is an unattributed photograph on the front cover of the 1998 paperback version of Thomas Popkewitz and Marie Brennan's edited book *Foucault's Challenge*. It is of light entering the window of what appears to be an otherwise unlit room. There is something suggestive of a prison cell about the room: the window itself, with its mullions reminiscent of bars; the apparent darkness of the room; the deep, soulless window ledge on to which the light falls, barely able to creep any further into the enclosed space other than to leave a barely discernible reflection on one of the walls. On the far side of the window there is, by contrast, plenty of light. So much, in fact, that it is dazzling, making it impossible to identify what actually lies beyond. Are there trees? Might we see sky? Other buildings, perhaps?

A problem is that the light only partially illuminates the darkness we are in, and yet it draws us to it, toward the barrier presented by the window with its small, leaded lights. We can see that there is light. We know that there is *something* outside to see, something bathed in that light. But the window, the internal darkness and the excessive brightness all combine not simply to prompt a desire to move beyond but to render immediately unknowable what we might find if we ever were to leave the confines of the room. Perhaps there is beauty and enlightenment out there. Perhaps there is danger and confusion. Perhaps all these things await us. So what do we – what can we – do? Are we at ground level? Does a precipitous, life-threatening fall await us? Are we better off remaining in the room? Or are we better advised to take a risk as our only hope of escape: to climb on to the sill, to press our nose to the glass, perhaps even to attempt to transgress the boundary that has, quite deliberately, been placed between us and that other world?

★ ★ ★

This book is mainly (though I hope not exclusively) for teachers and for those interested in the lives and experiences of teachers: not because I perceive teachers as living in the dark, so to speak (on the contrary, of all the professionals I have met and worked with around the globe, teachers are always among the most curious and open-minded, endlessly seeking out the light even when endlessly frustrated by circumstances that seem determined to deny their habitation within it) – or that I have the arrogance to suggest that the pages that follow will cast some kind of celestial light into the darkness of my unfortunate, incarcerated readers. The cover photograph I have described above is presented, rather, as a metaphor for one of the book's key explorations – that of the operations of discourse and of what we might call the discursive experience that is common to us all: an exploration, in this particular case, of how education policy – essentially, neoliberal education policy – seeks to change and remould professional subjectivities and relationships, and of the processes and practices whereby '[w]hat it means to teach and what it means to be a teacher … are subtly but decisively changed in the process of reform' (Ball 2003: 18). It is a book that is meant to provoke discussion rather than to seek confirmation. Its intention is to share some of the thoughts and ideas that have intrigued and stimulated me over the years (in the main, those of other writers who have similarly chosen to take part in such sharing) and that its illustrations of theory will be interrogated, challenged and compared with readers' own experiences of and thoughts about professional life in whatever way they see fit. In considering how policy can infect us individually, how it can modify both our practice and our sense of who we should be, it focusses on the matter of feelings: specifically, on the ways in which we experience and 'manage' feelings; on how, if at all – and with whom – we choose to share our feelings; on the role that feelings play in guiding us to undertake or to resist certain courses of action; and, most centrally, of how feelings can be manipulated by others in order to gain practitioner compliance within local and central education policy. To most readers such a discussion will not, I suspect, either appear unusual or be unwelcome. However, as Megan Böler has observed, despite the fact that '[e]motions are a feature always present in educational environments', we rarely 'find educational histories that systematically explore, or even mention, the significant role of emotions as a feature of the daily lives of teachers and students' (Böler 1999: xxii).

As with an earlier book, *The Good Teacher*, which might be seen as a precursor and companion piece to this one, I have been theoretically driven partly by my own pre-interests, pre-concerns and pre-beliefs, and partly by my research data, which I have tried hard to analyse as impartially and open-mindedly as is possible. It is from the data that two distinct themes have emerged, linked by a single connecting thread. On the one hand, I will focus on what I have come to call *resistant teachers*: that is to say, teachers who, in varying degrees and with differing levels of discomfort, find themselves working and thinking in partial but striking opposition to certain aspects of centrally or locally imposed education policy and its embedded ideology – often finding themselves having to do things which they may feel to be against the long-term (and in some cases the shorter-term) interests of their students. Resistance of this kind is best understood as an experience, a response, a condition or a set of feelings rather than as activity – although activity, in the form of disobedience, might follow on from it. My research suggests that this form of resistance is not a minority condition; indeed, if it were I would not have been prompted so pressingly to write about it in the first place. It is something, on the contrary, that has been raised with me by very many teachers, often, in the case of England (which is where my investigations have mainly taken place), expressed in terms of a tension between wanting to ensure that students do well within an imposed system and according to imposed criteria, while at the same time feeling that that system and those criteria are, in themselves, unfair, educationally inappropriate and potentially damaging. This is not, I should add, a phenomenon that is confined to class teachers. The evidence suggests that many headteachers and deputy headteachers, too, find themselves clearly and uncomfortably at odds both with aspects of government policy and with its apparent endorsement in much of the mass media.

This first strand that I will be pursuing, concerning opposition and resistance to key aspects of central education policy – its effects, and how it is or might be managed – has led me to consider issues not just of resistance but of (often reluctant) compliance: of how policy 'works', of how it is that teachers – including resistant teachers – become the bearers of policy discourse and ideology that appears to run counter to cherished social and pedagogical beliefs. Viewing resistance not simply in terms of action or orientation but of feeling and experience, I will explore the key role of language in this process and, centrally to the book as a whole, the ways in which imposed policy relies on affect[1] rather than on rationality for its successful implementation in the local domains of the school and the classroom. In exploring these issues, I have become particularly interested in the (inter)relationship between discourse, ideology and affect, and in how a variety of overt and covert feelings, including differing manifestations of fear and love, are deliberately conscripted and manipulated within education policy rhetoric and implementation.

My second strand (though dealt with first in the pages that follow) is also concerned with understanding feelings, but rather than focussing on tensions and issues related to mandated policy implementation, it turns its attention to what some might consider the more quotidian tensions that many teachers are likely to experience to a greater or lesser extent as they set about managing and responding to their own and their students' and colleagues' feelings and emotions in the course of simply doing the job. This strand, which, like the other, draws heavily on aspects of psychoanalytic theory, proposes a theory of reflexivity by which teachers might come to understand their own emotional responses differently and more productively, contextualising them historically, socially and biographically, with a view to becoming both better at and happier in what they do. This strand references Foucault's notion of 'care of the self', along with the work of various other theorists who have grappled with issues of self-image, self-worth and personal agency. It also offers suggestions as to how a more psychoanalytically informed understanding not just of our own but of our young students' behaviour might result in more positive, less confrontational interactions and outcomes – for though the book focusses principally on teachers, their students are never far from the action, and indeed at times take centre stage in the analysis.

The link between the two strands is precisely the theory of reflexivity referenced above. I will be identifying two kinds or aspects of reflexivity, one of which is concerned with critical dialogue with one's past and how it has come to influence one's self and one's experiencing in the present ('Reflexivity 1'), the other of which turns its gaze outward, so to speak, to critical exploration of the social and symbolic milieux in which we live and work ('Reflexivity 2'). This twofold nature of reflexivity finds its parallel in two kinds of resistance. The first of these is 'refusal' – not to be confused with denial or passive resistance, but, as will be explained later, as an internal rejection of subjective colonisation. The second is more obviously active in relation to the subject's interventions into his or her social world, comprising an act or acts of what we might call subversion. As with reflexivity, these two modes of resistance are not mutually exclusive, although I shall suggest that resistance of the second kind struggles to assert itself without the prior existence of refusal. Reflexivity, I shall argue, can help us to have more rewarding, more satisfying and less uncomfortable experiences when we are grappling with our own pedagogic identities and when we are managing and working through difficult relationships with students or colleagues, but it can also help us to manage the uncomfortable feelings we may have when obliged to teach in a way or take part in assessment procedures that we may feel fundamentally or broadly opposed to. While *individual* reflexivity can help in each of these instances, I shall argue in the final chapter that much is to be gained by breaking down the barriers that can exist in schools (in no small part produced as a result of neoliberal policies and ideologies that promote competition and individual over collective success) to *group reflexivity*.

Structure

The complexity of these issues has inevitably made the writing of the book a very difficult and equally complex business. Rightly or wrongly I took a decision fairly early on to divide it into three broad sections, adding, later on, a concluding section at the end. Part I, comprising the first three chapters, is mainly theoretical in nature, providing some shared understandings and questions to take into a reading of the next four chapters. These next chapters, Chapters 4 to 7, which comprise Parts II and III, are essentially case studies, the first two focussing mainly on primary-school teachers and student teachers (or 'beginning teachers' as I shall refer to them hereafter), the next two (Chapters 6 and 7) on secondary-school teachers. The empirical data drawn on illustratively comes partly from on ongoing study in which I continue to visit schools and interview teachers about their feelings, including those connected to public and local policy directives, and partly from previous empirical studies of teachers' lives and work. Those earlier studies include two ESRC-funded projects, 'Teacher Identities and the Consumption of Tradition' (Halpin, Moore *et al* 1998–2001) (also known as 'Pedagogic Identities and the

Consumption of Tradition') and 'Children's Learner-Identities in Mathematics at Key Stage 2' (Bibby *et al* 2005–2007), along with the University of London funded study 'Key factors in the promotion and obstruction of reflective practice in beginning teachers' (Moore and Ash 2001). Eighty-two interviews from these combined studies have been drawn on, with the testimonies of twenty-four teachers (sixteen secondary and eight primary), mainly taken from the ongoing study, being used for the majority of the illustrative material in the book. These respondents have been selected partly because of the amount of time and detail that went into their responses, partly because of the striking ways in which they raised and talked about issues that permeated the data as a whole, and partly because of the value they expressed as having resulted from our discussions. This same respondent enthusiasm on the part of the teachers I have more recently spoken to, after having completed the bulk of the book, has led me to add an additional chapter, Chapter 8, arguing the merits of what I have called group reflexivity. Each school visited, both in the main studies and for the more recent interviews and discussions, has been mixed in terms of the cultural and socio-economic backgrounds of its student intake, and none have been academies.

My original intention had been to write separately about the experiences of beginning teachers and those of more experienced teachers. However, I have rejected this proposal, and for two reasons. First, contrary to my initial expectation, I came to feel that, although there were obvious differences between the overall experience and practice of experienced teachers and those just entering the profession, those differences were not sufficiently striking *in relation to the particular issues I wanted to explore* to merit this kind of separation – differences here being more a matter of degree and contingency than of kind. Second, it felt more natural – and was certainly much easier – to separate out the primary school staff from the secondary school staff for analysis. Admittedly, there was not so very much, either, that was different in terms of the teacher experience between the two phases of formal education, as will become apparent in the reading; however, some kind of structure is necessary, and I hope this approach will make life easier for the reader in terms of finding a way around the text and in identifying key respondents. In the event, Chapter 4 sticks more closely to the originally planned structure, in that it does focus mainly on beginning teachers at Primary School One ('Primary One' hereafter) – though not exclusively so. Chapters 5 to 7 follow the revised plan much more closely, focussing on specific issues and events rather than on teachers at specific stages in their careers.

As indicated above, in addition to revisiting data from previous studies, I have made use of data from ongoing visits, including some that are very recent, drawing on formal and informal discussions with teachers both on a one-to-one basis and in small groups. In some instances, these conversations have been quite practical in nature (for example, discussions of specific classroom incidents and how they were dealt with, or issues related to national curriculum requirements), while others – particularly in schools where my own work was already known – have been more theoretical or philosophical (focussing, for example, on theories of learning, or on the nature and purposes of education and schooling). An interesting feature of these recent discussions has been how much they were enjoyed by the teachers taking part – a common response being that it made a nice change to be able to talk about their experiences in education and to share their views on policy issues. Toward the end of each group discussion, I have developed a habit of asking participants if they often get together for such discussions. Each time the answer has been a resounding 'No! Never!' – invariably accompanied by collective agreement that the session has been very useful. I am struck by how different this is from my own experiences as a classroom teacher between 1969 and 1987. Unlike the English teacher in one of the groups I spoke to, who told me, 'These days, as soon as the bell goes, I'm out the gate', I have fond memories, which I hope are not too rose-tinted, of sitting in the staff room at the end of the day or during the lunch break chatting with friends and colleagues about various of the day's more interesting events, or about education issues that intrigued or vexed us, or discussing possibilities for shared ventures. We were under so much less external pressure in those days and had so much more time, it seems, for thinking constructively and independently about our work.

Data and analysis

Given the ever-growing volume of data at my disposal and the fact that, as one measure of ensuring respondent anonymity, I decided for the ongoing study not to electronically record any discussions, I have found myself making far more extensive use of fieldnotes than in previous studies. In the spirit of the research, I have attempted to use these reflexively, thinking about my own choices and interpretations of what I have noticed and written down and why I might be focussing on some incidents while ignoring others. Given my emphasis on affect, I found that I was increasingly seeking out and prioritising the anecdotal and biographical in my questioning, and prioritising this over specifically seeking out views of teaching and learning *per se*. It also felt more honest to include myself as a research participant (or research 'subject') in the writing up, given the obvious and acknowledged futility, despite my best efforts, of seeking to exclude entirely my own emotional and ideological biography from the research process itself.

In my original notes and in the first draft of the analysis, the schools from the various studies were anonymised as Primary and Secondary One, Two, Three, Four, Five and so on. However, in writing the book I have 'collapsed' these schools into two virtual schools – Primary One and Secondary Two – initially with the intention of making it additionally difficult for any respondent to be tracked down other than of their own choosing, but also to make the book more reader-friendly. Ensuring anonymity was something I considered to be extremely important given the sensitive nature of the study and the level of honesty and personal revelation it required, and as a further measure I have, in the main, cited no more than one respondent from any one school. Names of quoted respondents have been changed as a matter of course, and for the sake of additional security, I have ensured that no school I have visited has known the identity of any other school included in the study. I have also changed or invented physical characteristics of my respondents, introducing a fictive element to the accounts – although I have been assiduous, as one would expect, in only making use of respondents' own words and thoughts in any direct quotations, in cases of doubt referring back to the respondent for confirmation of accuracy. From the reader's point of view, and without wishing to be presumptuous, the easiest response to this approach might be to forget that data from more than two schools have been drawn on, and to read the text as if Primary One and Secondary Two were the only schools visited. Further to this, it is worth noting that every one of the schools whose teacher testimonies I have drawn on had either recently undergone or was about to undergo an Office of Teaching and Standards in Education ('Ofsted') inspection at the time of my visit(s), and I was also able to be present at two of the primary schools on the day that Standard Attainment Test (SAT) results arrived and at two of the secondary schools on the day that General Certificate of Secondary Education (GCSE) results arrived. The reactions and responses of teachers on these occasions were sufficiently similar for me to be able to write about them as if describing single events – so that, for example, in Chapter 7, Zoë and Margo are cited alongside Mary, Abigail, John and James as if teaching at the same school, while Ruth and Miriam appear together in accounts of primary teachers' experiences of the pressures resulting from inspections and SAT scores.

Before leaving this short introductory section, it is important, finally, to make it clear that I make no claim to be writing and analysing ethnographically – that is to say, during the course of my studies, to have become a living ('live-in') member of each or any school community. Nor is my intention in undertaking the current study to 'ground' theory in data. Rather, it is to apply and to interrogate theory drawn from my earlier studies that would enable me to present a number of provocations – or 'things to think about (differently)'. My broad approach, then, was to identify pre-defined issues and questions that still seemed to have widespread relevance, to eliminate from my enquiries those that did not and to explore the ones that did through micro-scopic analysis of a small number of testimonies. I already knew from my previous studies that fear and love were very present, though not always obviously 'visible', in schools and classrooms, and it was with the aim of finding out more about the role and nature of such feelings that I initially undertook this new study – offering a record of sorts on which to hang developing theories and to help make better sense of our professional worlds and of our practices and experiences within them. I was certainly not out to present a complex picture of the workings, the experiences, or the micro-politics of any one particular institution. Instead, I wanted to pick up on a variety of experiences that seemed worthy of further exploration and analysis and that might be more widely applicable. In a sense, what I have settled upon might be described, after Seigworth and Gregg (2010: 20), as a series of 'moments', and it is around such moments that the book seeks its internal structure, giving it something of the nature of a collection of short stories. The task of taking the testimonies, the moments, the arguments and the conclusions from this book, and applying them to experience and practice more widely is, as always, that of the reader. It might be that some of the quoted data will resonate very loudly with the reader's own experience; it might equally be the case that it does not. The hope is that it will at least provide some useful and challenging suggestions that can feed into or provide alternative perspectives on the reader's own endlessly evolving understandings of classrooms, of learners and of learning, and of their own experience of being a teacher.

PART I

Contexts and theory: reflexivity, psychoanalysis and empowerment

1

REFLEXIVITY AND PSYCHOANALYSIS

The cutting-room floor: Pinar and Freud

Some books have a longer gestation period than others. Some may represent the final product of a long-term project (though of course these things are never truly final). Others may have evolved over months or years, almost by accident.

This book may be regarded as something of an accident in that it has emerged, so to speak, over a period of twenty-five years, drawing its material from a number of studies each of which had its own particular objectives: some undertaken at the beginning of that period, others during its course, and one – in relation to what follows, the most significant – still ongoing. It also owes much of its content to material not used in those earlier studies: material that in many cases was deemed at the time to be insufficiently relevant to the issues in hand.

From a purely theoretical perspective, the book's origin may be traced to a moment in the early noughties when, looking again at some original interview data from a research project into teachers' professional identities – a project entitled, variously, 'Pedagogic Identities and the Consumption of Tradition' and 'Educational Identities and the Consumption of Tradition'[1] – I became acutely aware of how much of the data the research team had overlooked or parenthesised in drawing its conclusions. This is not to say that the shelved data and any conclusions drawn from it had not been interesting or valid, simply that they were not felt to be significant enough to address the specific research questions we had pre-identified.[2]

My decision to return to our interview transcripts some years after the study had been completed had, itself, something of the accidental about it, being prompted in no small part by two readings I had happened to be absorbed with at the time. The first of these involved a return to Sigmund Freud, whose collected works I had been re-familiarising myself with in preparation for a short course I was running for research students at the University of London's Institute of Education, entitled

'Psychoanalytic Perspectives on Educational Enquiry'. Apart from reinvigorating an interest in adapting and applying elements of psychoanalytic theory to the analysis of research into education (specifically, research into how formal education is understood and experienced by those most directly involved in it), this return had reminded me of Freud's determination in (for example) analysing his patients' dreams, to include in his analysis every detail of the information made available to him no matter how small or insignificant it might seem or how little emphasis it might be given by its provider. (Indeed, it was often those seemingly insignificant, 'tossed away' elements which provided the psychoanalyst with the clearest window into what was actually troubling the person who had come seeking help.)

Coincidentally, I was also re-reading at this time William Pinar's intriguing book *What Is Curriculum Theory?* with a view to reinstating it to a 'Curriculum Development and Design' Masters module that I had become involved with at the Institute. I had been particularly struck, during this re-reading, by Pinar's metaphor of the cutting-room floor (Pinar 2004) to describe a stitching back together again into a new narrative those parts of a whole that may have been previously discarded. It occurred to me that this same metaphor – not just the cutting-room floor and what might be found there, but the importance of returning to it, and perhaps the reasons for the initial rejections and for not going back there previously – was particularly apt in describing research material and ideas that are, at least at the first pass, also treated as of little or no relevance to the task in hand but that might also offer up interesting insights on subsequent inspection. This same metaphor, partly, no doubt, affected by my re-readings of Freud, prompted in me a growing interest in adopting what might be called a neo-Freudian reading of some of the data at my disposal, that asked not just why we had originally 'cut it out' (whether this was more than simply a matter of perceived [ir]relevance), but also why I was resurrecting it for analysis now.[3]

Looking again at this rejected material, much of which comprised responses to an initial warm-up question – *'What brought you into teaching in the first place?'* – but also to a subsequent question regarding possible tensions between preferred practice and policy directives and to a number of asides, I was struck by how many direct and indirect mentions there were in it both of love and of fear. Given what now, at some distance, seems the very obvious relevance of such feelings in connection to central research questions in the earlier project regarding the development of professional identities, I began to wonder if our conscious elimination of this data might have had something more to it than just perceived irrelevance to the task we had set ourselves. In particular, I wondered if perhaps we had felt as obliged to parenthesise these data in our analysis as our respondents had in their accounts. In other words, could it be that it was not necessarily our respondents who wanted to acknowledge their feelings but not to explore them in any depth, but our researcher selves too? Had we, also, and the rationalist research traditions and parameters within which we had, almost without thinking, been working and constrained by, been vaguely acknowledging but actually marginalising our respondents' (and perhaps our own) feelings – of effectively ostracising what I shall later be referring to as *affect*? If so, what might we learn about how (in this case) teaching is understood and experienced, and about how teachers respond to and work with education policy, if we de-marginalise and *validate* affect – actually bringing it centre-stage in our analyses of teachers' testimonies and classroom observations? And what kind of research methodology might be appropriate to such an approach?

Psychoanalysis and society

In light of the above, it will come as no surprise that the approach I have adopted in this book is what is broadly known as a psychosocial one: that is to say, it is an approach to social enquiry that is fundamentally concerned with how the individual-personal and the 'psychic' are embedded in the collective-societal and the 'material', and *vice versa*. Very often, such an approach combines what are traditionally thought of as sociological approaches to studying and writing about such matters as social policy trends and effects with perspectives, understandings and concepts drawn from research and writing about the individual psyche: most typically, from the fields of psychoanalysis and psychotherapy. This may combine considerations of the material effects of (say) social policy – that is to say, by way of an example, the 'measurable' or readily describable effects on classroom practice or student or teacher experience or 'performance' of the introduction of a mandatory school curriculum – with a parallel focus on how such policy is not just practically but also psychically mediated and experienced by social actors (teachers, students, headteachers). This latter set of considerations tends to focus more on the role and nature of what are generally understood as personal feelings in the social process, seeking to expose and describe immediately less visible psychic forces at work, in the hope of encouraging more sophisticated, nuanced and helpful understandings of practice and experience – both for researchers and for the social actors whose experiences interest them.

In the case of the current book, I have barely drawn on sociological theory as such. The 'social' part of 'psychosocial' comes, rather, from the modified application of elements of psychoanalytic theory, mainly adapted from the theoretical writings of Sigmund Freud, Melanie Klein, Wilfrid Bion and Jacques Lacan, to interpretations and understandings of everyday social situations. Where I have drawn a little more heavily on sociological theory, it has been mainly on Basil Bernstein's conceptualisations of how commonly devolved education policy is modified, resisted or adhered to as it becomes 'recontextualised' (Bernstein 2000) from policy formation, articulation and direction to local implementation in the contingent, idiosyncratic sites of schools and classrooms. Psychoanalytically informed analysis seeks to explain this process in terms of affective appellations and attachments and, in particular, of how policy and its reception impact on teacher experience, outlook and practice – that is to say, how policy works, with varying degrees of success, to construct actually or functionally compliant teacher (and learner) subjectivities.[4]

I am aware that drawing on psychoanalytic theory in social research is always likely to be frowned upon by some and dismissed altogether by others – and for a variety of reasons. These range from easy accusations of 'quackery', 'psycho-babble' and 'pop psychology' to a very genuine concern that psychoanalysis' emphasis on understanding and treating the individual and the family unit can detract attention from critiques and criticisms of the wider social practices, policies and systems within which (and perhaps because of which) emotional suffering occurs – potentially placing the responsibility and the potential resolution for socially produced problems in the individual actor and thereby, albeit unintentionally, letting broader social policies and ideologies escape largely blameless and unchallenged. Understood thus, the use of psychoanalytic theory, rather than liberating critical thinking and challenging traditional ways of understanding human society and experience in the way that is often intended, can be seen to support repressive accounts and constructs of the individual. As Reid warns us, in relation to a popular construct of the 'resilient subject' within wider policy and ideology, such a mis-use can seek to produce a self-focussed subject which 'must permanently struggle to accommodate itself to the world' (Reid 2013: 355) rather than, as the psychosocial approach would wish to encourage, a subject engaging critically and actively with the social world – including what it perceives to be wrong with it.[5] The line I will be taking in the pages that follow is that, although psychoanalysis has the potential to focus our attention regarding society's ills on the individual and the family unit rather than (for example) on the failings in and of wider structures and systems, it doesn't have to – and that there is no contradiction in criticising psychoanalysis for its characteristics and applications in some situations while at the same time embracing it in relation to other situations and other applications. Related to this point, a major part of the psychoanalytically informed reflexive work that I will be arguing for concerns developing understandings about our own individual biographies, not just in relation to our personal encounters and experiences with family and friends, but in relation to how events and circumstances in the wider 'external' world have shaped us – including how they may have blinkered or constrained us as well as how they may offer up to us opportunities and affordances. Such undertakings invite us to a different relationship with our past than perhaps we are accustomed to: not as something either to be 'put behind us' (as it cannot be changed), or to be dwelt on nostalgically as a 'lost object', but as something to be explored for what helpful light it might throw on present situations, outlooks and difficulties, and to help us overcome obstacles to our ongoing process of becoming. As Mari Ruti puts it, in her emphasis on the value of constructive, critical engagement with our personal histories: 'Although psychoanalysis recognizes that the past shapes both the present and the future … an excessive faithfulness to the past can prevent us from gracefully entering the art of living'. We need, therefore, to learn to develop 'a more discerning relationship to our past', to embrace 'a way to go on with our lives without letting the ordeals of the past diminish our aptitude for aliveness in the present' (Ruti 2009: 148).

The idea that psychoanalytic theory has relevance and usefulness outside the clinic, in more everyday circumstances and situations and in relation to understanding experience and behaviour that is troubling though not particularly unusually so, is not new and has been recognised within psychoanalysis itself. Freud, for example, in *Civilization and Its Discontents* (1930), references the three common sources of suffering and potential anxiety that we all face as human beings[6]: those related to our own physical bodies (dangers and anxieties related to actual or potential illness, infirmity and disease, to growing older, ultimately to dying); those related to the external physical world (the temporary dangers and anxieties we might experience while in an aircraft or when walking through a dangerous part of town; and the more enduring ones, often experienced collectively, posed these days by such things as terrorism or climate change); and those related to our interpersonal relationships, linked to felt emotions such as happiness, fear and love, often concerning the threat of loss (for example, loss of love, loss of friendship or loss of esteem). More recently, Lacan's theorising (Lacan 1977, 1979) focusses our attention on the nature and effects of the subjectivising journey that every human being takes as it moves from the pre-symbolic, 'primordial' state of early infancy into the pre-existing symbolic world of language and custom (Lacan's 'Other') – a journey which has positive and negative consequences for us all, regardless of who we are, the only difference relating to degree and to the relative ease of our transition. Most pertinently in relation to this current book, Anna Freud, who may be seen as both a psychoanalyst and an educationalist, was of the view that, because psychoanalysis helps us to understand ourselves, others and our relationships *with* others, it is not only advisable but imperative that schoolteachers should have some understanding of the science: that via psychoanalysis 'the teacher's knowledge of human beings is extended, and his understanding of the complicated relations between the child and the educator is sharpened' (A. Freud 1931: 104).

Ruti's account of the value of psychoanalysis as applied in everyday experience emphasises its invitation to develop new relationships both with our past and with our *unconscious* – that place where many of our most powerful, most motivating and demotivating drives and determinations lie hidden:

> [N]o matter how resolute our efforts to modify our lives on the conscious level, we will fail to bring about genuine transformation as long as we are incapable of effectively arbitrating between our conscious and unconscious processes of making sense of the world. This is why one of the aims of psychoanalysis as a therapeutic practice is to enable us to develop an actively interpretative relationship to our unconscious motivations. It is when we lack an adequate understanding of these motivations that we get caught up in the meshes of the repetition compulsion – that we end up re-enacting destructive patterns in a passive and uncontrollable manner.
>
> *(Ruti 2009: 8)*

Of course, the unconscious can never, by definition, be properly accessed and 'known',[7] but it can be known about: that is to say, we can be aware of how it might be affecting our experience, our behaviour and the choices – sometimes consciously undertaken, sometimes not – that we make in our daily lives. As later illustrations will suggest, such awareness itself has some degree of empowerment, opening up new ways of seeing, understanding and approaching life's situations and circumstances, helping us to understand not only how – and why – we 'feel', but also how we 'work', and enabling us to dare to do things differently rather than remaining locked in rigid patterns of thought, feeling and action laid down in our infancy. As Ruti concludes:

> Once we come to see that we are not merely the helpless victims of these impulses but can take a dynamic role in deciphering them, we can begin to alter our lives. This is what it means, in Freudian terms, to move from a passive repetition of the past to an active working through of this past.
>
> *(Ruti 2009: 8)*

The idea that we passively, perhaps unknowingly, repeat past behaviours and responses, that we relive previous experiences that may themselves be unproductive and unrewarding, and that an 'active working through' of our past can help us to develop as individuals is one that will be explored in greater depth in Chapters 4 and 5, in a consideration of the repeated returns we might, in spite of ourselves, find ourselves making to specific roles and specific responses in previously unresolved conflicts. These chapters will also consider the associated Freudian notion of 'transference', which concerns the ways in which we may incorporate other people (in our present) into our re-experiencing of past encounters – in the process unknowingly (at least, at the time) ascribing to them and to ourselves certain relational roles. For example, in the classical Freudian clinic, the analysand might unwittingly ascribe to the analyst the role of parent, so that the analyst comes to 'represent' the analysand's parent to the analysand. I want to suggest that, just as there is a focus in much psychoanalytic theory on understanding and exploring the relationship between the analyst and the analysand (in lay terms, though the term is not always welcomed within psychoanalysis, between the analyst and the 'patient'), so might there be fruit in focussing in not dissimilar ways on the relationships in schools and classrooms between teachers and students, or indeed between teachers and teachers and between students and students, especially at times of conflict. In school, for example, might we not most noticeably and importantly find such role ascription in those situations in which a single child is in confrontational dialogue with a single, authoritative adult, discussing matters related to behaviour? If so, might recognising and understanding such ascriptions help us to understand *why* the ascription is being proposed by the child/student and/or by the adult/teacher, leading to a more accurate, more nuanced understanding of what it is that might be troubling them? I will suggest in Chapter 5, and later in this current chapter, that Kleinean and post-Kleinean theory and practice related to the analyst-analysand relationship might be particularly helpful here, impelling us to read rudeness, for example, as a form of empathy-seeking communication rather than as simple anti-social behaviour.

Such psychoanalytic understandings, whether focussing on the same analyst-analysand relationship or drawing on more strictly Freudian approaches which explore (for example) the ways in which past experience continues to colour our present socio-emotive responses, might also help us to understand how the adult teacher experiences life in the classroom, including confrontational dialogues with students, and how such dialogues might then be approached and understood in ways that are constructive rather than destructive to either party. As Brenman Pick puts it, accounting for the way in which 'an interaction of the past is re-enacted in the present' (Brenman Pick 1992: 27):

> Freud's great discovery [was] that feelings and impulses were transferred from earlier relationships, *not remembered but re-lived and re-experienced in the relationship with the analyst* – the transference.
>
> *(ibid.: 25, emphasis added)*

Such a relationship is not confined to the analyst-analysand relationship, for:

> We are all at times taken over by such states of mind. … We see things partly accurately, partly coloured by emotions, and partly by relationships we made in the past.
>
> *(ibid: 27)*

Of particular importance in relation to the studies I have drawn on in this book, and especially in relation to my previous and ongoing work with beginning teachers, is Brenman Pick's subsequent suggestion that, even in 'normal' life outside the clinic, 'maturity is being able to re-view these issues, knowing what distorted pre-views we may form' (ibid.: 27, emphasis added).

Psychoanalysis and empowerment

Anna Freud's suggestion that schoolteachers will be better teachers with some knowledge of psychoanalysis is particularly interesting when explored in the context of recent government distillations in the UK and elsewhere of what teachers need to know and what skills they need to have, in lists of 'standards' and 'competences'. 'Knowledge of ourselves and others as complex human beings' or 'understanding of the complicated relations between the child and the educator' are unlikely to figure with any degree of prominence on such lists, while the very suggestion of 'complicated relations' may be seen to run counter to the rather uncomplicated picture of classroom interaction that these lists so often appear to suggest. While Anna Freud promotes a knowledge of psychoanalysis as a practical classroom tool aimed mainly at helping teachers to help students more effectively and sympathetically, Ruti's broader claims for the benefits of psychoanalytic theory suggest the possibility of a *therapeutic and empowering* facility for teachers themselves that is not directed exclusively to the learner's benefit. In contrast to the universalising, somewhat reductive lists that teachers these days are so often presented and charged with, Ruti's account pleads for the development of understandings of the social world that resist universalising tendencies and that seek to re-insert into our under-standings of our own and others' experiences the very contingent, idiosyncratic aspects of experience and practice that lists of competences and standards generally eschew. Psychoanalysis, Ruti suggests, 'makes a *virtue* out of life's contingency', for

> the more we cling to the notion of predictability, the less dexterously we are able to deal with life as the erratic and capricious stream of unanticipated events, encounters, and developments that it often is. ... No matter how carefully we strive to organize our lives around certain centers of security – ideals, ambitions, or relationships, for instance – it is our lot as human beings to learn to survive less than secure circumstances.
>
> *(Ruti 2009: 4–5, emphasis added)*

Ruti's emphasis on the power of psychoanalysis as able to help us in an ongoing project of becoming,[8] emphasising its refusal to accept simplistic, universalising answers as it promotes our 'active and lively engagement with life' rather than our 'passive response' to our circumstances (2009: 2), is worth referencing at some length, not least because it looks forward to the matter of reflexivity which will be examined in more detail in the following section. In contrast with the criticisms sometimes levelled at psychoanalysis, that it distracts us from critiquing problems that are systemic in nature, in the process promoting self-blame, Ruti's argument is that psychoanalytic approaches can effectively be applied, albeit in non-clinical forms and contexts, in assisting and developing our understandings not just of the circumstances and systems of the social world we inhabit but also of ourselves as thinking, feeling, agentic beings. The notion of personal empowerment at the heart of Ruti's defence of psychoanalysis' wider relevance and applicability, with its focus on the development of the individual not as a neoliberalised subject willingly accepting responsibility for its life experiences but as a critical thorn in the flesh of dominant, fundamentally dis-empowering policies and ideologies, has applicability both to our wider social engagement with policy and political action and, more locally, in how we engage with the conditions of our working lives: for example, how we engage with mandated agendas such as a centrally imposed national cur-riculum, regular compulsory national testing or sets of standards and competences. Rather than seeking to identify responses and strategies that may be deployed by anyone in any situation, the application of psychoanalytic theory promoted by Ruti (and in this book) argues that we can benefit by developing the capacity and the confidence to behave flexibly and resourcefully in the face of a variety of sometimes unpredicted and unpredictable circumstances: in short, to have trust in ourselves as social actors rather than feeling obliged always to reach for the nearest guidebook. If 'standards' are about attempting to impose order, coherence and definition, to provide simple answers to life's complex and often troubling challenges, the psychoanalytic approach suggests, instead, a project of conveying 'something constructive about coping with their intrinsic incoherence' (Ruti 2009: 4) – emphasising the (assisted) identification of and engagement with personal issues and troubling or positive *experiences*, as opposed to merely reflecting on one's *practice* in line with criteria that have been established by others. Ruti continues:

> Psychoanalysis at its best – when it curtails its dogmatic and prescriptive tendencies – can empower us to embrace the unforeseen with a measure of resourcefulness. To put the matter differently, psychoanalysis can help us to envision what it might mean to be agents of our lives in a world that questions the very possibility of agency. ... [P]sychoanalysis promotes our capacity to feel effectively connected to the here and now, to the tangible (yet also fleeting) density of living our lives.
>
> *(5, 7)*

This is an approach which invites us not to seek to 'rise above', to 'transcend' or to 'overcome' the 'constraints of our positionality in the world', but which encourages us 'to view it as a matter of our ability to inhabit our actual circumstances in ways that allow us to make the most of those circumstances' (ibid: 6–7).

There are, undoubtedly, difficulties with such a view, some of which will become apparent in the testimonies of teachers and students in Chapters 4–7 of this book. They include difficulties that return us to the broader criticisms of psychoanalysis, that it can be counter-revolutionary and overly personalising. Making the most of one's circumstances can certainly be rather easier said than done, and there is a substantial difference between someone in the position of an academic or a teacher seeking to make the best of the hand they have been dealt, and expecting or inviting someone without a home or a job (or for that matter a young student) to do the same. The call to help oneself personally through psychoanalytic strategies, too, while it may provide some assistance to the individual, does little in itself either to challenge the 'actual circumstances' that might confront us (individually and/or collectively) or to promote the kinds of collective activity that might be required to modify or overthrow circumstances that are (a) manifestly unfair and (b) *can* be changed through collective action.

The issue here essentially takes us back to Ruti's observations concerning agency. My own research, both previous and ongoing, particularly with teachers who find themselves in a position of crisis, is that (re)connecting with their past in the way promoted in Ruti's analysis can be extremely beneficial, not least, as she suggests, in restoring a sense of agency that has previously been lost. An example of what I am getting at might be helpful here. It is one I have often used in the past in discussions of the potential value of psychoanalytically theorised approaches with both qualified and beginning teachers. It concerns a previous student of mine – Emily – who effectively saved herself from withdrawing from teaching altogether as she became overwhelmed by a conviction of – and acute embarrassment in – her own enduring inadequacy in the face of her young students' refusal to comply with her lesson plans and classroom behaviour rules. 'There is nothing I can do', she would say to me. 'I've tried everything in my locker and I've failed abysmally. Either I'm just not up to it or these classes are unteachable'. My work with this teacher encouraged her to undertake critical, often very difficult re-engagements with her own past experiences, both of home and as a school student herself, including working through specific childhood experiences of difficult and fractured adult-child relationships. It transpired that she had had a particularly difficult experience of school herself in her formative years. Her middle-class parents, 'for mainly political reasons', had sent her to the local secondary school which had had something of a reputation as being 'very tough', and she had struggled to fit in and to forge lasting friendships there. Her recollection was that in most lessons very little teaching and learning had taken place, as the teachers had had their work cut out merely to retain some semblance of control. She had come to feel sorry not just for herself but for some of her teachers, one of whom in particular had on more than one occasion broken down in tears and had had to leave the room. Eventually, partly in an attempt to make herself more acceptable to her peers, she had pretty much stopped working herself, as a result of which her grades had dropped and letters had been sent home. Her mother in particular had given her a hard time about this and had tried to push her (unsuccessfully) into therapy as she had started to become increasingly uncommunicative. After almost two years – 'wasted years' – her parents had taken her out of the school and sent her 'to the school they should have chosen for me in the first place'.

The exact nature of the possible connections between these past experiences of schooling as a student and her current experiences as a teacher were never fully articulated by this beginning teacher, though she was to assert on a number of occasions that she had 'almost forgotten about them' and had 'never really thought much about them'. However, it was clear that this revisiting of the past – and its sharing with a sympathetic other – had had some therapeutic effect, given that it appeared to precipitate an almost immediate change in her outlook – not least, in her understanding and assessment of herself. This observable therapeutic benefit encouraged me to persist with my slightly unorthodox approach (one which temporarily set to one side the lists of competences that had been presented to her at the start of her teaching practice), enabling her to occupy a space in which she could examine more circumspectly her emotionally dominated responses to unsatisfactory classroom interactions and to reassess her teaching approach in the light of this examination. Specifically, she came to focus less on the negative feelings she was experiencing *in themselves*, more on why she was experiencing them and how this experience might connect with previous conflicts which, for all her emotional response to current events, she had never fully engaged with on an emotional level or in a more analytical way. Such engagement, she observed later, had had a 'strangely liberating' effect on her, seeming to free her up to think practically about alternative strategies she might try, enabling her to treat failure as a failure in her successful interrogation of the approach and materials she was adopting rather than failure in and of herself as a subject. While she continued to experience feelings of unhappiness, still 'taking things far too personally' as she put it, she no longer blamed her own inherent inadequacies for her problems, no longer perceived them as insurmountable, and no longer found her emotional responses so overpowering as to effectively render her incapable of constructively addressing them. The more we talked together, the clearer it became to both of us that her obsession with student behaviour and classroom control had powerful links to her own behaviour as a school student – that she had found herself occupying, in a sense, the position she had helped place her own teachers in (specifically, that of the teacher who had cried), that her experience of being – or feeling – an outsider and her resentment at finding herself in an environment that she hated had never really left her, and that, as with some of the other teachers whose stories we will consider later on, she had chosen to re-enter the classroom partly by way of an expiation.

Adapting psychoanalytic techniques in order to help move oneself out of despair and beyond an *impasse* – an approach which may be self-initiated or might be suggested and prompted by supportive colleagues or (as in the above case) by an experienced teacher educator – typically draws on the Freudian theories of repetition and transference described earlier (see also Moore 2004; Britzman and Pitt 1996): in particular, the idea that when we think we are reacting to the behaviour of one person or one group of people we may in fact by experiencing a delayed and hitherto repressed reaction to some other(s). In the case I have quoted, the self-analysis carried out by the student clearly gave her a greater sense of agency, resulting both in a change of approach on her own part (which in the event had positive results) and a decision to remain in the teaching profession. It is certainly a limited form of agency, but I would suggest it is no less worthwhile for that. In effect, it may be understood as a form of, or one aspect of reflexivity, related to improving one's own professional practice and experience through enhanced understandings of how one has been shaped historically. As I have already suggested, there is another form or aspect of reflexivity that has a more outward-facing and potentially more political character, in that rather than stopping at understanding and making the best of one's inherited circumstances it seeks to challenge those circumstances – and is prepared to endure greater psychic pain in the process. This includes confronting and critically analysing the impact on us of those wider 'events of contemporary history' that 'mark' us in various ways (Guattari 1972: 154).

Since I have used the term 'reflexivity' several times now, and am aware that the brief gloss I have given is becoming increasingly wanting, it is to a fuller account of the concept that I will turn next.

Reflexivity: exploring subjectivities, problematising the ordinary

What do we understand, then, by 'reflexivity'? And why (and to whom) might it prove helpful?

As I am using the term in this book, reflexivity is best understood as a particular form of reflection (Moore 2004) that adds an extra dimension to what might be called technical reflection. To develop a definition begun in the previous section, it has two interrelated and equally important strands: one informed by the kind of psychoanalytic theory that we have already been considering, which promotes understandings of one's (and others') feelings, reactions and responses to social

situations ('Reflexivity 1'), the other that looks outward, so to speak, to acknowledge and make sense of the wider social, economic, cultural and political world in
which we and those around us are positioned and experience life ('Reflexivity 2').[9]
The first strand is aimed at helping us to understand why we feel things the way
we do, and why, for example, we react in certain ways to school and classroom
experiences, as in the example in the previous section. It attempts to promote more
nuanced and perhaps more reliable understandings both of ourselves and of our
students and colleagues, enabling us to understand them better by developing more
complete and complex understandings of our own reactions in specific situations
– not least, those involving confrontation and reconciliation. The second strand
invites us to uncover the hidden or disguised roots, causes and interests that lie
beneath and behind the *circumstances* in which we might find ourselves (and might
find ourselves [re]acting), in addition to the personal histories of social, physical,
economic and psychic situatedness within which these circumstances arise and are
experienced – a process undertaken not simply for our own individual interest
and development, but because, as Sameshima has argued, '[t]he *teaching profession* is
dramatically strengthened when teachers understand who they are, know how their
experiences have shaped their ideologies, and find and acknowledge their place of
contribution in the broader context of the educational setting' (Sameshima 2008:
34, emphasis added).

Britzman and Pitt have argued that the first of these strands can be particularly
helpful in relation to the well-being of teachers and beginning teachers as well as
to understanding the behaviours and experiences of their students, given the highly
charged emotional circumstances in which teachers work and the ever-present
reminders, in the already-familiar school and classroom setting, of experiences gone
by. As they put it:

> The classroom invites transferential relations because, for teachers, it is such
> a familiar place, one that seems to welcome re-enactments of childhood
> memories. Indeed, recent writing about pedagogy suggests that transfer-
> ence shapes how teachers respond and listen to students, and how students
> respond and listen to teachers. ... [T]eachers' encounters with students
> may return them involuntarily and still unconsciously to scenes from their
> individual biographies.
>
> *(Britzman and Pitt 1996: 117–118)*

Such an argument suggests that it is unreasonable to expect of teachers the impossible: that is, to deny their feelings and emotions, to 'leave them at the school gates'
as it is sometimes put. On the other hand, it is important to note that the invitation
to reflexivity is not an invitation for teachers to display their feelings openly and
habitually in front of their students. It is, rather, a matter of accepting and including
one's feelings in thoughtful, informed considerations of how one is teaching and
experiencing classroom life, and of knowing how, when, where and (perhaps) with
whom to manage one's feelings and emotions so that they do not impact negatively

on practice or on one's sense of self. Unlike what I sometimes call (without any note of criticism) *basic reflection*, which is largely focussed on the analysis of matters of technique and practicalities and which encourages reflection during the event as well as after it, reflexivity, precisely because it is more affect-oriented, more 'personal', takes place more profitably at a temporal and spatial distance from the event. Teachers will always and inevitably be making thoughtful, reflective real-time decisions regarding the content and structure of any and every lesson, not least in analysing as they go along the extent to which what they have prepared is actually working. Reflexivity influences practice too (and development, and our sense of self). However, it does so in accordance with a somewhat different brief. Whereas reflection undertaken simultaneously with practice may focus on the teacher's 'performance' in purely technical terms, which can result in instant modifications to an intended plan or pedagogy, any attempt to reflexively analyse performance in the same way is likely to lead only to unhelpful self-consciousness: that is to say, it may result in an unhelpful focus on the self rather than in a more objective focus on the mechanics and technicalities of the lesson. Rather than facilitating real-time modifications, which themselves can be further reflected on *post hoc*, the intrusion of reflexivity in the classroom, bringing with it a less than welcome eruption of affect, is more likely to lead to conflict, to panic or to despair.

All of this is not to deny that, even when one is focussed simply on doing the job, there will be moments – perhaps more than moments – of unhappiness and anxiety, a sense of failure (as well, indeed, as of pleasure, contentment, joy, a sense of success), as experienced by the beginning teacher in the example I gave a little earlier. It is, rather, that just as these feelings must not be allowed to impinge negatively on pedagogy at the time in which they are experienced, so they must *be allowed* to have a more positive effect on how we do things and how we feel about ourselves once we have found a space away from the classroom in which to re-experience and interrogate them. Nor should we be afraid or suspicious of the feelings we[10] experience in the classroom, or seek to eliminate them. As Edna O'Shaughnessy observes in relation to the psychoanalyst, though it applies equally, I think, to the teacher:

> Anyone who has tried to work with a psychotic personality knows the anxiety and invasiveness which must be expected and carried by the therapist. *We can be fortified by Bion's opinion that these are not necessarily due to our bad work, but are inescapable if we are doing our work.*
>
> (O'Shaughnessy 1992: 96–97, emphasis added)

In the classroom, as in the clinic, reflexivity offers a new way of looking back on our experiences, including those that disturb us. Anxiety is not wrong or to be avoided; what is important is how we understand and make use of it.

Britzman and Pitt's reference to how teachers 'respond and listen to students' offers another argument in favour of promoting this kind of reflexivity: that is to say, it does not only help the teacher to overcome personal difficulties in the professional context; it also works to develop more subtle, appropriate and helpful understandings of one's students and their cognitive and emotional needs. The 'effective' teacher, whose competence is judged according to observable and 'measurable' learning 'outcomes' and against pre-specified professional criteria, becomes, too, the 'affective' (as well as the 'affected') teacher, willing and able to interrogate and understand circumstances, situations and experiences in ways that are sophisticated and open enough to make individual and collective pedagogic judgments more secure – potentially leading, itself, to a more positive learner experience. As I have pointed out elsewhere (Moore 2004), and as Britzman and Pitt go on to observe, Anna Freud herself felt so strongly about this issue as to suggest that psychoanalytically informed reflexivity of this kind is not simply desirable but, rather, an 'ethical obligation' on the teacher's part:

> Such an exploration requires that teachers consider *how they understand students through their own subjective conflicts.* … The heart of the matter, for Anna Freud, is the ethical obligation teachers have to learn about their own conflicts and to control the re-enactment of old conflicts that appear in the guise of new pedagogical encounters.
>
> *(ibid.: 118, emphasis added)*

The value of understanding one's own affective responses in relation to teacher-student interactions – and the potential dangers brought about by an imperfect or absent understanding – can be seen in Chapter 5 of this book, in the brief case study of Archie, a 'troublesome' (and evidently troubled) student at Primary One, where an alternative and, one could argue, more complex reading by teachers of their own responses to a child's behaviour might have resulted in a different and perhaps rather more successful approach to dealing with a particular set of events. In this case, I shall suggest, a particular post-Kleinian psychoanalytic theory might have led to a different set of understandings, not simply in relation to the event in question, or even just to a more helpful understanding of one 'deviant' child, but to the behaviour and experiences of children more widely. This particular theory, which is a development of Klein's work on projective identification and object relations, insists on the psychoanalyst's (and, we might add, the teacher's) paying attention to the ways in which their own reactions and responses might be deliberately, if not necessarily consciously, prompted or manipulated by the analysand (or young student): specifically, to understand their own feelings in the analytic situation in terms of communication and information from the analysand, rather than (for example) as deliberate provocation. Elizabeth Bott Spillius advises:

> [U]nlike Klein, we are now explicitly prepared to use our own feelings as a source of information about what the patient is doing, though with an awareness that we may get it wrong, that the process of understanding our response to the patient imposes a constant need for psychic work by the analyst … and

that confusing one's feelings with the patient's is always a hazard. ... [T]he analyst is always affected to some degree by his patient's projection, there is always some 'nudging' by the patient to push the analyst into action, and inevitably there is usually some acting out by the analyst, however slight.

(Bott Spillius 1992: 62–64)

One suggestion mooted by such theorising is that, when an analysand's behaviour is overtly insulting toward the analyst (as it often can be), the analysand might be deliberately, though not necessarily consciously, attempting to engender in the analyst the same feelings that they are experiencing – a sense of worthlessness, perhaps, or of rejection or neglect: that is to say, 'Now you really know how it feels to be me, perhaps you can understand better what I need'. Alternatively, or additionally, they might be casting the analyst in the role of another, less approachable, perhaps more frightening person, whom they may feel *responsible* for their own low esteem but are unable or unwilling either to challenge or to identify in more direct communication (a parent, perhaps, or a child or partner).

Confrontations or reconciliation meetings between teachers and individual students are not the same, of course, as interactions between psychoanalysts and their patients: teachers are not psychoanalysts, any more than a 'digressing' student can be considered a patient, and it is probable, though not inevitable, that neither party will have taken themselves into the confrontational or remedial situation voluntarily. However, there are distinct similarities in the relationship and in its context, which typically involves a 'problem' (usually identified as within the student/patient) coupled with the requirement, if at all possible, for a mutually beneficial solution. The expectation in school is not that the teacher will attempt to psychoanalyse the student or the situation. However, they might, if minded, adopt the same kind of reflexivity as the psychoanalyst described by Bott Spillius, who suspects that their patient might be communicating a feeling rather than simply being unpleasant and confrontational.

A brief example from my own days as a schoolteacher, very reminiscent of the story of Archie to be returned to in Part II, illustrates the potential advantages of a school or teacher adopting such a perspective, and the potential negative consequences of not doing so. This concerns a female Year 7 student I once taught who, almost from the moment we first met, openly expressed a strong and unremitting dislike for me – such that it had a profound effect on my self-esteem. (*Why* did she not like me? After all, I was a decent enough person – wasn't I? I had done nothing to offend her.) For the most part, this dislike expressed itself in glares, heavy exhibitions of reluctance at every written assignment I set, and an exaggerated turning away from me and looking the other way whenever I tried to sit near her to explain something or to ask her how she was getting on. Matters reached a head one day when she decided to leave the classroom, ostensibly to use the toilet, without asking permission, ignoring my calls to return to her seat. Incensed and humiliated, feeling that my authority had been undermined, I sent another student to find the girl's Head of Year, with a note saying that I did not want the girl back in my class until she had apologised for her behaviour and had agreed to some basic ground rules in order to allow me to teach her. Later in the day, there was a reconciliation meeting involving myself, the girl and the Head of Year, at which the girl replicated the behaviour I had become used to in the classroom, refusing to acknowledge either my presence or the Head of Year's, spending most of the interview turned away from us looking at her fingernails and ignoring the Head of Year's repeated warnings of what would happen if she persisted in refusing to engage with us – every so often casting a look in our direction that appeared to speak of disgust and contempt. Labelling this behaviour as unacceptable, the girl was sent home by the Head of Year and told she could only return by prior arrangement and if accompanied by a parent. In the event, she did not return, and we heard little from or about her until several weeks later when it emerged that she had run away from home and that her current whereabouts were unknown. It was only some time afterwards, when she finally did return to school, now living at a new address with an aunt and uncle, that we learned that she had been experiencing an extremely troubled home life which had made her feel worthless and uncared for: feelings not unlike those her behaviour had attempted (with some degree of success!) to produce in myself and the Head of Year.

It is impossible to know for sure whether an alternative approach to dealing with this issue, based on an alternative reading of the girl's behaviour *as communication*, might have brought about a happier outcome – or indeed to know whether the theory proposed by Bott Spillius and others is actually valid. (As Bott Spillius herself acknowledges, 'we may get it wrong'.) It is true, too, that a school is bound to demand certain behaviours of its student body and to have at its disposal clear sanctions for mis-behaviour if it is to function properly for the benefit of all. Not attempting such an alternative reading, however – partly because that alternative was *unknown* to us, but partly too, I think, because we had allowed our personal feelings of outraged indignation to predominate – seems, with the benefit of hindsight, to have been at the very least an unfortunate omission that had left us with too narrow a range of behavioural and situational readings and related strategies. If the alternative reading *had* occurred to us, it might also have opened up more persuasively the possibility, which I think had hovered in the background all through our joint meeting, that the root problem had nothing much to do with school itself, or indeed with this student's apparent feelings about us, but more to do with an unresolved issue outside of it – alerting to us to the possibility that there might have been more serious safeguarding issues for us to address. The readings/approaches we *might* have chosen required us, as adult-teachers, not only to be aware, via self-analysis, of the complexities of our own subjectivities, but to remind ourselves that the child-learners we worked with were likely to be (and to feel) equally complex, if not more so – in ways that may not have been too dissimilar. To quote Ruti again:

> [W]hen we perceive the other as a living subject – as a singular creature absorbed in its own relentless and at times confusing process of becoming

– rather than as someone who either meets or fails to meet our ideals, we gain access to deeper levels of intersubjective possibility.

(Ruti, ibid.: 147)

In the case of Archie, in Chapter 5, I will be suggesting that a less-than-helpful form of *love*, in which the other is essentially understood as different and in need of special help (to be sought not in his teachers' own experiences and feelings but from agreed 'procedures'), coupled with an articulated *fear* of his perceived capacity to subvert, combine to resist the alternative understandings and approaches that psychoanalytically informed reflexivity of this kind might have brought. I will also float the idea that the very act of adopting a reflexive, psychoanalytically informed reading of such situations can divert the adult teacher's own immediate sense of anger or inadequacy, enabling less confrontational and less defensive engagements with a troubling student.

The second aspect of reflexivity ('Reflexivity 2'), which is by no means dependent upon the first (for reflexivity of the kind we have so far considered, aimed at personal development, does not have to be the precursor to acts of individual or collective resistance), returns us to the possible point of departure referred to earlier: the point, that is, at which a reflexive, psychoanalytically informed version of heightened self-awareness and self-empowerment looks 'outward' as it were, to critical analysis of the impact of material structures, systems and circumstances on our own and others' subjectivities – with the potential, perhaps even the invitation, to a wider, more overtly political personal or collective project that may be practical as well as psychical. In this other kind of reflexive project, which will be examined in more detail in Chapters 2 and 8, exploration of one's past life does not confine itself to interrelations with specific, identifiable others (for example, family members, ex-teachers, friends and enemies) but of interrelationships with society and its systems more widely, and of experiences of power in that wider context. As Foucault puts it, in arguing for 'radical reflexivity' as a practice of freedom, the subject within this reflexive turn is incited 'to learn to what extent the effort to think one's own history can free thought from what it silently thinks, *and so enable it to think differently*' (Foucault 1985: 9, emphasis added). Though such reflexivity can be essentially therapeutic for the teacher, it also brings with it the possibility of changed attitudes leading to changed *action* – directed not just toward improving one's students' learning and helping to make their experience of school more positive on a day-to-day basis, but to challenging the givens of a socio-economic, ideological status quo within which a classroom, a school and an education system are situated. This second, more outward-looking form or aspect of reflexivity requires our critical engagement not just with the social systems and cultures within which our lives are lived and experienced, but with custom and with what might be called the ordinary: the everyday, whose status as normal is conferred, principally, by familiarity. While this does not of necessity involve what might be called direct action on the individual's part, it can help us to situate or envisage ourselves differently within the relations of power that contain us, so that 'active resistance' comes to be seen as a possibility, while non-active yet still subversive resistance may be experienced less troublingly. To quote Bailey, we may learn, via this reflexive process, to 'render more visible the complex "topology of power" (Collier 2009) in order to inform ways of subverting it' (Bailey 2015: 29). In this sense, this kind of reflexivity might be understood in the same terms as Foucault's notion of 'critique': that is to say, as 'the art of voluntary inservitude, of reflective indocility' (Foucault 1997: 386).

Reflexivity as theory and practice

Before leaving reflexivity – though leaving is perhaps not the right word since the concept will re-emerge repeatedly in the pages that follow – there are some further points that require clarification. The first is that psychoanalytically informed reflexivity is both a theory (related to understanding our selves and the world) and a strategy or practice (related more to overcoming specific challenges and problems in our professional and personal lives). The theoretical aspect does not require justification, any more or less than any other theory, although we might note, in passing, Falzon's observation that our concern as researchers and theorists attempting to make sense of the present 'is also a concern to *interrogate* the present, to undermine the self-evidence, necessity, and universality of its ruling forms, to eventualize and defamiliarize them, and open up the possibility of changing them' (Falzon 2013: 293). In short, the situation we are in needs to be recognised, artic- ulated, understood and examined if and before we are going to seek to take steps to challenge and change it, but also if we are going to be able to manage significant tensions in our professional lives. As a beginning teacher in one of the earlier studies I have mentioned (e.g. Moore and Ash 2001, 2003) put it:

> The pressure to do this and do that and prove to someone that you are doing it can make you forget what you actually believe is right and what you're doing here in the first place. You're so pushed into a position of responding that you just treat the status quo as the natural way of things and forget that actually it's run by people with maybe a completely different agenda [than] your own].

I want to suggest that the very same rationale identified by Falzon in relation to research and theory – to *challenge* the present, so to speak, and to 'defamiliarize' dominant 'ruling forms' in order to open up the possibility of a different future – applies equally to the reflexive project undertaken by individuals, and perhaps groups of individuals, in the practical context, regardless of which aspect or version of reflexivity we engage with. In making this challenge, the reflexive project attempts to '[bring] to light what was held in obscurity' (Pinar 2004: 55), in its 'refusal to forget the question of origin' (Pinar 2004: 57, referencing Lukacher 1986). It will be clear from what has already been proposed that the same princi- ple applies to 'inward-looking' reflexivity', in its encouragement to see 'ourselves as caused' rather than as somehow transcendental – revealing the true nature of reflexivity, that, although it might sometimes appear to be unidirectional, it actually looks inward and outward at the same time, always concerned with how the outside is 'internalised' and how, through the understandings of self brought about by this action, we can look differently at the outside – whether this outside is our own or others'. To reprise an earlier argument, the whole point of this form of reflexivity for the teacher lies (a) in its therapeutic potential, (b) in the changed perspectives and actions that are made possible as a result, which themselves can result in both improved practice and a more positive outlook. Negative feelings, rather than being understood as symptoms of failure, become windows through which to look at a difficulty from a different viewpoint. Rather than feeling that our Fate has been fixed, we recover a sense that our future, and who we might be(come) in that future, can, at least to a significant extent, still be written.

I have made a point of stressing the potential benefits of reflexivity, and its beneficial *intentions*, knowing that there is a criticism, not without connection to the one previously rehearsed in relation to applying psychoanalytic perspectives to everyday practice, theory and experience, that reflexivity can lead not to liberation and empowerment at all, but simply to a heightened feeling of inadequacy, failure and self-blame: in short, that it has the potential to do more harm than good, resulting in painful and/or self-indulgent introspection. It is true that close self-examination *can* have such negative effects – and also true that there exists a powerful counter-discourse, embedded within a wider neoliberal ideology (see Chapter 6, below), in which individuals are often encouraged to feel guilty, anxious and fearful: the other side, in essence, of the golden 'personal freedom/personal responsibility' coin that neoliberalism dispenses.

The difference between the kind of positive reflexivity I have been promoting and what we might call negative reflexivity (though I would suggest that the latter does not qualify as reflexivity) is neatly summed up by Pinar in his concept of '*currere*' as an 'intensified engagement with daily life' (Pinar 2004: 37) and in Lasch's broader distinction, cited by Pinar, between 'anxious self-scrutiny' and 'critical self-examination' (Lasch 1978: 94). Though he does not use the term, Pinar's *currere*, or more specifically what he refers to as its 'regressive phase' (regressive here in the sense that it takes us back into our history, rather than with any negative connotation), bears a marked similarity to the form(s) of reflexivity we have so far considered:

> There is, I think we can say, a relatively 'authentic' self, or selves, or elements of self. This is the person I was conditioned and brought up to be. When I am in touch with that 'self', and act in accordance with him or her, I feel congruent, integrated, 'right'. The regressive phase of *currere* is about uncovering this self, and in psychoanalytic fashion, experiencing the relief of understanding how one came to be psychically, which is to say, socially. For, as in psychoanalysis, bringing to light what was held in obscurity represents, in part, the therapeutic potential and consequence of self-reflective study.
>
> *(Pinar 2004: 55)*

Pinar adds: 'It is to oneself one comes to practice the autobiographics of self-shattering, revelation, confession, and reconfiguration. Self-excavation precedes the self-understanding, which precedes self-mobilization' (ibid.).

This 'regressive phase' of Pinar's is reminiscent of what is, effectively, another account of reflexivity offered by David Blacker (1998), in which reflexivity comprises 'not self-absorption, but being absorbed into the world: a "losing-finding" of the self … that avoids the pitfalls of both narcissistic aestheticism on the one hand, and the alienation of political obsession on the other' (Blacker 1998: 363) – to return to Pinar, one which precedes and subsequently interacts with a second, 'progressive' phase of *currere*. This second phase, moving us on from a re-engagement with our past in order to see how we have 'become', looks forward toward possible alternative futures (for ourselves, but perhaps for others too), which one is now able constructively and imaginatively to envision and to engage with. The possibility of this phase, Pinar says, 'is to discern how who one is hides what one might become', producing and embracing 'fictive representations of who I might be, what world I might inhabit in the future'. These fictive representations are 'the means by which we midwife what is not yet born, in ourselves, generated by others. They change where we are, how we feel, what we think' (ibid.: 55–56). Following such changes, and dependent upon them, is the third stage of *currere*, 'self-mobilisation', which resonates to a degree with what I have called Reflexivity 2, leading the individual from becoming changed to seeking to effect change – not necessarily alone but in the company of like-minded others. *Currere* as a whole is then understood as 'an ongoing project of self-understanding in which one becomes mobilized for engaged pedagogical action – as a private-and-public intellectual – with others in the social reconstruction of the public sphere' (ibid.: 37). From the point of view of *curriculum* theory and practice, *currere* in its fullness imposes on us the following challenge:

> Curriculum theory asks you, as a prospective or practicing teacher, to consider your position as engaged with yourself and your students and colleagues in the reconstruction of a public sphere, a public sphere not yet born, a future that cannot be discerned in, or even thought from, the present. So conceived, the classroom becomes simultaneously a civic square and a room of one's own.
>
> *(ibid.: 37–38)*

If the processes of – and moves between – self-excavation, self-understanding and self-mobilisation sound straightforward, they most certainly are not. The suggestion in *currere* is that, in order to enable self-understanding to develop most profitably, it is necessary to remove oneself, as much as possible, from carrying out that understanding within the limitations and limited affordances of externally imposed, pre-existing discourses. As I shall argue at greater length in Chapter 8, this requires, at the very least, an act of *refusal* (refusal, that is, to accept or to be colonised by these terms of engagement), but it might also, to return to Reflexivity 2, lead us toward more active *resistance*: that is to say, not just refusing to accept and internalise dominant discourses and ideologies but actively seeking to oppose and subvert them through some kind of action.

Neither refusal nor resistance comes easily, any more than Pinar's vision of the classroom as 'simultaneously a civic square and a room of one's own' – in each case having to confront the material obstacles of potential consequences and reprisals that active resistance brings, as well as the psychic obstacles of counter-resistance from many of those with whom and for whom we work. (Whether it is even possible to engage in genuine critique, given the extent to which criticism is inevitably conducted within the constraints and affordances of existing *language*, is a question over which philosophers continue to disagree.)[11] A particular difficulty returns us to a central preoccupation of this book, which concerns the nature and role of affect in how we lead and experience our private and professional lives: in particular, how affect can serve both to influence and to constrain our choices and how, without addressing affect as it operates within ourselves and within others with whom we come into contact, our endeavour to be reflexive, to be critical, to be resistant, to 'refuse', to 'imagine' and to 'become' in the way suggested by Pinar, is unlikely to meet with a great deal of success.

The problems of refusal and resistance will be returned to in subsequent chapters, but I will close this chapter with another quote from Pinar, serving as a reminder that for all these difficulties it is important for critical voices, including those of teachers, along with alternative ideologies and discourses, to be kept alive – that one should not be deterred when change does not happen quickly or appears to have little chance in the present conjuncture, and that sometimes it is necessary to play the longer game:

> Through remembrance of the past and fantasies of the future, I am suggesting, we educators might write our way out of positions of 'gracious submission'. Not in one fell swoop, not without resistance (both inner and outer). But creating passages out of the present is possible. We know that. That is why we believe in education; we see how powerfully schooling crushes it, and yet, still, there *is* education, despite the schools. There is God despite the church, justice despite the government, and love despite the family. We educators must prepare for a future when the school is returned to us and we can teach, not manipulate for test scores.
>
> *(Pinar 2004: 127)*

2

DISCOURSE, IDEOLOGY AND AFFECT

It is a wet, cool, overcast October day. Everyone is complaining about the weather and about the latest proposed changes to the National Curriculum – almost as though there is some connection between the two. Everyone, that is, except Susan, who tells me that she 'loves' this kind of weather, that it makes her feel 'safe' and 'contented'. 'I think it's because I have a couple of particularly fond memories from when the weather was just exactly like this', she tells me. 'Maybe that's why it makes me feel so … comfortable … and satisfied. I can worry about the government tomorrow!'

(Susan, Primary One: Fieldnote Entry)

What is affect?

I am aware that I have already used the term 'affect' several times without a proper gloss, in the hope (a) that it will either be familiar already or, if not, that its meaning will be partially discernible from the contexts in which it has occurred and (b) that my provisional, sketchy account in the first section of the previous chapter will suffice as a temporary measure. In order to make sense of what follows, though, it is necessary to offer a more precise explanation of how I will be using what is, indisputably, a somewhat slippery term.

To a degree, affect, like another term I will be using – 'discourse' – can mean what we decide it will mean from a smörgåsbord of possible meanings. This is not to say that its meaning is necessarily contested, but rather that it is understood from the start as negotiable. If this results in a certain slipperiness about some accounts of affect, it is partly because slipperiness is, in a sense, characteristic of affect itself. Indeed, the use of the term only partially disguises the resistance that the concept has to identification in the symbolic order, given that its concealed nature means that its presence is only demonstrable inferentially through observable *e*-ffects in physical and mental pleasure and pain.[1] As Gregg and Seigworth observe:

> There is no single, generalizable theory of affect: not yet, and (thankfully) there never will be. If anything, it is more tempting to imagine that there can only ever be infinitely multiple iterations of affect: theories as diverse and singularly delineated as their own highly particular encounters with bodies, affects, worlds.
>
> *(Gregg and Seigworth 2010: 1)*

If Gregg and Seigworth's suggestion seems immediately unhelpful, it at least underscores the importance of anyone using the term to be clear about how they are using it! My own use, and its distinction from emotions, is best summed up by Gregg and Seigworth themselves:

> Affect arises in the midst of *in-between-ness*: in the capacities to act and be acted upon. Affect is an impingement or extrusion of a momentary or sometimes more sustained state of relation *as well as* the passage (and the duration of passage) of forces or intensities. That is, affect is found in those intensities that pass from body to body (human, nonhuman, part-body, and otherwise), in those resonances that circulate about, between, and sometimes stick to bodies and worlds, *and* in the very passages or variations between those intensities and resonances themselves. Affect, at its most anthropomorphic, is the name we give to those forces – visceral forces beneath, alongside, or generally *other than* conscious knowing, vital forces existing beyond emotion – that can serve to drive us toward movement, toward thought and extension, that can likewise suspend us (as if in neutral) across a barely registering accretion of force-relations, or that can leave us overwhelmed by the world's apparent intractability. Indeed, affect is persistent proof of a body's never less than ongoing immersion in and among the world's obstinacies and rhythms, its refusals as much as its invitations.
>
> *(Gregg and Seigworth, ibid., original emphases)*

There is a lot to get to grips with here, and it's easy to see how hard the concept is to pin down – or rather how unwise it is to attempt to pin it down too firmly. The account offered by Gregg and Seigworth includes an understanding of affect as a 'hidden' (in the sense that it does not dwell in the realm of the conscious) *force*, that is also a *relation* (to some external 'impingement' or some internal 'extrusion') and a 'passage' of that force-relation. It is a force, a passage, a relation that is experienced at times as an *intensification* – of what we might call 'heightened feelings' – but also producing noticeable physical effects such as shaking, sweating, palpitations or psychosomatic pain, which might be either momentary or sustained over time (in the same way that a product of affect, a feeling or emotion such as fear, might be momentary or sustained over time). While affect in itself may be hidden from us and elusive, and therefore beyond conscious control, its effects – certainly, at those times of intensification – may be experienced and acknowledged in the conscious world. Affect is 'beyond' emotion, in the sense that it lies prior to the experience of an emotion, not just in relation to any given manifestation but also, perhaps, chronologically, in relation to the individual's development as a human subject. As Massumi (2013: xv) puts it, inviting both a comparison with and a distinction from instinct, affect is a 'prepersonal intensity'. That is to say, affect is 'within us' from birth, or even before birth, prior to our subjectification – not, however, as a hardwired and immutable entity but rather as a 'visceral', 'vital' life-force that is neither purely physical nor purely psychical, both being and existing in an 'in-be-tween-ness' – a central cause of its elusive identification. Affect can 'drive us toward movement' – energise us, push us to take a course of action that may itself be consciously taken – or 'suspend' us, perhaps rendering us incapable of a consciously experienced and determined response given its relation (as that of the physical body) to an ever-changing external/internal world of 'obstinacies and rhythms' which both invite us to action (at times, and of sorts) and obstruct our action (at and of others). As such, affect may be understood as a permanent *disposition* or set of dispositions (Shouse 2005; Sacks 1984) that orients and prepares us for action and for experience without requiring, and indeed without accepting, any conscious prompting or decision-making.

This notion of intensity, of heightened awareness, of affect being beyond conscious control, and of affect's 'alarming' effects on us physically and psychically – including its habit of impelling us to action (or even apparent in-action) – is neatly summed up in Tomkins' comparison between the affect mechanism and the pain mechanism:

> The affect mechanism is like the pain mechanism in this respect. If we cut our hand, saw it bleeding, but had no innate pain receptors, we would know we had done something which needed repair, but there would be no urgency to it. Like our automobile which needs a tune-up, we might well let it go until next week when we had more time. But the pain mechanism, like the affect mechanism, so amplifies our awareness of the injury which activates it that we are forced to be concerned, and concerned immediately.
>
> *(Tomkins 2008: 620)*

In other words, affect, always there within us latently or as potentiality, becomes manifest ('visible') as a wordless form of communication from the self to the self – in essence, from the body to felt experience. This intrusion of affect will either prompt some kind of responsive/reactive engagement with the situation or cir-cumstance or, if the engagement is, for whatever reason, unforthcoming, leave us in a state of numbness and inactivity that may result in anxiety or surrender. (As we shall see in the case study chapters, affect does not only come into play in relation to threats to our physical-psychic well-being; it also plays a central role in relation to our responses to and experiences of situations and circumstances that may appear to offer us potential benefit.)

If affect lies beyond our own conscious reach, this does not mean that it cannot be 'reached' or 'touched' – and thereby manipulated and taken advantage of – by forces in the 'external' contexts of our lives. Indeed, it is the capacity of affect to be manipulated, or to be touched by way of manipulating our consciously known choices of thought and action, that is one of the central concerns of this book. This is an issue that will be further explored in the following sections, as we consider the role of discourse in public education policy imposition and implementation, and the relationship between affect and ideology. In relation to developing under-standings of how central education policy (and, in passing, other central policy) 'works' – how it is received, made sense of, recontextualised and managed – within schools and classrooms by teachers and students, I am particularly interested in the impact of affect in relation to what we do (how we act), how we are acted upon (by circumstances and by the policies and actions of others), and how we inter-act with a world, and with events, that remain to a great extent beyond our control. I will be exploring, through the testimonies of teachers, the tensions that may arise when what we wish to do (what we *feel to be right*) does not chime happily with what we are told to do (what we are *told is right*) – not just at the level of consciousness and rational choice, but because affect, wherever it comes from, and whether it is understood as constructed or as natural, will guide us, direct us, orient us, in ways that we may never have known about or understood.

The limiting or enhancing/encouraging effect of affect on one's capacity to act is crucial here, but also the way in which affect can be used and manipulated in the conscious world of emotionality and rationality by one actor or set of actors in relation to another or others: a manipulation that takes place through something of a linguistic/discursive assault on affect's visible and conscious products: that is to say, on our feelings and emotions. What is it that attracts some people to certain roles and discourses, that makes them relish certain events and situations? What it is that repels others – or perhaps repels the same people at other times – in relation to those same roles, discourses, events and situations? What is the nature of the interaction between whom one has 'become' as a result of previous experiences (as a child, at home, at school, in the wider world) and whom one is encouraged or persuaded or coerced to become within political, cultural and hegemonic discourse?

If there is a theory lurking here, it is that emotions and feelings – most notably, fear and love, but also guilt, shame, embarrassment, feelings of being personally responsible – all of which may be momentary or chronic, one-off or repeated – act as drivers to educational work in both teachers and students, and that affect, which lies behind such feelings and emotions, can be manipulated via linguistic/discursive intrusions in order to produce forms of active and passive compliance. Of particular interest in this regard is how even manifestly resistant teachers – that is to say, teachers who are ideologically, philosophically and emotionally resistant to imposed education policy or aspects of it – are manipulated into becoming the willing or unwilling bearers of public policy *and of public policy discourse and ideology*, not just out of a practical and understandable need to survive (to remain in work, to continue to receive an income, to support students to succeed within whatever system is imposed upon them), but also in more subtle ways that are connected to psychic issues such as wanting to fit in or not wanting to be seen as causing difficulties.[2]

The affected teacher: Abigail, Simonetta and Marsha

This is all rather abstract. Perhaps the best way of clarifying things is to offer some concrete, albeit somewhat speculative, examples.

The first of these illustrates the simultaneously hidden and powerful nature of affect, including its power to impose reluctant repetition. It concerns the kind of personal experience that most of us will be familiar with when we find ourselves embarking on a course of action or taking an important choice in relation to something that we simultaneously do and do not want to do or to happen – or find ourselves experiencing what is sometimes called 'guilty pleasure' when there is a mismatch between the negative *thoughts* we may have about some thing or event or attraction and the positive *feelings* it can nevertheless, in spite of ourselves, engender.

One of the main respondents from my current study, Abigail, is a senior leader at Secondary Two. She informed me that all through her teaching career she had found herself repeatedly applying, usually very successfully, for management-oriented positions that would take her away from the things that she most enjoyed doing and that she felt 'reasonably good at' – in particular, the various elements that make up teaching:

> Why would I do such a thing, not once but over and over again, each time knowing that I don't like management posts, and they don't play to my strengths, or give me the job satisfaction I need? In my more rational moments I could tell myself I didn't want to do it, but I went ahead anyway. Why? There seemed to be some hidden force pushing me. I could feel it there … something saying 'Do it. Do it', even though I knew it wasn't right for me.

Although on one level, which we might call the cognitive level, in which she could make considerations consciously, Abigail did not want to take management posts (which were nearly all promotions), on another level, which we might call the affective level, in which decisions appeared to be made by forces over which she seemed to have no control, she did. In other words, affect had primacy over reason in the decision-making process.[3] Aha, we might say: But could it not simply be that it was actually the promise of greater financial rewards offered by these promotions that was the main reason for Abigail's applying for them, and that it was this essentially practical concern that had primacy over her deep-seated reluctance to do something she did not, at this other level, want to do? Well, yes, it is possible. However, Abigail's subsequent accounts indicated very clearly that money (seen as spending power) had never been an issue for her – particularly given that her husband earned a six-figure salary from his own job and that she already enjoyed what she described as a 'very comfortable and actually very privileged lifestyle'. The issue for Abigail seemed to have had far more to do with the higher *status* offered by the promotions and what this meant to her:

> To put it crudely, I suppose it made me feel better about myself. It was an indication that I was 'somebody'. I'd been, you know, 'recognised'. I'd arrived! [Laughs] Again! … I actually wanted to do something I didn't like doing, if that makes any kind of sense. I mean, for one thing, it actually took away my capacity for independence. It took away the distance I'd always tried to maintain from systems. I mean, I've never really liked what's been going on politically, with all this results-driven stuff and, you know, I can see other people getting really happy when their kids do well and I can feel that a bit I suppose, but there's always this nagging voice: 'Yes, but what are they actually achieving that makes it so wonderful and worthwhile?' And that does make you feel like a bit of an outsider too. Worse: an outsider who is actually in charge of supporting the system. … So I knew each time the job would give me all kinds of grief, but at the same time it would justify my existence. … Maybe I've just had to accept the grief as the cost of feeling better about myself – even though these jobs actually don't make me feel any better about myself at all, and I'd really be much more happy on a day-to-day basis spending most of my time in the classroom.

Whenever we feel uncertainty in the face of such life-shaping choices, the roots of that uncertainty will almost certainly lie in the realm of affect, even though we may not be fully aware of it – masked, as it is always likely to be, by apparently analytic thought in the conscious, articulable world of rational conversation. Abigail appeared to recognise the existence of something we might call affect (a 'hidden force') impelling her to make a choice that in the conscious, rational world she was inclined to reject, but the recognition of its existence was not enough to reduce its power and its primacy, and, as she started to explain, it carried with it a certain resistance to critical engagement: she either could not or chose not to learn more about its nature, and perhaps, therefore, to seek to override it. It was not that she did not want the management posts; it was more that a part of her did not want them while another part, that remained stubbornly removed from rational engagement, did. Her subsequent acknowledgment that she may have been repeatedly and with reservations driven to take a course of action because her fragile ego demanded some form of recognition and validation is one that will be familiar, I suspect to many readers, and that was certainly evident in my discussions with many other teachers, as well as, in other ways, in previous studies, with young students. It is also something I can identify with in relation to my own private and professional biographies!

The desire for validation, to feel a sense of socially and symbolically belonging, to have evidence from 'outside' of one's worth, is one that emerged very strongly in my earlier studies, and one that has been reported on elsewhere (see, for example, the case of 'Bill' in Moore [2004, 2006] and below in Chapters 3 and 6, where it is discussed in terms of Lacan's and Žižek's accounts of symbolic and imaginary identification). It also resonates with Judith Butler's account, summarised by Amy Allen, of how subjection 'works at the psychic level by exploiting our primary narcissism, our basic desire for recognition' (Allen 2008: 173). Another useful lens into understanding such feelings and behaviours comes from Sara Ahmed's theorising around the idea of social – and in this case institutional – *alienation*. Ahmed writes, in relation to 'objects' imbued with 'happiness' that circulate as 'social goods':

> When we feel pleasure from such objects, we are aligned; we are facing the right way. We become alienated – out of line with an affective community – when we do not experience pleasure from proximity to objects that are already attributed as being good. The gap between the affective value of an object and how we experience an object can involve a range of affects, which are directed by the modes of explanation we offer to fill this gap.
>
> *(Ahmed 2010a: 37)*

In one sense, Abigail's understanding of promotion – related to higher status embedded within what she calls 'the system', and reflected in the financial rewards it attracts – was that promotion was a 'good object' from which could be derived genuine pleasure and lasting happiness. The reality, the felt experience of the object once (re-)attained, produced a misalignment which rendered the object unappealing but that was nevertheless insufficient to render it durably 'bad'. Each time the object appeared in the guise of a different post, it could be perceived as intrinsically different from its previous incarnations, bringing with it again, albeit temporarily, the prospect of a happiness that was, inevitably, bound to be elusive.

Abigail's apparently perverse pursuit of something she said she did not want is by no means an uncommon occurrence in my research data, repeating itself in very similar ways in the written and spoken testimonies of several teachers, both in the present and in previous studies. It was most prevalent in middle and senior managers – deputy or assistant headteachers, or heads of secondary-school departments – who would often link comments like 'I should have just remained a class teacher; there would have been much less stress' (Peter, Head of Year at Secondary Two) with what sounded like a simultaneous glorification and mourning for a lost golden past. To quote Peter again: 'I could just get on and teach, you know. Would it be the same if I took a step down now? I'm not sure. I'd give it a try, anyway. It could hardly be worse than this!' – the 'this' referring both to his current job in general and to a particular incident he had been recently struggling with involving a series of complaints about a member of his Year team.

Others, however, were in pursuit of something they felt they *did* want: something that had the appearance of a fantasy and was therefore quite unachievable in spite of their relentless pursuit of it. One respondent, Angus, spoke repeatedly of how he found it impossible to remain for more than two or three years in any one school, always seeking out the position from which he was 'actually able to achieve something positive'. Another, Rosemary, would tell me of her endless reworking of a scheme of work, whose perfection constantly eluded her. Perhaps the most striking examples, however, were provided by Simonetta, a young Italian teacher and Head of Subject at Secondary Two, and by Marsha, a teacher at Primary One who talked passionately about how the job had changed and how the only thing stopping her from quitting altogether was her unpaid mortgage. My fieldnotes relating to Simonetta include the following:

Simonetta is surprisingly open about things with me, happily sharing personal issues that many might feel are more appropriately kept to themselves. Whether she is always like this, or whether she simply sees in me a harmless confidant, I don't know. Like most of the other languages teachers at Secondary Two, she tends to spend any non-contact time in the office of the languages suite. However, she comes into the staffroom Period 2 on Wednesdays to do some marking, when I am often the only other person in the room, catching up on my own notes. It's on these occasions that she will sometimes share her frustrations with me.

I have learned that there are two problems that particularly disturb her. One is that she has been registered for a PhD degree at Central University,[4] which she has been following on a part-time basis for eight years, including various approved interruptions to cope with life events such as changing jobs, moving house and the serious illness of a close relative in Italy. It seems that she is no nearer to completing her thesis than she was six or seven years ago, even though it appears, from what she has told and shown me, that everything she needs for it is in place. She talks repeatedly of needing to get it finished, of how it will change her life, opening up for her possibilities for moving into higher education, which, she says, is where she eventually wants to be. But she needs time, she says, and everything else always gets in the way. I ask her why it is so difficult to prioritise the PhD work, and it becomes clear from her replies that she feels that life and life's events control her, that she is perpetually being 'done to', having to respond to an incessant flow of demands related to paid work and family. She tells me that her current partner, whom she had initially hoped and planned to marry, does not understand this, feeling that she should take more control of events. He complains to her that she does not contact him to tell him she has been held up at school by meetings that overrun or were unplanned, or simply because she has lost track of the time doing her marking. He does not understand the nature of her working life, she tells me. He feels that her failure to keep him in touch is disrespectful, that it is indicative of a lack of love. She feels he is childish in this regard, that he is insecure and not the man she had thought he was. An assiduous perfectionist in her marking and lesson preparation, she is equally so, it seems, in her academic writing and in her expectations of her partner. From the outside, it seems highly unlikely that she will ever complete her thesis or find in her partner the man she would like him to be, and so the unfulfilled desire for both lives on, the quest for perfection continues. I speculate privately that it is precisely because the desire lives on and the quest continues that 'completion' in both areas of her life might always evade her, that in fact there is something about and within her that has silently, invisibly, rejected completion.

I wonder if Abigail's and Simonetta's optimistic quest, their belief in the possibility of a better present-to-be than the present they currently inhabit, is self-sustaining – if it is necessary to keep on failing to find something approaching perfection, as with Peter and his constant changes of job, that if the ideal present ever were achieved the quest would no longer have any meaning. I'm reminded of Lauren Berlant's account of such faux optimism:

> Whatever the *experience* of optimism is in particular … the *affective* structure of an optimistic attachment involves a sustaining inclination to return to the scene of the fantasy that enables you to expect that *this* time, nearness to the thing will help you or a world to become different in just the right way.
>
> *(Berlant 2011: 2)*

In the conscious, rational, everyday world of getting up, going to work, doing the job, it may well be that teachers like Abigail, Simonetta and Peter believe not only that things can be better but that every fibre of their being (to use a favourite expression of Peter's) *wants them to be bette*r. The presence of affect suggests otherwise, inviting a more Lacanian account (Lacan 1977, 1979): that what drives them is not the attainment of a better future, but the pursuit itself.

Another teacher in the current study, Marsha, who works at Primary One, revealed herself to be likewise less than contented with her current lot. Unlike Abigail, Simonetta and Paul, however, she had little faith that things would ever get better, either for her or for public education generally. In Marsha's case, optimism was directed more to a belief that, if she could not realistically hope for a better future, she could at least hope for a more comfortable subjectivity. Shortly after my initial meeting with Marsha, I learned that she had recently taken up yoga again – something she had been very keen on as a younger woman. In interview, she had been one of the teachers most passionately and vociferously opposed to a great deal of current government education policy, not least its insistence on over-emphasising phonics in the teaching of reading and in what she saw as pointless, waste-of-time handwriting exercises and spelling tests. She found resistance difficult and painful, however – a perpetual and often isolated struggle. She told me that attending a yoga class on Monday evenings at a local sports centre had given her back the strength she needed to cope with and perpetuate her resistance. Talking to her, though, it felt as if the yoga classes had simply made her more relaxed about things, giving her what she called 'a different perspective on things'. Having told me that she had previously stopped going years ago because she had felt her fellow attendees were overly competitive, she added:

Going to yoga again's actually been fantastic, more than I ever thought it would be. I'd forgotten how good it was. Every Monday night, it just takes me out of myself. It makes me realise there's a lot more to life than work, and I really need to look after *me* a bit better. Did I say? I've joined the Saturday morning class now too.

I felt that yoga may have helped Marsha's general sense of well-being, but it had not helped her at all to fight against the things that troubled her. Indeed, it appeared to have effectively withdrawn her from the fight, taking her away from the pain and stress of the battlefield to a calmer, more comfortable place in which to experience life. What had been a site of ideological struggle had now, it seemed, been simplified, characterised and domesticated as just 'work'.

In each of these examples, there appears to be a conflict between the choices taken in the realm of consciousness, in actual life so to speak, and the less overt but more dominant choices made by and in the realm of affect. Abigail's part-recognition of her difficulty – that she required some form of validation – calls to mind again Lacan's and Žižek's theorising around imaginary and symbolic identification, and the need we may have of a 'symbolic mandate' (Žižek 1989: 106; see also Chapter 8 below), whereby we seek not only the affection and acknowledgment of others but also to acquire a sense of justification for the life-roles we have chosen for ourselves or that have otherwise befallen us. If this part-recognition did not result in a change of action or an obvious reduction in the tensions Abigail experienced, this may have been because she remained (like Simonetta, perhaps) wedded *to* the tension, perceiving it as an almost inevitable feature of her life. Perhaps to challenge her affective choices was simply more demanding and, at least in the short term, more debilitating than the effort required to continue to live *with* tension. Marsha, meanwhile, who had re-adopted yoga ostensibly by way of strengthening her resolve in her battle of resistance, appeared to have found a way of coping better with the uncomfortable tensions she was feeling, in that yoga helped her achieve a calmer, less tense, more accepting professional existence – not so much because of the claimed physical and spiritual effects of yoga itself but because yoga provided a new source of focus for her, along with an illusion of renewed psychic strength: a diversion, rather than a renewed engagement, involving a certain re-capture of past pleasures ('I had forgotten how good it was'). Marsha, it seemed, had found something else to think about, that may not have completely displaced or replaced her concerns about 'what education policy is doing to children', but that had rendered it less pressing and less de-pressing – something that she (perhaps euphemistically) described as giving her a 'new perspective'.

There is nothing wrong with any of this, of course, and we might argue that Marsha was simply, perhaps even wisely, taking care of herself. Nor is there anything particularly unusual about therapeutically seeking to restore a past feeling. However, it does shed some important light on the power of affect not just to drive us to critical activity but to curtail or to block it. Of particular interest in Marsha's account, not just of her yoga classes but of her repeated references back to the way education 'used to be', is the feeling of retrieval, of resurrection, of preservation that appeared to comfort her. As we shall see in subsequent chapters, loss, and the fear of loss, has a very powerful affective effect on people. Equally important, however, is the possibility of the retrieval of that-which-has-been-lost – so much so that even if that-which-is-lost was never actually lost at all (or perhaps never actually existed at all), even if it is pure fantasy, the lost object, along with its potential return, may still be embraced and believed in. (In the UK, this is something we have seen in recent years, in certain politicians' repeated attempts to restore a 'lost' traditionalist education of the past, but also in many teachers' recollections of a golden past of lost progressivist education. We have seen it, too, on the wider political stage, in 'Brexiteers' in the UK and in Donald Trump and his followers in the USA, promising voters to, respectively, 'get our country back' and 'make America great again'.)

A psychoanalytically informed approach to understanding tensions such as those experienced by Abigail, Simonetta and Marsha is not the only one, of course, and it does not necessarily provide a solution (although, as is implicit in what has been argued thus far, 'solution' might not be quite the right word anyway). We may never know if Abigail's desire for validation might have been removed, reduced or replaced as the result of such an understanding, and whether, if so, this would have enabled her to embark on a revised – not so much more comfortable as more fulfilling – engagement with her present, or if Simonetta, likewise, might have broken off her quest for the mythical perfect partner or ideal job. What the approach does do – and this is the only claim that is made here – is that it makes such understandings *possible and valid*, opening the way for new conversations with ourselves and with one another that might just help us see a clearer, more productive way through some of the professional and personal difficulties that may beset us.

'Sticky attachments': policy, discourse and affect

I want to turn now to considering in a little more detail the inter-connectedness between affect and *policy*, including the role of discourse in encouraging teachers to become not just the mediators but the bearers of dominant ideologies. In so doing, I will elaborate further on the nature of that affective 'stickiness' (Ahmed 2010a) that attaches us to certain ideas and practices – even those we may be consciously and openly critical of. It is my hope that this will, in turn, encourage readers to explore, in the contexts of their own experience, the nature of affect – including the manner in which affect can be manipulated to promote compliance – as well as why resistance to imposed policy, even when such resistance is felt rather than actioned, can make us feel so very uncomfortable. (As one respondent in the current study, John, put it: 'Logically, I shouldn't feel so bad about disagreeing with [elements of mandated policy]. It's hard enough having to do stuff that I fundamentally disagree with, but I can't even feel comfortable with my opposition – like I almost feel there's something wrong with me: especially when I see other colleagues just getting on with it without complaining'.)

I want to suggest that there are at least two ways in which anybody may be manipulated affectively, even though the power *to* manipulate may not be evenly distributed:

1   Through a direct appeal to deep-seated affective states and orientations: for example, our orientation or disposition in relation to how, both consciously and unconsciously, we experience, anticipate and respond to *loss*, or our deep-seated desire to 'belong', to be accepted.

2   Through language and discourse less directly – in processes whereby words and phrases become attached or attach themselves to positive and negative feelings (or vice versa), such that the feeling remains even if the actual/original meanings or understandings of the word or phrase change, or even if it comes to express something we may continue, consciously, to find repugnant.[5]

An illustration, introduced very briefly in the previous section, of the first of these manipulations can be found outside the field of formal education in the UK's recent referendum on whether or not to remain in the European Union. It was widely reported at the time that the voting public were furnished with very few facts and details on which to make a sound judgment on this very important matter, and indeed it has since transpired that some of the information that *was* supplied was false. This might be seen by some as a matter of incompetence or poor communication. However, it was very clear during the course of political campaigning leading up to the vote itself that the main appeal to voters, on the part both of those urging us to vote leave and of those urging us to vote remain, was an affective one. Those arguing to 'remain', for example, tapped into *fear* – particularly, our fear of the unknown, of what might happen if things were to change: concentrating this fear around material fears and concerns about potential loss of income and jobs. Loss and fear also featured in much of the 'leave' campaign, whose proponents tapped into existing deep-rooted fears about loss of control as an unchecked army of Eastern European immigrants was said to be flooding into the country under current arrangements, and even of loss itself – the fantasised loss of a whole country, and the opportunity now to seize it back into 'our' ownership. (In reality, of course, the UK had never been 'lost' or stolen, or 'taken away' or gone missing. Since joining the European Union, it had carried on pretty much as it had always done. However, once the myth had been sold to enough people that the country was, indeed, gradually being taken away from 'us', that 'we' were being run and dictated to by other countries and other organisations, the vote to leave was relatively easily secured: 'Your country is being taken from you. Are you happy with that, or do you want it back?' Surely, only those rejecting the initial premise and focussing their attention on other issues would be likely to vote to remain![6])

   This affective appeal of policy does not only apply to specific, individual policy initiatives. It also applies to the wider political ideologies within which such initiatives occur and are framed. As McChesney argued, writing in 1999 of a particular political and economic ideology – that of neoliberalism – as practised and experienced at the time in the United States (though clearly little has changed in the intervening years):

> [N]eoliberal initiatives are characterized as free market policies that encourage private enterprise and consumer choice, reward personal responsibility and entrepreneurial initiative, and undermine the dead hand of the incompetent, bureaucratic and parasitic government, that can never do good even if well intended, which it rarely is. A generation of corporate-financed public relations efforts has given these terms and ideas a near sacred aura. As a result, the claims they make rarely require defense, and are invoked to rationalize anything from lowering taxes on the wealthy and scrapping environmental regulations to dismantling public education and social welfare programs.
>
> *(McChesney 1999: 7–8, emphases added)*

Policy's widespread appeal not just to positives but also to negatives has already been touched on in relation to the testimonies of Abigail, Simonetta and Marsha and will be returned to in the case studies that follow. It is there also, in a different way, in McChesney's citation of 'incompetent', 'bureaucratic' and 'parasitic'.[7]

McChesney's account offers an introduction to the second kind of affective-discursive manipulation I want to consider, one which will be very familiar to teachers in England, bombarded as they are with terms like 'professional[ism']', 'aspiration[al]' and 'social mobility', typically embedded within central government policy and discourse related to 'raising educational standards' – a manipulation which very specifically and in a very focussed way uses language as its major weapon in seeking to ensure ideological compliance.

We need look no further for illustrations of this technique than McChesney's references to the positively and negatively charged terms 'enterprise', 'choice', 'reward', 'bureaucratic' and 'parasitical', or to the following pronouncement, emanating from the recent UK Conservative-Liberal Democrat Coalition government, in relation to proposed developments in Higher Education:

> [The Coalition *vision* for Higher Education] is a simpler, more *flexible* system which gives students *better value* and *greater choice*. That means a *more diverse* range of providers should be able to play a role. It means funding for teaching should follow the *choices that students make*. And it means *empowering students* to make their own choices based on *better, more transparent information*.
>
> *(David Willetts: 2012, Minister of State for Higher Education and Science,*
> *emphasis added)*

Naturally, we all want to sign up to these ideas, to embrace and endorse the terminology – and our very affective attachment may push us into using them ourselves, even to 'identify' with them, drawn in by affective attachment to their positive inflections to such an extent that we come to use the language independently (a crucial first step to our becoming the bearers of its embedded ideology), rather than to challenge it. Who, after all, would not want to support and identify with freedom and choice? Isn't it good to have 'vision', to keep things simple, to be flexible within systems which are themselves flexible enough to allow us to be, to have better value, more diverse options, to be empowered and informed by more 'transparent' government?

The use of such positive language is by no means confined to Higher Education policy discourse. Teachers working within the compulsory education sector will be all too familiar with the same terms deployed by Willetts, along with many others such as 'resilience', 'challenge' and 'responsibility' – and also, perhaps, with how such concepts can animate an affective and 'neuronal' conception of the *self* (Pitts-Taylor 2010; Bailey 2015; see also Worsnip 2012, on 'pragmatism'). As Apple (2006: 8) put it some years ago, current ('rightist') education policy refers to and promulgates 'an assemblage of … words that have an emotional valence and that provide support for the ways in which differential power works in our daily lives'. It is only when – and if – we take into account the wider political, social and economic contexts within which such positively saturated terms are sold that we can feel justified in *not* signing up to them – or rather, not signing up to them in the particular guise in which they are being advertised: although even here affect may work against our conscious efforts. As Allen, after Judith Butler, observes, reminding us in the process of the limits and potential limitations of reflexivity:

> [P]ower and subjection take hold of subordinated subjects at the psychic and affective level, producing an attachment to subordinating modes of identity that is capable of surviving even after such modes have been rationally demystified.
>
> *(Allen 2008: 183)*

In other words, even though we may 'see behind' and expose to ourselves the affective manipulations with which we are managed, we may still behave as successfully manipulated subjects. To flag the example of current discourses of 'professionalism' (elaborated in Moore and Clarke 2016, and below in Chapter 6), in which professionalism is effectively [re]cast in terms of carrying out mandated policy as intended, we might find ourselves falling in line practically and rhetorically with a revised, rebranded concept of professionalism – perhaps criticising colleagues or ourselves in relation to its revised meaning – even as we continue to believe in, to talk about and to adhere philosophically and ideologically to other, previous meanings of the term.

Affect, discourse and ideology

We are now in a position to trace the beginnings of an understanding concerning the relationship between affect, discourse and ideology as played out in the education policy context – one to which I shall return later on in considerations of what we know as *propaganda*: that is to say, an investigation into the ways in which public policy constructs, deploys and naturalises discourse (and indeed individual and popular opinion) to substantiate ideology through a direct appeal to and reliance on affect.

As elsewhere (e.g. Moore 2004), I am using the term discourse throughout this book to denote a system of representation, largely expressed and promoted through language but being 'more than language alone', in and through which dominant ideologies are conveyed and disseminated – in the same way that words may be seen as conveying and disseminating ideas. Dominant *ideologies*, meanwhile, are understood as systems of ideas 'that promote the interests of a particular group of people' (Holliday 2011: 98), who utilise discourse as a way of presenting, packaging and selling those ideas. Though we might speak with justification of *alternative* discourses and ideologies, or of *counter*-discourses and ideologies, I am focussing on *dominant* discourses and ideologies (Moore, 2004) and on the exercise of power to which they are conscripted. Fundamental to these understandings of ideology and discourse is that they do not represent 'reality'; rather they construct reality, or particular, partial versions of it (see also Ball 2008: 5). As Eagleton (1991: 223) argues, ideology represents 'the points where power impacts upon certain utterances and inscribes itself tacitly within them' – a process by which words (and not only words, but images and practices too) are invested with ideas that lurk virus-like, almost invisibly, within them, their presence masked by surface meanings as understood and used in the simple act of practical communication.[8]

Sometimes – often, indeed – an ideology and a discourse can be identified in terms of the same language, so that, for example, a discourse of 'competition' (in which competition is to be understood as intrinsically good, saturated with positivity), which promotes competitiveness in education and in economic practice and policy, can be said to be the bearer of an *ideology* of competition. What makes competition (and competitiveness) an ideology is its necessity in materialising free-market capitalism – a system which, in line with Holliday's definition quoted above, serves the interests of particular groups of people at the expense of the interests of others. Competition is thus, in a sense, a notion of how society should be organised and indeed self-perceive – one which must have its parallel in the life of each individual subject. Competition and competitiveness are not the only bases upon which society might be structured. Nor are they intrinsically 'good'. However, we must be persuaded to believe not only that they *are* intrinsically good – and 'healthy' – but also that they are *naturally* so, and that 'normal people' will recognise them as such. Teachers and school students in many countries will need no reminding of the dominant role played by competitiveness and competition, latterly morphing into a wider ideology and discourse of performativity, in their daily lives at school – not only in relation to public tests and examinations, through the abiding dominance of competitive sports in physical education and through the promotion and resilience of pedagogies in which students are predominantly required to learn and work on their own rather than in groups, but in relation to competition *between* schools, often underscored and encouraged by externally imposed grades and 'league tables'. While many teachers may struggle to embrace such competiveness, students are encouraged to love it and to succeed within it – to get a positive feeling when they do better than their peers, to embrace it and absorb it even as they may experience, on a regular basis, the negative feelings – the anxiety, the fear, the stress – that it can also produce. What they are not encouraged to do, any more than are their parents and teachers or for that matter any of us, is to challenge the story they are often told about the relationship between hard work and obedience on the one hand and social and financial betterment on the other: in particular (to anticipate a point to be raised later on in an account of *Results Day*), that although some of us may succeed 'beyond our station', not all of us can: the System simply does not allow it.[9]

Discourse (of course) is not, as Foucault (1994) argues, the only thing that operates to persuade us to do or not to do, to think or not to think. The actuality of an Ofsted inspection, for example, such as that described in more detail in Chapter 7 below – the viscerally experienced presence of inspectors in school, the physical and mental effort involved in preparation and performance – serves as a poignant reminder that discourse is but one element, albeit a key element, in a wider technique and politics of control, a collection identified by Foucault in the expression '*dispositif*'.

Dispositif comprises a 'heterogenous combination of discourses, institutions, architectural edifices, regulatory decisions, laws, administrative measures, scientific pronouncements and philosophical, moral and philanthropic propositions' (Foucault 1994: 299) – all working in combination to prompt direction and to maintain high levels of social and psychic conformity. The various elements of *dispositif* not only combine to contain discourse, but are also impregnated by it and render it operational ('le mettent en oeuvre': Veyne 2008: 19: see also Veyne 2010) – so that discourse has a triple function within the *dispositif*: as an element working in combination with others, as a powerful force in its own right with its own particular character and *modus operandi*, and as an element that can colour and give character to the *dispositif* as a whole. As Bailey (2015: 38–39) elucidates, the *dispositif* can include a whole range of institutional and discursive, but also regulatory and moral elements and practices. In public education, for example, it might comprise the regulatory element of inspection and public examination systems, along with the moral imperative for us to achieve the greatest success for the greatest number of students within those given elements, within a given system, and within a plethora of dominant but interconnected discourses of performativity, aspiration, equity and so forth. *Dispositifs* can be either 'molar' (broader, more universal in application, less contingent) or 'micro' (relating to more specific programmes, events or local practices):

> Whilst a heterogeneous, productive and 'singular' formation of discursive and non-discursive elements of education policy can (albeit partially) be plotted (a *molar-dispositif*), it is also possible to identify within this ensemble hegemonic codifications and configurations, and also individual mechanisms and tactics, such as organisations, programmes, or events (*micro-dispositifs*).
>
> *(Bailey 2015: 39)*

Teachers will immediately be aware of their own insertion in *dispositif*, as soon as they begin to describe schools and classrooms and the various elements that combine to create formal education: the pre-selected curriculum, the encouraged and/or adopted pedagogies, the physical arrangement of desks and chairs in the classroom, the wall displays, the school's architecture, the various school policies, the codes of dress and behaviour, the structure of the school day and year, the means of communication of information, the staffing structure, the decision-making processes, the agenda selection processes for staff meetings, the test and examination criteria, the performance management process, the very *existence* or otherwise of a performance management process, and so on and so forth. All of these elements combine to make the teaching and learning experience what they are and to ensure that a pre-defined model and set of practices of education are complied with by both teachers and students. Both jointly and severally, they are reflective of, supportive of and underpinned by key – sometimes apparently contradictory – discourses and preferred models or understandings of society, of humanity and of social behaviour – most typically, perhaps, a dominant neoliberal view that favours competition between individuals in line with a wider free market 'globalising' world.

3
FEAR AND LOVE

Fear

The pursuit, via reflexivity, of visibility and subversion referenced in previous chapters is made especially difficult by two particular affective aspects of teachers' lives which themselves may need to be rendered more visible before any wider advances can be made. These, which will feature prominently in the pages that follow, are fear and love: in particular, the fear that is engendered by failure and by a new zero-tolerance culture in relation to perceived 'weakness', and the love for others and sometimes for our self that pushes us to do things that we feel are in the immediate material interests of our students even when we may feel that they are not helpful at all – and possibly damaging – in the longer term. (As an example, this is a love that may find us ceaselessly pursuing a didactic, front-of-class pedagogy in order to ensure good SAT or public examination grades for our students, even though we may feel that this represents a rather poor form of education for them and a less than adequate preparation for their future lives.) This short chapter will explore the effects of fear and love in teachers' lives in a little more detail, by way of introducing and providing more context for the data-driven chapters that follow. If more space is devoted to considerations of the nature and role of fear, this should not be taken as a suggestion that love is less important than fear, but because fuller discussions of the nature and power of (teachers') love occur more naturally in the case studies in Chapters 4–7.

The presence – we might say, the role – of fear in public policy and the operations of national governments, including its role in Foucault's notion of 'governmentality (2000a)',[1] is well documented. It is an essential element of what Naomi Klein (2008) has called 'disaster capitalism', whereby governments create and take advantage of national crises and exploit the fear and distraction engendered by such crises to push through potentially unpopular policies. It is also an aspect of what Rose (2001, 2006), Žižek (2009) and others, after Foucault (2010), have elaborated in relation to 'biopolitics'[2]: in Žižek's words (2009), 'a politics of fear' whereby central government's prime role becomes one of the physical protection of its electorate in the face of real or imagined threats.

Fear also has a long history when it comes to the lives of school teachers and students. Almost a century ago Mark Starr, in his excellent but little-known book *Lies and Hate in Education*, described school teachers as living in a 'dangerous atmosphere of "Safety First"', in which they were afraid to experiment or be innovative as they carried out their work within an oppressive dominant ideology in which such deviant behaviour as '[a]cknowledged possession of heterodox opinions, refusal to distribute medals on Empire day, and any similar action' was likely to have potentially (and negatively) life-changing consequences, including ruling out any chances of ever obtaining a headship (Starr 1929: 23–24).

Thankfully, we do not live in quite the same educational world today as that described by Starr, in which, in England at least, the Church of England and Central Government combined so effectively in an overt mission to 'keep socialism out of school' (ibid.). However, if the evidence of my own research is anything to go by, fear of a not entirely dissimilar kind continues to stalk the classrooms and corridors of many schools: not generated simply by a politics of conservatism but also, increasingly, by one of change or 'reform' – a circumstance which has led Coffield and Williamson (2011: 48) to propose that: '[t]he main driving force for [educational] change in England has become fear: fear of poor exam results, fear of poor inspection grades, fear of sliding down the national league tables, and fear of public humiliation and closure' – adding, in an echo of Starr's reference to the negative impact of such fear on the quality of teaching and learning, 'Fear is inimical to learning'.

The implication in Coffield and Williamson's account that fear is not simply a consequence or an effect but that it is a deliberate policy strategy is endorsed by Stephen Ball's analysis of educational life in schools and universities in the public sector in England, which identifies the deliberate creation and utilisation of fear as a key strategy of wider discourses of performativity and judgmentalism. For Ball, performativity itself is 'a culture or a system of "terror"' in which 'the teacher, researcher and academic are subject to a myriad judgments, measures, comparisons and targets' (Ball 2008: 49–50). Lest we attribute such analyses (as some politicians and journalists are apt to do) to the ideological partiality of a small band of critical academics, it is worth reminding ourselves that politicians themselves are not always backward in coming forward when it comes to this matter. Not so long ago, the Conservative politician Oliver Letwin, in his role as Policy Minister in the UK Conservative-LibDem coalition government of 2010–2015, went on record as pronouncing:

> You can't have room for innovation and the pressure for excellence without having some real discipline and some fear on the part of the providers that

things may go wrong if they don't live up to the aims that society as a whole is demanding of them. … If you have diversity of provision and personal choice and power, some providers will be better and some worse. … Some will not survive. It is *an inevitable and intended consequence* of what we are talking about.[3]

> *(Letwin, quoted in the Observer newspaper, July 30th 2011,*
> *emphasis added)*

This kind of fear – the fear of very real economic and practical consequences of falling foul of government policy (for example, the fear of losing income or one's job) – we might call material or practical fear. It is typically related directly to an object, such as a judgment call or a policy demanding redundancies, but it may continue to exist in the form of anxiety when that object is not immediately present or observably imminent. Rather in the manner of Foucault's 'panopticon' metaphor of the workings of discourse and the development of self-monitored social behaviour (Foucault 1977), this material fear does not require the immediacy of the feared object in order to influence the subject's behaviour, since the object lurks ominously and perpetually in the form of a possible or likely future manifestation or event for whose possible existence and arrival one must always be prepared. It is the product of what Starr (ibid.: 11) called 'mental dictatorship' – a dictatorship that becomes so habitual as to efface itself in the eyes both of its agents and of its victims.

Whether we are talking about fear or anxiety (for a discussion of the proposed distinction, see Chapter 7 below), the actual or ever-impending event of a school inspection by a centrally appointed and managed team of school inspectors from the Office of Teaching and Standards in Education ('Ofsted') is known to generate a great deal of teacher stress (see, for example, Perryman 2009) and has certainly featured as one of the most talked-about experiences in my own studies. In her fascinating study of developments in teacher professionalism in the UK, Chun-Ying Tseng writes of teachers' perceptions of Ofsted inspectors and their parallel in the field of initial teacher education (the then 'Training and Development Agency') as being experienced as 'educational police', capable of spreading fear not only among practising teachers but among those charged with their training and education (Tseng 2013: 152). Drawing on her interview data, Tseng cites a former 'Additional Inspector's'[4] own felt sense of inspectors' presence in schools:

> People are always very frightened about inspections because of the impact they can have on their reputation. I mean Ofsted inspections are hugely important because of the power to shape your reputation. You know beyond your own institution … they are significant in shaping your funding, not directly because of Ofsted but because of what the [government] then does with the grades.

> *(Tseng ibid.: 154)*

A similar picture is drawn by another of Tseng's respondents, also a former Additional Inspector, talking of her own previous experience of being inspected and remembering what the atmosphere was like when her institution was graded as a 'failing' training provider:

> There was [a sense of] failing, there was a very punitive atmosphere … you know it's really terrible, very de-motivating de-moralising for everyone.
>
> *(ibid: 156)*

To return to the Foucauldian metaphor of the panopticon, in which behaviour is controlled via self-policing as a result of our not knowing whether or when we are being 'watched', such fears do not only exist for the duration of the Ofsted inspection itself; they continue after it and in anticipation of the next inspection – fears that are only heightened by recent developments in which inspections may occur at extremely short notice, creating an unrelenting feeling of anxiety. Within such an inspection regime, Ofsted is always 'there', ever-present, 'always in your head' as one of my respondents put it – constantly influencing the ways in which practitioners set about their work and (importantly) construct themselves as professionals (Moore and Clarke 2016): in short, inspection becomes 'the panoptic metaphor made real' (Perryman 2009: 617).

It is important to note that anxiety of this nature is not only experienced on an individual level; it may also exist as a form of *collective* concern, which is, so to speak, experienced institutionally.[5] During my time at Secondary Two, the school was in a state of unrelenting anticipation of an expected Ofsted visit. They had no fixed date for such a visit, and the senior leadership team had relied on educated guesses on the part of the headteacher as to when it might happen – these guesses repeatedly (and somewhat painfully and frustratingly) turning out to be false alarms. All the while, an atmosphere of anxiety and pessimism seemed to grip the school, like an epidemic against which no one had immunity. Talk of a potential, dreaded 'RI' ('Requires Improvement') judgment often dominated staffroom discussion, and even the students seemed to have caught the Ofsted virus. When the date of the inspection finally did arrive, giving the school very short notice to prepare itself practically and psychically for it, I wrote in my notes:

> It's Monday, and at Secondary Two the Ofsted phone call has finally come – just when everyone was beginning to think it never would. Despite the incredible levels of detailed preparation, everyone goes into instant hyperdrive. It seems that no amount of preparation will ever be enough to produce confidence and optimism. Always, there will be at least one stone left unturned. It's as if everybody knows deep down that whatever they do, however good they actually are, the report has already been written, the result already irreversible and unalterable – and yet they are still driven to do their best to achieve the impossible.

It would be misleading, and over-simplifying things, to suggest that the fear of Ofsted is *solely* about the fear of material consequences (e.g. closure or imported management of the school, or potential loss of earnings), even though this may be the principal mode of fear individually and collectively experienced. As we shall see, there is another kind of fear, too, which concerns how we are perceived, judged and valued by other people – even those whose opinions and criteria we might individually and collectively dispute. One striking feature of responses to actual or impending inspections among teachers in my own study was the extent to which they felt hurt or upset by what they saw as negative comments, not so much by inspectors (who these days are instructed to keep such things to themselves) as by teacher colleagues charged with ensuring that Ofsted criteria will be met if and when a formal inspection takes place – even when they rejected the criteria by which such judgments had apparently been made. An example of this comes from an informal discussion I had with one of my respondents, John:

> John sought me out today. It's the first time he's initiated a discussion with me, even though we regularly find ourselves sitting virtually opposite one another eating our packed lunches in the staff room during lunch breaks. Normally (at least, so it has seemed) a very self-assured, outgoing kind of person, John is clearly suffering a crisis of confidence. He tells me it goes back to a previous Ofsted visit, when an inspector visited one of his lessons and he was told it was 'good' – or, in John's words, 'only good' – rather than 'outstanding'. His opinion at the time was that the lesson deserved an outstanding grade and that the inspector did not know what he was doing; but his immediate anger at what he felt to be the injustice of the assessment quickly converted into a sense of personal failure. Over time, these negative feelings gradually dissipated, and his old confidence in his ability was restored – at least, until now. John reminds me that Ofsted inspectors no longer grade lessons they observe ('not overtly, at any rate'); however, there is a practice at Secondary Two of ongoing lesson observations, usually carried out my members of the senior leadership team, in which the old grading system is still used and still shared with the teacher whose lesson is being observed. What has happened is that earlier in the week a member of what John and some of his closer colleagues calls the internal observation team has again adjudged one of his lessons to be 'only good', when he considered it to be one of the best he had ever given. He tells me: 'In a moment, it all came back to me: that same feeling of injustice, but also of being useless. But possibly worse this time, because it's not an inspector judging you, it's one of your colleagues – so you start to really doubt yourself, as well as feeling. … I don't know … betrayed, I guess. Certainly unsupported.' Once again, as happened after the official Ofsted judgment, John appears to have lost faith in himself and become unhelpfully introspective – and the shadow of Ofsted, which he thought he had escaped following his previous unhappy experience, has returned: 'It's that same feeling, of being watched, being judged. And even

when you know who's doing the watching, you still can't really localise it. It gets inside your head. It's been there every other lesson I've taught since the observation – not helping me, because obviously they tell you why they think the lesson wasn't great – but all the time feeling self-conscious.' I ask him who is doing this watching, given that no one else is now observing him. He tells me he doesn't know. 'Perhaps it's the students' he suggests; perhaps he's wondering if they are judging him in a way that hadn't occurred to him before; or perhaps 'it's just paranoia' – perhaps it's nobody other than himself, 'some critical self that's split off from me and is continually shaking his head in disappointment. … I don't know if it is Ofsted or if it's SLT, or if I've just been listening too much to you talking about Foucault.[6] … Maybe it's a bit of everything – but it really does feel like there's an Ofsted inspector taken up residence inside my head. … Maybe not an inspector as such. Maybe just the whole inspection process'.

Later, I ask John if he has discussed his feelings with his Head of Department or anyone else on the staff that he feels he can talk to. He says he hasn't, other than to a colleague James with whom he has become good friends. He doesn't want people to think he's being 'wet', he says – or 'a whinger'. Despite his current lack of confidence and low self-image, he still, he says, has ambitions to run his own department one day, and he doesn't want to say anything that could sow seeds of doubt in the minds of potential referees. I'm half expecting him at any moment to beg me: 'You won't say anything about this conversation to anyone else, will you. It's just between the two of us, right?' But in any event I jump in first: 'I'm wondering, John. … If at some future point I might talk about our discussion in my writing? You would be rigorously anonymised, of course'. John chuckles at this. 'Rigorously anonymised', he mocks. 'Sounds like something a Dalek would say. Yeah. Of course – fine to use, if you think it might help. As long as you know I'll deny it – rigorously! – if anybody ever traces it back to me'.

John's concern clearly extends beyond a fear of being inadequate: it is also about being *perceived* as being inadequate by an-other, even if one would not normally value that other's opinion or capacity to judge. His fear appears to be twofold, in fact: a fear of material consequences (not simply of his Ofsted evaluation, but of being perceived as 'weak' by potential referees) in relation to future job prospects, coupled with – and perhaps inseparable from – a fear that he might actually not be as good as he wants to be and might lose or not have the respect of (certain) other human beings. This conjoined kind of fear was expressed by others in my research, one striking instance of which concerned another Secondary Two teacher, Zoë, whose testimony chimed uncannily with John's:

Zoë sought me out in the staffroom to tell me about a problem she was having with a particular class: one that was giving her sleepless nights and reducing her to tears. She is an experienced teacher, and is clearly not used to this sort of thing. Equally clear is her difficulty in coping with it or finding a way out of it. My immediate advice was to talk to her Head of Department about it, but she quickly told me this was a non-starter. She had already spoken to me about the dangers of revealing what she called 'emotional weakness' to the students: 'Sniff that, and they'll go for you like sharks smelling blood'. I had had some sympathy with her on that score. As an ex-teacher myself, I knew all too well that, as one of my old PGCE students once said to me, 'If there's anything at all making you feel unhappy in any way, just don't expect to get the sympathy vote [from the kids]!' I now discovered that what had seemed like a reasonable and acceptable fear of displaying emotions – including perhaps fear itself – to students applied also to Zoë's relationships with senior colleagues. She had lowered her voice and looked about the staffroom before explaining: 'You can't tell some people about these kinds of thing. It'll be construed in terms of failure. You're weak. You can't cut it any more. And then one day you're going to need a reference, or apply for an internal promotion, and it comes back to bite you. Or maybe you do a duff lesson during an Ofsted visit, and what might have been passed over as an aberration suddenly becomes something else … like a confirmation that yes, actually, you aren't very good at your job any more – or people forget that once upon a time they thought you were brilliant and even sent student teachers to you to see how it was done. . .' .

Zoë's observations worry me, and have led me to ask other teachers at Secondary Two how confident they would feel about sharing problems with their line managers. I have managed to question a dozen teachers about this, of a variety of ages and experience levels, across a range of subject disciplines and year groups, and overseen by colleagues with what I knew already to be a wide variety of management styles. In all cases but one – that of a teacher nearing retirement age – the answer has been similar. They would always think twice about approaching a line manager for emotional support, even though in most cases they would be happy to ask for more technical support and advice. It would be a last resort, if that.[7] They would sort it out themselves, maybe with the help of friends outside of school. One teacher was particularly adamant about this. She had a long-term illness that from time to time made her feel very unwell. Everyone knew about the illness, but what they didn't know was that she had frequently come into school feeling sick and dizzy. As far as most of her colleagues knew, her episodes of illness always managed to occur during the longer school holidays. What struck me was not just that she was afraid (as she put it) to share these recurrences of illness with her line manager or anyone else on the senior leadership team; she was also afraid of taking a day off in case it 'went on her record'. She felt she had to have a 100 per cent attendance rate in order not to 'project a negative image'. When I asked her if she meant by this that it might hinder any chance of promotion, she replied: 'Yes, that. But also I just don't want people to think of me as someone who's always ill'.

Material fears such as those identified by Starr and by Coffield and Williamson include not only fears for oneself or one's school, but also for one's students. A commonly expressed fear, particularly among secondary school teachers, where public examination results take on such great importance, was the fear of letting down one's students – that is to say, of the material consequences that might befall one's students rather than oneself directly, should one's teaching fail to measure up to the task of achieving with them ('for them', as it was often put) the best possible examination grade(s). An example of this is offered by the testimony of one of the secondary school teachers in my current study, Margo, who self-described herself as 'a bit of a neurotic'. Margo was beset by all kinds of fears, including that of losing her husband who, she told me, had threatened to divorce her 15 years previously (a threat she seemed unable to dismiss) unless she could sort out her work-life balance. Margo's greatest fear, though, was of failing her students – a fear inextricably linked to, and perhaps originating in, an unfortunate event which had occurred even longer ago (some thirty years ago, in fact) but which still felt to Margo 'as though it was yesterday'. It was a feeling, a fear that was never far from Margo's mind but that returned with particular intensity, as something approaching terror, every time the public examination season came around again – an intensified fear coupled with an intensified experience of guilt related to how she had 'let down' (as she saw it) one particular student and how it was, still, 'something I will always have to live with':

> I had an A level group. They had three [English Literature] papers to sit: an unseen and then two on set texts. They were on consecutive days. I don't know how it happened, but I managed to mix up in my head which exam took place on which day. I told the students the wrong order, so they turned up on Monday morning expecting a set text exam and they were confronted with the unseen one. I can still feel today the shock and despair I felt then. I didn't know what to do. There were only eight students sitting the exam, and they were all in one classroom on their own, so I could at least address them all together in situ. I told them I had made a mistake, and that they shouldn't worry; there was not much they could have done to revise for the unseen anyway, and it meant they'd have an extra day to revise the set texts. But it clearly threw them. So the next day one of the students' parents came into school, demanding to see me. Ironically, she was probably the weakest of the students taking the exam that year, and she would have struggled to achieve the lowest pass grade anyway – but perhaps that was partly why her parents came in: you know, they knew it was going to be hard enough for her anyway, without any additional obstacles being put in her way. I was devastated. I had already been thinking about it all night, hardly sleeping, and when they told me how devastated their daughter had been I just burst into tears. All I could do was keep on saying sorry, telling them I would contact the Board and ask them to take special consideration in marking the scripts. They threatened me with all sorts, and for months

I was in a state of permanent anxiety and misery, waiting for the results to come through in August. I was a bit relieved that everyone had achieved their predicted grades, including this particular student who, as we had hoped, had passed, albeit with the lowest grade. But the parents were back in again in September, threatening me and the school with all sorts of action. Solicitors, newspapers, demanding my resignation – all sorts of horrible stuff. You see, I was Head of Department in those days, so the buck really did stop with me.

Fear and identity

Margo's account, as in John's testimony, reminds us that there is a psychic as well as a material dimension in such fears. The fear of students failing while on one's watch is not only a fear on the students' behalf, so to speak; it is also likely to attach itself to a sense of one's own personal inadequacy, and perhaps to a loss of love or respect in the eyes of those students and maybe of one's colleagues. But there are other fears that are more directly and obviously psychic in nature and origin. These include, in particular, that same fear of either losing or not winning love, the fear of losing control and, related to each of these, the fear of losing or not securing one's place in the socio-symbolic order of the school.

The fear of absence – or loss – of love is one that will be returned to in the pages that follow. It is one aspect of a wider desire to 'fit in' in an institution, in society, in a social grouping, allied to a deep concern about what other people might think of us. These are feelings I have described elsewhere with reference, after Lacan and Žižek, to the notions of 'imaginary and symbolic identification' (Moore 2004), but since these concepts are so important in so much of the analysis that will follow (and in particular, in Chapter 6), it is helpful, I think, to say a little more about them here too.

Put simply (I hope not too simply) imaginary identification concerns the way(s) in which we see ourselves as subjects: how we would wish others to see us, how we make ourselves likeable to ourselves and the measures we take to make our likeable selves likeable to others. Symbolic identification is more about how we understand our selves in relation to the Symbolic Order: its social systems, structures and conventions – including the reassurances we demand that we have successfully fulfilled certain named roles that we find ourselves occupying. (What must I do to merit the title of [good] parent, child, teacher, and so on?) Both imaginary and symbolic identification are saturated with affect, but it is through symbolic identification, and specifically by commandeering and deploying the language and discourses through which symbolic identification is inscribed and articulated, that policy's appeal to affect and its consequent capacity to enthral takes place. This is not to say that policy makes no appeal to imaginary identification. On the contrary, the language and discourse of policy can reach and generate such feelings in the borderlands between affect and its physical manifestations as shame, guilt and a need to 'belong' – feelings that might be more appropriately described as imaginary (that is, related to matters of [self] image). This seepage suggests that there are no fixed, non-permeable boundaries between symbolic and imaginary identification, but that the two modes of identification are in constant interaction and negotiation with one another. The question to and of the Symbolic Order, 'What does it mean to be a [good] teacher?', for example, is inseparable from the other question, apparently directed to the self, 'Why does this question matter [to me]?'

What must I do to merit the title of (good) teacher? How do I wish to be seen and understood and responded to as a person? On the basis of my own research, these are questions that teachers frequently ask of themselves and of others as they seek to do their best for their students and to achieve a sense of wider satisfaction in a job well done. Often, the uncertainty and lack of confidence embedded in the question 'What must I do to merit the title of (good) teacher?' is inextricably linked to another question: 'In whose eyes must I be judged to deserve the title, and by whose criteria?' In his fascinating account of two groups of Mexican and Spanish teachers attempting to 'find' or perhaps rediscover themselves by participating in an out-of-school group therapy course, Charles Keck describes one teacher, Dora, as she struggles with a not unfamiliar problem of feeling a profound unease, a feeling that things are not as they should be, as she attempts to meet externally implied or imposed professional criteria in her lesson planning:

> Today I realized why I always wanted the children to be quiet, because I'd get so worked up about – for example in my head I was all prepared, that from 9:00 to 9:15 we would do such and such, and then from 9:15 to 9:45 such and such. … [I] was very programmed. [And it was like things weren't] really bearing fruit in that way, because I was very rigid. According to me it was so the children learned and were prepared – they are little things, 4 or 5 years old. I implemented some activities, but they were based in my neurosis: they weren't based in love, not based on their learning and growing, but that they *had* to learn, this group *has* to do well, we shouldn't even hear a fly in this group, nothing should be disorganized.
>
> *(quoted in Keck 2012: 108)*

Dora's fear is that, unless everything is strictly controlled (by her), the children won't learn, and therefore, by inference, she will have let them down – even though she has a strong feeling that the children are suffering from her over-control. This same (hegemonically endorsed) fear that without strict control adequate learning will not take place was experienced by many teachers in my own study. However, the fear of loss or absence of control had a significantly different inflection in some teachers. Yanick, for example – a student teacher at Primary One – frequently expressed his concern, in the early weeks of his second school practice, not so much that the children needed to be strictly controlled, but that the loss of control would impact negatively *on himself* regardless of its impact on his students, making him feel he had failed – that, to refer back to John, he was 'weak' simply because he had lost control:

Being child-centred is all very well, and, yeah, I approve of all that. … But at the end of the day you have to show them who's in charge. I remember that from my own school days. I was not a good student. At primary school I was in a class and one year we had a teacher, Miss Simms, who was weak, and we just ran rings round her and we didn't hardly do any work. So I know – I'm not saying [my class here] are like that, but I know if I let up for one minute they're gonna be in there, you know, and it's gonna be a hell of a job getting them back to where I want them to be. And I know that too well, because at my last [teaching practice] school I did go in thinking ah, I'll be all student centred and all that, and get them doing collaborative learning and stuff, and I lost them from Day One and never got them back. Losing control. It's one of my worst nightmares. I'm always thinking to myself: keep on top of them, don't ever let them think you're a soft touch. That's possibly the most important lesson I've learned from my teacher training course.

Yanick's fear of losing control appears to have arisen at least in part from a previous experience of having lost control and from the lingering, still painful memory of the personal psychic consequences of that loss of control. He was by no means the only teacher in the study for whom a past experience would precipitate fear in the present – often described, in what might be seen as a process of mis-recognition, as 'learning from experience'. Other teachers, however, displayed such fear without any apparent – or at least any remembered, identifiable – past experience. While Yanick had been fearful of losing control *again*, others feared losing control for the first time. Not surprisingly, perhaps, it was the teachers who were most visibly controlling in their pedagogy, who insisted the most stridently on peace and quiet and order in the classroom, who were the ones most likely to express this fear, just as it was often the teachers who were most highly regarded by colleagues and students who expressed the strongest fear of losing respect or of not being valued. There is no room here to explore the complexities of these issues (why it is, for example, that some people are more likely to fear losing control than others); however, it is worth noting, in passing, Keck's suggestion that losing control, being out of one's depth and insufficient to the task in hand, is an ever-present threat in teaching and that we might need to contextualise the pressure to maintain control, even though it may be typically experienced as coming 'from within', with reference to wider drives and pressures in society and social policy and to a dialectical relationship between policy as imposed and policy as implemented. As Keck puts it:

> The attempt to maintain a tireless order and stamp a directionality on educa-tion [might] be regarded as a reaction to [a] public and private fear of a loss of 'civilization' and collective and individual sense of meaning.
>
> *(Keck 2012: 125)*

What is particularly intriguing in Keck's analysis is that it is not just practice but policy too that is infused with affect: that is to say, policy itself is driven by psychic as well as by material or practical fear – in essence, by a profound sense of insecurity, of a fear that 'civilisation' is precarious and that at any time it might dissolve.

Love

As with fear, I want to suggest that love can be politically conscripted, and that it can act as a force for promoting compliance *alongside* fear (indeed, I would argue that these two affective responses – love and fear – have a tendency to operate and to be utilised in tandem). But I am also concerned to explore how love might prompt or support teachers in *resistance to* or *management of* fear, including resistance to aspects of public education policy that they may feel to be harmful to their students even as they are compelled to implement them. Just as different kinds and sites of practitioner fear are explored and discussed in the pages that follow ('material' fears such as losing one's job or being denied promotion or having one's school taken away and put under some other control), as well as 'psychic' fears (such as the fear of being unpopular with colleagues or students, or of failing to live up to one's own or others' expectations), of equal importance is love for one's students, and perhaps love (or non-love) for ourselves. Strongly connected to these loves is an abiding human desire *to be loved*.

Fear may appear to us as a relatively straightforward concept – but love less so. We certainly like to use the word a lot, even though it resists definition. But perhaps we prefer it that way, choosing to invest it with an air of mysticism, of otherworldliness, of being somehow above and superior to the mundane world of dictionary definitions.

When I talk here of the love that teachers have for their students, the love that brings them into teaching in the first place, the love they have for the job, I refer essentially to a kind of altruism: a desire to do good for other people, a warm glow that can ensue from successes in turning such desire into some form of observable reality, and, accompanying that warm glow and in part bringing it about, a sense – not necessarily articulated – of *self*-love and even self-congratulation.[8] To return to an earlier point, this feeling, perhaps the whole idea of 'being a teacher', can be described as a sort of object: we might say again, after Ahmed (2010a), a 'happy object'. But it is a feeling, an experience, that has an added element, in that the warm glow is in response not just to what we can do for others; it also concerns others' recognition of our what we give to them, leading them to see us as loveable people. It is, thus, more than simply the love we may have for others, and different again from the desire for others to respect us. Unfortunately (so it might seem), although this love may be underscored by a desire for reciprocity in one sense, it is not always or necessarily a love that is shared. The teacher may love and demand love from students, but might not necessarily feel love for colleagues, even while desiring love *from* them – even from those who may not be held in the highest regard. We might argue that the feeling of being loved that we may crave must be understood as internally produced (despite any corresponding, independently produced feelings in the other), but that it is actually mis-recognised as being received. The experience and belief in the 'receipt of love' may thus, as Harris (1989) implies in his study of the emotional development of young children, be illusory though nevertheless very powerful. Whether imagined or not, this receipt of love is crucially important to our sense of well-being, and is consequently related to a corresponding fear: the fear, that is, of losing or of not receiving love – of being symbolically and affectively cast out, avoided or rejected, of being seen as 'trouble', or of losing the affection/love/respect that one has already gained, which can feel so precarious.

Once again, the inclusion of some illustrative examples is in order, and I'll begin with a brief return to two teachers, Shay and Graeme, interviewed in an earlier study (Halpin, Moore, *et al* 1998–2001), whom I have written about at greater length elsewhere (e.g. Moore 2012a, 2006) – teachers working at the same secondary school as one another in Inner London. The first of these, Shay, told me a very moving story of being involved in a terrorist bomb attack in Northern Ireland and of feeling forced to move to England to work in order to escape both the memory of that event and the possibility of a repeat experience. He had taken up teaching, he said, 'almost therapeutically':

> There was something about teaching that suddenly appealed. It was one of those 'good' professions. Good stuff was going on, you know: preparing young people for a better life, maybe for a better world. Doing something about that – helping turn out decent human beings with love and respect for one another. I was always drawn to the Humanities side of things, and to the pastoral side. Education, school, that was going to be the nice side of things, the better face of humanity.

Shay's colleague, Graeme, had had what was, in some respects, a not dissimilar tale to share, telling me of his own 'appalling' schooling when, as a child, he had been sent away to a boarding school where he had been made to feel so inferior that he had failed all his exams and dropped out at an early age – only to return to formal education some years later and to go on to train as a teacher so that he might draw on his own negative experiences and 'perhaps … make it better for others'.

It appeared to me that both Shay and Graeme had been attracted to teaching at least partly by way of an expiation. There was a sense in both their testimonies of wanting to atone for the wrongs of others (in Shay's case, almost for the sins of the world): of wanting to make things better, or to show how they could be better, of helping to give others a more positive life experience than they had had in their own younger days. They were, each of them, both owed and owing: owed a second chance to experience and perpetuate the 'good' in life, owing others that same experience themselves. Significantly, Graeme was shortly to leave the profession after many years of service – his decision taken on the basis that he could no longer fulfil this atoning role, that changes in the system, and in particular a perceived trend in education policy back toward the 'bad old days' of high-stakes pen-and-paper testing and the 'them-and-usness of front-of-class teaching', had simply made it impossible. A man who had once prided himself on his capacity to empathise with his students, to be able to help them through 'the strains and stresses of puberty', at the age of 49, Graeme had found himself being pushed from his chosen 'progressive', 'liberal' approach to education and pedagogy toward one that was more 'reactionary', more 'abrasive'. As with Shay, the project of 'getting it right' that had led him into teaching seemed to have been scuppered, and he was now being forced, as he saw it, to get it all wrong – to be just like the distant, undermining teachers of his own school days. Shay, on the other hand, had decided to carry on at the school, though he could 'not say for how long'. Like Graeme, not only his philosophy but the very rationale for his having become a teacher had, he felt, been 'totally undermined' by government policy. But he didn't know what else to do, he had been left with a feeling of 'numbness':

> 'Sometimes you feel like the rabbit caught in the headlights. You know, I feel paralysed. I'm going to have to do loads of stuff I don't just not believe in, I actually, fundamentally believe to be wrong. I don't know if I can pull that off. Or if I even want to. … I'll do my best to keep going the way I always have with my classes. Better me I suppose than someone who actually signs up to all the crap. But I'm not happy. I'm really not happy. For the first time since I started teaching I don't enjoy coming in to work in the morning. It's depressing. The more I think about it. …'
>
> 'It depresses you?'
>
> 'It depresses me. I just have to live in hope that one day someone in power is going to see sense and at some point everything'll switch back to the way it was. Until then I suppose I'll just carry on being Benjamin the donkey'.[9]

Both Shay's words and Graeme's subsequent actions – Graeme's self-removal from the symbolic order of the school to adopt a new identity as an antique furniture dealer; Shay's acceptance of 'going through the motions' as the compliant cynic – call to mind Ahmed's notion of 'alignment' and proximity to 'good objects' and Ruti's summary of Lacan's elaborations of conformity and desire – of how 'when the subject is estranged from its desire – when it allows itself to be overrun by the desire of the Other – its existence feels empty, apathetic, and devoid of meaning' and of how, 'in the throes of such life-deadening conformity, the subject goes through the motions of life in a defensive manner, sacrificing the intensity of its desire for the convenience of an easily classifiable social identity' (Ruti 2009: 104).

Shay and Graeme, of course, are not 'typical', in so much as very few teachers will have experienced such negatively infused early backgrounds as theirs. However, many of the teachers I have spoken to have expressed not dissimilar reasons for entering the teaching profession and, in many of these cases, a not dissimilar experience in finding their educational convictions thwarted or undermined by policy. Large numbers of teachers are also drawn into the profession by what I have identified (and 'found' in Shay and Graeme) as love: not the love of a parent for a child (or children), but rather a feeling of love for large numbers of young people – perhaps for the majority of humankind – experienced and expressed in terms of caring, of wanting to offer help, of experiencing deep pleasure when that help proves fruitful, but of wanting to carry on helping even when it does not. Both Shay and Graeme, I would suggest, were drawn to teaching by this kind of love, this desire to do good in relation to other people, in each case, in different ways, gaining something in return for the giving that had made them feel positive about themselves: not so much in terms of the symbolic and imaginary identification we have already touched on, but a different kind of affective justification to set alongside these others and in constant interplay with them. Graeme in particular, feeling unable to continue to give this kind of love, receiving negative feedback in return, came to feel so badly about himself as to have no option but to remove himself from the profession. It was as if the happy object of teaching, of being a teacher, of doing something good, the feeling of self-justification, had been snatched away from him.

These examples of love for one's students, and the desire to be able to receive the fruits of that love in return (not necessarily through displays of student affection, but more often through the successes and happy experiences our students enjoy partly as a result of our labours), need to be set beside that other kind of love – and of desire – referred to earlier: the desire, that is, *to be loved*, both by our students and by our colleagues. As I have implied, love is not the word that everyone might consider appropriate in relation to these feelings, since it concerns, principally, a desire we have to be liked and respected by others, to be affectively accepted by them, to be, regardless of any differences we might have, a validated member of the social group in which we find ourselves.

An example of the possible impact on *practice* of such love and desire, including its capacity to render us both more and less compliant toward – and accepting of – central or localised policy that we may initially have responded to with hostility, concerns a policy recently introduced by the headteacher at one school – 'Secondary Two' – of the 'spot examination' of exercise books (see also Chapter 6 below). This policy, though internally devised, was introduced by the headteacher as a direct response to the spot checks undertaken by Ofsted inspectors and the increased attention paid during Ofsted inspections not simply to the visible evidence of the quality of students' work but also to evidence of the quality and regularity of teachers' written feedback to students – that is to say, of (one aspect of) their teaching. It was a policy, the Head had argued, which other schools were already adopting, and it would be foolish of Secondary Two not to follow suit. It involved senior and middle leaders at the school randomly approaching colleagues to demand sight of equally randomly selected exercise books at unpredictable times, to ensure that everyone was, in this regard, in a state of perpetual 'Ofsted readiness'. Despite the fact that members of the senior and middle management teams were not exempt from these checks (a deputy head with a mathematics specialism, for example, might expect to be checked by the head of the mathematics department – and vice versa), one of the school's deputy heads, Abigail, talked of the problems she had both felt and expressed to colleagues prior to the policy being rolled out:

I wasn't at all happy with it. I'm still not, if I'm honest. I didn't object to it in principle. In fact, I always thought it was a good idea. But I was very aware of how it would be received by colleagues and how they would think about the [senior leadership team]. Some of them already have us cast as the fascist Ofsted collaborator wing of the organisation. Some of the [senior leadership team] couldn't give a toss about that. But some of us are more sensitive to it. So in the beginning I did actually argue quite strongly against it, just for the sake of unity, you know. … Well, not just that. I mean, no one wants to be misunderstood, or type-cast as the demon. So we're doing it, and actually most people seem OK with it. But there are some, some of them, I know, really resent it, and probably resent me too for being part of it even though I have someone checking my books too. I think the English department have the biggest gripe. And you can't blame them really given the amount of marking they all have to do.

If Abigail's opposition to the spot-check policy had been based on issues of staff morale along with her own fear of how some colleagues might construct her in her senior leadership role, a young history teacher James, also at Secondary Two, had found the policy objectionable on rather different grounds:

'It just felt wrong, on so many levels. There's the lack of trust, which completely undermines your professionalism – like we're potentially naughty children that always have to be monitored and kept in line. But there are pedagogical issues too. You know, the kind of checking they are doing implies a completely different way of teaching and learning than many of us are trying to model here. In maths, OK. Tick, tick, tick, cross, cross cross. Couple of sentences at the end. Heads down for most of every lesson. But when you go into the Humanities it ain't like that. Sometimes there's a pile of marking to be done, but other times it just isn't there. They might not have done any individual written work for a week or two, at least none that would impress Ofsted. There just isn't this regular, same-same-same kind of production-line quality control that you can, possibly, have in some subjects. So like a lot of us who are more active [in the teachers' union] I was very strongly opposed to it at the start. But the trouble is, there just wasn't enough opposition generally, so you started to feel like a small band of mostly younger troublemakers, getting in the way of progress – like "Don't you *want* us to get a good Ofsted?" kind of thing. So I've kind of had to change my mind and go along with it'.

   'Change your mind? Or change your practice?'

   'Well. … Yeah, change my practice I suppose, giving [the students] a lot more shorter pieces of written work. But … not my mind, as such. … I still don't like it. But I guess you could say I've changed my … view, if that makes sense'.

   'Which is?'

'We all have our own ideas about what's right and wrong. But in the end you have to respect the wishes of the majority. Maybe that's what I mean. Not exactly changing a view. … More like, I don't know … reminding myself of a different view that I should maybe be taking. A bit like the referendum [on whether or not to remain in the European Union]. I voted to remain, like most people I know. But if most people say leave, you have to respect that. It's democratic. I can't say I liked [the result] or that our democracy is perfect, but you wouldn't want a dictatorship. I certainly don't want to be cast as a "remoaner" as they like to call it'.

James, it seemed, had done what many teachers are compelled to do when confronted by enforced change with which they are not in agreement: he had put his initial feelings and views to one side, and gone along with the change reluctantly – pragmatically, we might say, to flag a later discussion – rendering his immediate professional experience less happy, but simultaneously offering him his only hope of long-term survival. In order to justify his change of position, and perhaps to express his discomfort with it or to render it more acceptable to himself or to others, he interestingly (particularly in light of a not dissimilar discussion to be had in Chapter 6) explained and simultaneously rationalised his shift of attitude with reference to a discourse and ideology – one affectively saturated with positivity – of democracy. His understandable capitulation to a policy that he did not like is, in itself, of interest and importance, and examples such as this have much to tell us, I think, about the increasingly coercive effects of public policy on resistant individuals as policy becomes part of institutional hegemony. However, in order more fully to understand the *mechanisms* of such forms of local policy enactment, it is important to recognise and understand the part played by the individual psyche and the ways in which the psyche interacts with – and perhaps is manipulated by – the policy imperative. In this regard, James's testimony immediately brings to mind, along with echoes of 'Social Network Analysis', Michael Billig's discussion of the predisposition we all have to regulate our feelings in order to fit in with situational norms, and our shared understanding of the potentially damaging impact of conflicting demands (Billig 1997). It might also, depending on the reading we take, illustrate the same writer's comments (ibid.: 143) on how individuals will '[resolve] a neurotic conflict through fantasies about the ideal self' (in James's case, the consistent democrat). From my field notes at the time:

> James seems to have been compelled to subordinate one set of feelings – to do with educational and political *ideology* – to another set, to do with not wanting to lose popularity through giving offence to the developing ideological and symbolic order of the school: that is to say – though at first sight the reverse may seem true – in the struggle between ideology and desire, it is desire (the desire for acceptance, for personal and institutional equilibrium) that wins. As Billig expresses this in considerations of conversation analysis and discursive psychology:

'It is as if speakers find themselves inhabiting a normative structure which is more powerful than their individual feelings and to which they have to conform for interaction to proceed'.

(Billig 1997: 146; see also Mulkay's [1988: 79] argument concerning the avoidance of disagreement)

This reference to the powerful gravitational pull of normative structures is one that will be returned to later, in discussions of what I have termed the allure of normalcy. It speaks of a particular kind of pragmatism and compromise: not just about conscious, rational(ised) choices related to material fears and concerns (for example, of the kind expressed by many teachers, along the lines 'I need to keep my head down if I want to get on'), but a more affective pragmatism in which much more than job security or even the relative comfort of daily acceptance by one's peers is at stake. As with more conscious, more 'visible' pragmatism, pragmatism in the affective domain comes at a cost, but it is a somewhat different cost, and it assuages somewhat different fears and concerns. It may result in compliance, compromise, perhaps the sacrifice of cherished ideals in the domain of action – but such loss might at least be compensated for in the currency and embrace of love.

PART II

Repetition and transference: reflexivity as personal and professional development

4

NEW EDITIONS OF OLD CONFLICTS

Primary One: Yanick and Caroline

The previous three chapters have attempted to lay much of the theoretical ground-work for what follows, introducing some of the theories drawn from psychoanal-ysis that I think may be helpful to practising teachers (indeed, to us all) – at the same time arguing for the general benefits of adapting aspects of psychoanalytic theory by way of achieving more helpful understandings of ourselves and of others. I have suggested that this usefulness arises in no small part from the fact that it impels us toward critical and constructive considerations of the often ignored, overlooked or simply unseen effects of affect on how we experience life and how we construct and experience our sense of self. In relation to reflexivity, which is a central concept in this book, I have proposed two kinds or aspects of reflexivity, referencing these to William Pinar's conceptualisation of *currere*. The first of these ('Reflexivity 1') is essentially (though not exclusively) therapeutic in nature and purpose, aimed at helping us to overcome emotional difficulties we may experience in relation to our professional and private lives, but at the same time, through the richer understandings of our own subjectivities that reflexivity can bring, helping us to develop more helpful, perhaps more sympathetic understandings of those we work with, including, as teachers, our students. This kind of reflexivity draws quite heavily on Freudian notions of repetition and transference (Freud 1968) and on Kleinian notions of projection, as well as on Lacanian conceptualisations around identification.

It is this first kind of reflexivity that this chapter and the next will explore in a little more depth, drawing mainly on teacher testimonies at Primary One. This chapter will focus on how reflexivity might promote our own self-understanding and development, while the next will consider how more nuanced understandings of our selves might help us develop similarly nuanced understandings of others and of their behaviours, leading perhaps to more constructive relationships. The second kind of reflexivity, which concerns itself more with developing understandings of the ways in which policy, ideology and discourse work on us affectively with the aim of obtaining our compliance ('Reflexivity 2'), will be explored in more detail in Chapters 6 and 7, where the analysis will focus more on the experiences of secondary school teachers.

Most of these later chapters will emphasise the experiences of qualified teachers, but this current chapter concerns itself mainly with two beginning teachers, Yanick and Caroline, who were both undertaking the second of two teaching practices at Primary One and both completing a one-year PGCE course at the same university. Analysis will focus on the impact of elements of past experience on the ways in which these beginning teachers practice and experience teaching in the present, inviting readers to consider how re-engagements with past experience might produce a beneficial impact on present experience and practice – but also to consider the ways in which affect can inhibit and constrain reflexivity when it engenders a reluctance to undertake such re-engagement. I have chosen to focus on Yanick and Caroline not so much because they are beginning teachers as for a number of other reasons. First, mainly because of their lighter timetables, I was able to have longer and more frequent discussions with them than with other teachers at Primary One. Second, they both made a point of telling me how useful – in Caroline's word, how 'therapeutic' – they had found our discussions. Finally, they had both, at the time of our initial interviews, struck me as having been stuck in something of a psychic *impasse* that appeared to be standing in the way of their adopting the kind of reflexive approach to professional learning and development – to 'becoming' – that I have been advocating. In Yanick's case (in an echo of Dora's testimony), the impasse I had tentatively identified involved being stuck in an idea that classroom silence, seen by him as an indicator of discipline and control, was the key measure of professional and personal success – at the cost, I felt, of his young students' learning. In Caroline's case, it was a profound lack of self-confidence and self-worth that had appeared to be standing in the way of her development, making her nervous of attempting to replicate with her students the kinds of creative, student-centred learning that she had enjoyed herself and benefited from as a child. In each case, I was additionally struck by the extent to which not only previous experiences of formal education had impacted on their present experience and understandings, but also of the profound effect of childhood relationships with their parents – and how, in a sense, the classroom had become for each of them a site for the experiencing and playing out of 'new editions of old conflicts' (Freud 1968: 454).

Yanick's story: keeping it cool

We have already met Yanick, briefly:

> Being child-centred is all very well, and, yeah, I approve of all that. … But at
> the end of the day you have to show them who's in charge. I remember that

from my own school days. I was not a good student. At primary school I was in a class and one year we had a teacher, Miss Simms, who was weak, and we just ran rings round her and we didn't hardly do any work. So I know – I'm not saying [my class here] are like that, but I know that if I let up for one minute they're gonna be in there, you know, and it's gonna be a hell of a job getting them back to where I want them to be. And I know that too well, because at my last [teaching practice] school I did go in thinking ah, I'll be all student centred and all that, and get them doing collaborative learning and stuff, and I lost them from Day One and never got them back again. Losing control. It's one of my worst nightmares. I'm always thinking to myself: keep on top of them, don't ever let them think you're a soft touch. That's possibly the most important lesson I've learnt from my teacher training course.

My second meeting with Yanick took place after a day's teaching, soon after my arrival in Primary One. Like most of the other teachers I have met, Yanick seemed, at least on the surface, to be calm, confident and happy in his work in spite of his 'worst nightmare' comment. His mood was positive, even at the end of what I knew from experience would have been a tiring and testing day, and he was clearly pleased at what he had achieved. We talked a bit more about Miss Simms and Yanick's own earlier negative experiences at his first placement school. He jokingly told me that he had adopted Miss Simms as his 'official anti-role model'. I asked him who his actual role models were – if he had any. A little to my initial surprise, he nominated Mark, another teacher at Primary One, who had qualified three years previously at Primary One, had opted to stay on when a vacancy had arisen, and who now had responsibility for PE at the school.[1]

Yanick told me that Mark was the sort of teacher he aspired to be: one that 'just gets on with the job' and 'doesn't get sucked in to all the emotional stuff or take things personally' – one who 'just keeps it cool'. He liked Mark's 'strength' and was rather dismissive of the occasional public emotional displays of some of the other Primary One teachers. He also said that he tried 'like Mark' to 'keep a professional distance from the other teachers', so that although he did join in with some social events he tended to sit and work on his own in the staffroom during non-teaching time and had made a conscious effort to avoid making strong friendships with other students on his PGCE course. I wondered if his fear of losing control, which was clearly deep-rooted despite the apparent confidence with which he went about his work now, had not only driven him toward a somewhat un-empathetic, teacher-led approach to pedagogy but had also prevented him from feeling the love for his students, for the job and for himself that other teachers at the school seemed to experience. As indicated in his previous testimony, he had not been a good student himself at primary school and had only buckled down 'to an extent' when he had moved to secondary school. As a child, he had been particularly hard to control and at school had often been the ringleader of active disruption. It was not only Miss Simms who had struggled to contain him, even though she was the only one he had ever reduced to tears:

'I kind of feel sorry for her in a way. No, I do. I actually do feel sorry for her'.

'And guilty?'

'Um. ... Yeah, I guess. A bit. Yeah, guilty too. I shouldn't have been so horrible in class, I know that. And it didn't do me any good in the long run anyways. Miss Simms ... she tried and tried *everything* with me. Yelling, sending me out, sweets and stuff ... even if I was good. But the thing is she always backed down. She was so *nice*'.

'Too nice?'

'Yeah. *Too nice*. Yeah. And too emotional'.

Yanick smiled at this, and I asked him what else he was remembering.

'She was the complete opposite of Mr Hunt. He was one of the Deputies, I think. No one would ever mess with him. If Mr Hunt said he was going to get your parents in or exclude you or whatever you knew he meant business'.

'A bit like Mark?'

'No. ... Yeah. In a way. A not such nice version of Mark'.

Later, I asked Yanick how his parents had felt about his misbehaviour in school, during the course of his answer to which his mood changed noticeably from amusement to what appeared to be extreme sadness:

Oh my days. ... My dad. ... He was just like 'Go to your room' – sitting down for a long talk, which was actually more like a lecture. ... You know, trying to reason it all out and stuff, and asking me why I hung out with this or that bad kid 'cos I was like good really. But my mum. ... That's a different story. I tell you, parents' evenings. ... Oh no, they were *not* a happy time for any of us.

It transpired that Yanick's mother had more than once gone in to Yanick's primary school to berate the headteacher for Yanick's poor academic progress and on one occasion had embarrassed him by going directly to his classroom and briefly confronting Miss Simms at the door in front of the other children. He also talked of her sadness and despair at his behaviour – sometimes expressing incomprehension, sometimes blaming his friends or the school, sometimes blaming herself or his father. This had, at times, driven her to tears and to beating the table with clenched fists – but also to angry exchanges between his parents that had, to use his words, torn at his insides and made him silently scream. None of this appears to have effected any speedy improvement in his behaviour or academic progress, and it was only when he went to secondary school, 'which was actually like a couple of miles away from where we lived and all of my friends had gone to the more local school', that he began to 'knuckle down'. As my fieldnotes at the time record:

It's clear to see the sadness and guilt Yanick still carries from the pain he feels he caused his mother, who is now dead. As he talks of her trials, I see and hear a Yanick very different from the one I've become accustomed to. The brash, surface confidence has temporarily gone. In its place there is regret, humility and self-blame.

With Graeme's story of redemption still very much in my head, I found myself wondering immediately if Yanick might be transferring his own previous bad studentship, for which he clearly felt some remorse, on to his class – their potential badness being diverted, in a kind of rescue act, by his own 'firmness' and 'strength'.[2] He would not be another Miss Simms. Nor would he ever again be the Yanick he was on his first Teaching Practice. As he talked, weakness and student-centredness seem to elide into one another, so that by association or attachment student-centredness, 'collaborative learning and all that stuff' was 'bad' while teacher control and directed study were 'good', and control – maintaining control – became almost the sole measure of professional success. But control itself also took on a somewhat narrow meaning – again, I felt, linked to Yanick's own past as a schoolboy. I suggested to him that collaborative learning and class discussion *could* be controlled, and indeed had to be. But he would have none of it. Children, it seems, were always on the lookout to undermine the adult in their midst and must never be shown the slightest sign of weakness. I wondered if *absence* of a (desired) quiet, orderly, respectful classroom – experienced by Yanick as a child and again in his first teaching practice – had come to be perceived by him as the *presence* of something else: that is to say, of potentially malevolent, misbehaving children waiting to pounce, leading to a fantasy that, by abolishing dis-order, personal and professional success had been achieved.[3]

Yanick's comments took me back to my own time as a teacher educator when it was common to equate professionalism with rationality and detachment and to advise would-be teachers (rather absurdly and impossibly, I now realise) to leave their emotional baggage outside the classroom. Yanick denied *having* any emotional baggage, even though he had talked of his 'nightmare' of losing control, suggesting that this was not a problem for him. But It seemed to me that his assertion masked a denial of a huge and very important aspect of who he was – one that might come with a cost not only for his students but, in the long run, for Yanick himself. By effectively denying affect, it felt as if Yanick was demanding of himself a 'strength' and a personal responsibility that might prove unsustainable and fragile. Like his role model Mark, Yanick seemed to be in the process of constructing himself as the different, almost superior, professional teacher, who might accept personal responsibility for the (compliant) conduct of his students but might also, unwittingly, be constructing himself as the repository of that very guilt he sought to overcome through his reparatory practice. Primary One, I felt like pointing out to him, was a relatively easy place to teach in. Would he still be able to 'play it cool' in a rather more challenging environment? And if he couldn't, what then?

I decided I wanted to find out more about Yanick's idea of control – to see it in action – and after slight prompting he invited me, toward the end of my stay at the school, to spend a day with him in his Year 5 class. I squared this with the school and with Yanick's tutor at the university, and shortly afterwards I did get to spend the entire day with him. It proved to be, for me and, I suspect, for most of the children, a sadly unedifying experience – a judgment which a later incarnation of Yanick, interviewed again at the end of the school year and now much more reflexively critical, would find himself 'sadly agreeing with'. He was certainly in control – of sorts. But this control consisted of long stretches of silent working from the children, punctuated by lengthy, often apparently gratuitous interruptions in which Yanick's own voice filled the room with further advice and explanation, or to stamp on the slightest deviation from a pre-set noise level. Only on two occasions did I see Yanick sit down with individual students, in each case inviting them to his desk from where he could continue to keep a weather eye on the class as a whole.

At the end of the day, he asked me, with barely concealed pride, what I thought. I felt I couldn't say very much. Instead I decided to take a bit of a chance, telling him about a past secondary-school student teacher of mine who had been through a similar experience to Yanick's – i.e. of feeling a loss or absence of control – at his first placement school and of his unsuccessful efforts to turn it around with a particular class. I was interested to find out if reflection on this story might result in Yanick critically revisiting his own position.

The student in question, I told Yanick, had got himself locked into something of an *impasse* with a particular class of 12- to 13-year-olds. A confident, assertive character himself, quick to dominate in conversation with his peers, he could not understand, come to terms with or apparently do anything to change the fact that almost the entire class refused to listen to him or obey his instructions to work, seemingly content simply to muck around and waste time in his lessons. I had observed him with this class on two occasions, and each time it was the same story. He would stand at the front barking orders and instructions; the class would pretty much ignore him, carrying on with their own conversations or throwing sweets and scrunched up notes to one another, or asking the teacher to intervene on their behalf as they were being bullied; and his response would be to repeatedly put them in detention and to 'refuse to teach them' until they were quiet and attentive. This onus on the class to sort out the problem by behaving differently had appeared, at least in his own eyes, to absolve him of having to adopt alternative strategies or to challenge his world-view – or, indeed, his view of himself-in-the-world. The situation had clearly made him unhappy, but it was all, he had insisted, the class's fault. As with the beginning teacher described in Chapter 1, the children were 'unteachable'; he had never encountered or expected to encounter or (a dig at his university- and school-based tutors, perhaps) been *prepared* to encounter such unreasonable behaviour. He had done everything any responsible adult could be expected to do. There was nothing for it but a continuation of trench warfare in which, so it appeared, there could be no winner.

I had suggested to him on my first visit that he might do things differently: for example, he might enter the class early, before the students, and put worksheets or activity sheets with any relevant resources on the students' desks, backed up perhaps by instructions on the board, and then go around the class addressing students individually or in small groups, getting them on task. He might also consider imposing a seating plan, perhaps enlisting the help of the Head of Year or Head of Faculty in putting this in place, and in the process maybe move the desks around so that they weren't all in rows facing the front: a horseshoe shape, perhaps, which might enable more effective surveillance of and communication with the students without the excessive threats and shouting that he customarily used which served merely to heighten their excitable resistance.

Yanick listened to my tale with interest. 'Well, that could be me', he offered – and on brief reflection 'or the me I was. It sounds like the trouble with your student is that he just wasn't tough enough. He should have instilled a bit of fear into them. Maybe sent some kids out to the Head of Year'.

I asked Yanick if he thought the children in his own class were afraid of him, and he suggested that to a degree they were. He indicated that this was how things should be and that there should be a distance between the teacher and the students, though he preferred the word respect to fear. It's all part, he said, of keeping it cool. My own impression was that that the children were not so afraid of him – that they did not 'live in fear', nor indeed did they display evidence of the respect he talked of, but that they were very aware of the potential consequences of being naughty, and made a largely pragmatic choice not to be. I could not help feeling as I sat in with the children, afraid myself of speaking to any of them lest I disturb the perfect, near-silent world that Yanick had created around himself, that the fear that was most oppressive and most obvious in the classroom was Yanick's own fear of losing control: of the shattering impact on his idealised self should his class (as he put it to me) 'defeat him'. I suggested that maybe the problem with my student was not that he was too 'soft' or 'weak' at all but that he was too confrontational, too obsessed with the issue of control, with keeping intact his own idealised ego, with not challenging the responses he was making, or questioning why he was having the feelings he was having; and not concerned enough about the children's actual *learning*. Yanick disagreed with me, reasserting that it was my student's weakness that was the problem. So I asked him another question, concerning his motivations for entering the teaching profession, half wondering if learning would be mentioned at all. His answer took me by surprise, indicating again that Yanick, for all his apparent lack of love for the children in his classroom, was at heart a good man who wanted to do some good in the world. The trouble was (though this was obviously a matter of opinion), he seemed to have lost sight of what that 'good' was, as if simply becoming a teacher – a teacher who could control a class – was enough in itself to merit the qualification, as if the (illusory) winning of the symbolic mandate was all that mattered:

> 'It's partly because of my own education, which you would have to say is not good. With proper teaching, I could have done much better. It all came together in the end, but that was probably more down to my parents and me

making a decision that I wasn't going to end up like a lot of the other kids on the estate. When you've seen something done not well, you sometimes want to do it well yourself'.

'So you wanted to help young people, to kind of give them what you missed out on?'

'Sure'.

'Not out of some kind of debt to society or that sort of –'

'No, no. I don't think so. None of that. You know, I was wild. And kids can't be wild. They want to be, but in the end it's not … no good for them. It will end up giving them pain … and grief. They need to knuckle down, and work for it. That's in school anyways'. (He laughs.) 'If they want to be wild, they can do that outside school. But even then, I'm not so sure. …'

Just as Graeme's story, involving a similar desire to give to others something that had previously been denied himself, has provided some context for analysing Yanick's, so Yanick's calls Graeme's to mind again. Though Graeme's negative experiences as a schoolboy had been caused more by personal circumstances than by perceived bad teaching, and although they had led him to adopt a more empathetic rather than a more authoritarian approach to his teaching, there are, I think, strong parallels between the two testimonies:

GRAEME: I dropped out of the sixth form at school and had five years wandering, doing all sorts of jobs of this and that, selling things and getting a motor cycle. Eventually a friend who was going into teaching suggested that I might be good at it. I thought about it and having had such an appalling school experience myself, which I hated, I think that led me to think perhaps I would like to make it better for others. That's what took me into it: I think it was that eventually.

INTERVIEWER: Those negative experiences – you say they helped you?

GRAEME: Those negative experiences have helped me as a teacher I am sure.

INTERVIEWER: Is that in the way you respond to the kids?

GRAEME: I think the way I respond to them, yes, because I do understand to an extent, I understand all that they feel.

It appeared that Graeme's students had as much of a function in Graeme's professional life as he had in their socio-academic lives: they, too, like a student in one of Anna Freud's case studies on transference and repetition [reported in Britzman and Pitt 1996: 118] 'served as a representation of a condensed version of [his] own childhood' – and I have suggested elsewhere that in rescuing theirs Graeme was, effectively, rescuing his own (see Moore 2004).

Unfortunately, in Yanick's case, this did not really feel like rescue at all, at least not from the perspective of his Year 5 students. Yanick may have been able to feel better about himself as a result of his successful seizure of control; however, I could not help feeling that his class might be footing the bill for this therapeutic programme and that a more reflexive approach, in which Yanick critically confronted his own obsession with control, might have been better for all concerned. To his great credit, Yanick *was* to adopt such a reflexive approach as the year wore on, leading to him telling me at the end of the year, on a return visit to the school, that I must have thought him 'a complete idiot'. By this time, I had thought a lot more about our earlier discussions, becoming increasingly convinced that Yanick had in a sense, like Graeme, been involved in an atonement of sorts: of a re-editioning, so to speak, of past conflicts, in which his current class had been cast as – at the same time as being constructed as a more positive alternative to – his own class, experienced as a child, enabling him to cast himself as a kinder version of Mr Hunt, or a stronger, more confident version of Miss Simms, or a copy of his role model Mark the PE teacher. At the same time, by way of re-engagement with the guilt he had expressed in relation both to his mother and to Miss Simms, he was also, perhaps, becoming the son his mother would have been proud of and the teacher she would have approved of – reproducing in his current charges the kind of quiet, hardworking student that she (and Miss Simms) had always wanted him to be. I did not put any of this analysis to Yanick himself; nor did I re-float that other question regarding his motivations for wanting to be a teacher, and how much his childhood experiences may have had to do with this decision. (Yanick had already advised me that it was the last profession he would have wanted or anticipated as a child.) My job, after all, was not to offer Yanick some kind of psychoanalytic interpretation of his experience and his feelings or (despite Caroline's observation) to expect some kind of therapeutic benefit to emerge from our discussions, but rather to record his story in order to share it with others by way of provoking discussion. That said, it did appear that our discussions about the impact of past experience on present experience and practice, coupled with a growing confidence as the established order of his classroom had shown no obvious sign of imminent collapse, had led to a marked modification in Yanick's relationship with his class, which, in his own words, had become 'much warmer', resulting in him – and, I imagine, his students – being 'much happier: more fulfilled'.

Caroline's story: never good enough

On the face of it, Caroline, the other beginning teacher at Primary One, could hardly have been more different than Yanick. While Yanick was still very young and had come from a relatively poorly off background, brought up on a London council estate, with no previous experience of extended employment and no long-term partner, Caroline had come from a relatively comfortably off family, had spent several years working in HR in the retail trade, was one of the few married students on her course, and had come into teaching much later in life, now being in her early forties – a fact which, she said, had made her feel uncomfortably different from the other students on the course and 'something of a fraud'. Unlike Yanick, who sought to distance himself somewhat from the other beginning teachers on his course, Caroline clearly craved a greater closeness, and felt distanced against her wishes:

> I mean, they have all decided straight away: this is what I want to do. I'll be a teacher. Nothing else. This is it. Whereas me, I didn't even really seriously think of it for years. To them it must feel like, Oh, here's another one, a do-gooder come over from the Dark Side in the hope of gaining salvation.

I suggested that it was possible that some students may initially have been suspicious of her because of her background in business, and might have made false assumptions about the way she understood and approached education, but that they surely would by now have realised that she was not 'that kind of person' and would certainly not reject her on account of her age and experience. I wrote in my notes after our initial interview: 'It might sound strange, but Caroline appears to have a determination to feel this (negative) way about herself and about how others on the course perceive her, almost as if unable or unwilling to *allow* herself a more positive sense of self'. I might have added: 'Just like Emily [the beginning teacher referenced earlier], she appears to continue to self-perceive as not fitting in, adopting an outsider identity almost by default'.

Caroline also differed from Yanick in her response to current centralised education policy and what she saw as a growing culture of 'testing, discipline and rote learning'. Although she had had a less-than-happy childhood experience of primary education herself, she talked fondly of the periods and days she remembered most warmly, when her class would be taken out to the park for Nature Study, or when they would write stories or paint pictures. Despite the liberal approach to teaching and learning taken by her university tutors, she still felt under pressure to go against her better judgment and fall behind Primary One's own more didactic approach to pedagogy:

> I think we had a lot more freedom then, even though it's not so long ago as all that. And the creativity side of things. Did we have SATs then? I don't think we did. If we did, I can't remember it. There was far less pressure on children then to perform. I'm sure we were happier – and no less well educated or capable. … I hate the pressure that's put on children these days. I hate myself sometimes for putting it on them. … Sometimes I just want to do things the way they used to be, but it's not easy is it. You're afraid that they won't cover all the stuff they're supposed to cover, or that you'll be failed and won't get [Qualified Teacher Status]. And then again, what if you try to be a bit more progressive and child centred and it doesn't work. I'd be even more depressed then. So that stops you doing it. You know, if you don't try it you can't fail. … I sometimes I wish I could be a child again, in spite of all the bad stuff. But I often wonder what it must be like to be a child today. Could I still even be that same child, today?

Caroline's concern that she might be complicit in making her students unhappy, and the feelings of guilt that this engendered, was accompanied, again in seeming contrast to Yanick, with a concern about what the children might think of her: in particular, whether, because she was putting them under pressure, they would view her negatively, or whether they would simply not like her as a person in spite of her efforts to be as nice to them as she felt the job would allow. She felt that being older did make them less likely to take advantage of her student status, but simultaneously wondered if they would prefer 'someone younger, all-singing-all-dancing', that they might find it easier to relate to. She was also racked with guilt – though it was of a different kind and had a different source than Yanick's. If Yanick felt some measure of guilt for his past behaviour as a child, a guilt which he might have sought to assuage by becoming a teacher himself, Caroline experienced guilt related to the present: guilt linked to the same sense of failure and weakness that Yanick sought to avoid. She was constantly berating herself for not doing as much as she felt she should, for not working harder; and she told me that every morning she woke up with a sense of fear and foreboding, believing that she had insufficient control over and respect from her students. This came as a surprise to me, and appeared almost perverse. Like the vast majority of other teachers I have met, it was clear to me that Caroline worked extremely hard, paying far more attention to detail and following up issues far more assiduously than I think most of us ever did when I was a classroom teacher, and she seemed to manage her students very well too. I wondered why she felt such a failure. I had not spent time in her classroom, but I had passed by many times and the children had always seemed happy and engaged. I wondered if her self-doubt had something to do with her own childhood. When I asked her about her experiences at primary school, she grimaced. The teachers, it seemed, were all likeable and sympathetic, but she had been the younger of two sisters, the older of whom, who had attended the same school, had been outstanding 'in every way: academically, artistically, musically, in school sports' – something which had clearly made life very difficult for Caroline. This past had consequently become a two-faced object for her: an idealised past of progressivism and child-centredness, whose remembrance brought a smile to her face, along with a miserable past that haunted her mercilessly and that she wished would simply go away:

> They never said so in so many words, but the elephant was always in the room. [My sister] was the smart one, the child my parents would always have dreamed of having. I was never going to be as good as her … never good enough, no matter how well I did. I'd get A grades, oh but she had got A pluses. I eventually got to Grade 6 on the piano, oh but she had got to grade 8. I could never measure up to her at home or at school. I knew some of the teachers there had taught her too, including my own class teacher which is never a good idea, and I knew that under[neath] their kindness they'd be thinking the same thing and probably always thinking I was under-achieving. … Then of course [my sister] went on to get a first-class degree at Cambridge

and ended up landing a top job at [a well-known charity] and I got an upper second and ended up in a [HR] job I hated.

I asked Caroline if all of this really mattered, reminding her that she had told me that she had always wanted to be a primary school teacher and that she was now doing what she had always wanted to do – that it wouldn't have made any difference if she had got A pluses at school or Grade 8 piano or a first-class degree at Cambridge, and that she had shown considerable strength of character to turn her back on the HR job at quite substantial financial cost.

> Yes, right from primary school I knew it was what I wanted to do. But things have definitely changed since then and it is proving very hard for me … much harder than I had ever imagined. The elephant's still there, too. [She smiles] The elephant in the classroom! I ought to bring in a picture of one and put it up on the wall. Confront the elephant! It's a confidence thing, I know that. But even now I'm thinking 'How would [my sister] have got on if she had decided to become a teacher?' 'What would she do to put across this point or deal with this problem?' It's hard to be myself with that going on.

I wanted to tell Caroline that her half-joking suggestion about bringing an 'actual' elephant into the room might not be such a bad idea, but I was interested to know if she had felt able to talk through her difficulties with her school- or university-based tutors, which seemed more to the point.

> Not really. I think [my school-based tutor] thinks I'm a bit of a wimp anyway, and that I should just get in with it and not keep bleating on about every little thing – as she sees it. I've obviously spoken to Yanick, in strictest confidence. Not sure if that's wise, on reflection! He told me I should complain to [my university-based tutor], but it's the politics of it all. It's just really difficult'.

I asked her what she by meant by 'the politics of it all'.

> 'I don't want to tell [my university-based tutor] in case she thinks I'm not getting enough support from [my school-based tutor] and takes it up with her, and then my relationship with [the school-based tutor] deteriorates even more and, you know, in the end she's the one who's mainly going to decide if I pass or fail. For the same reason I have to be really careful about how much I say to her. In the end you have to make a judgment call. Will things be better for me if I pursue the matter, or will they be better if I pretend everything is going fine and just carry on suffering every time I go into the classroom, hoping in time it will get better?'
> 'It sounds like you're saying it's the lesser of two evils'.
> 'It is. I've decided that in the long term it's probably best, or least bad, to pretend I'm doing OK'.

'And continue to suffer'.

'Yes. And continue to have sleepless nights. … Cry in secret'. [She smiles.]

A quick coding of Caroline's testimony speaks of ambivalence in relation to a personal past (including to her own childhood experiences of school); of feeling pressed into teaching in ways that she is uncomfortable with because there is no alternative; of fearing, in consequence, that she might be harming her students as well as being disliked by them; and of guilt in relation to her present practice – rather than, as with Yanick, guilt on account of past misdemeanours. Here, it seems, is someone who worries a great deal about others' perceptions of her, who cannot trust other people's motives (as evidenced in her assumptions about the 'politics' of her PGCE course), and who consequently finds it extremely difficult to 'be herself' – or perhaps to be true to herself. What strikes me most forcefully about Caroline, however, is the impact of her childhood experience on her present experience and practice – in particular, the way in which childhood feelings of never being good enough, of never working hard enough (no matter how many hours she might put in) are carried over into adult life. It seems not only that Caroline doubts her capacity ever to work hard enough, but that she recognises that the consequence of not working hard enough is failure – so that, in effect, the conviction that she has not worked hard enough creates itself the fear, the *expectation*, even, of failure. Fear of not being good enough, of losing or failing to command respect, of failing her PGCE course if she does anything that might be considered to be troublesome or unconventional, all combine to make her a dutiful, pragmatic, and in her own words 'rather uninspiring, if I'm honest' teacher in practice, even as her theoretical stance maintains its progressive roots and as the more golden aspects of her childhood continue to lap warmly against the shores of her consciousness.

Not everyone carries quite the same past into the present as Caroline and Yanick. But there are clearly pressures, both from 'within' and from 'without', not to address repetition and transference in our daily (in this case, our daily professional) lives, either on our own or in the company of others, and even discussing personal difficulties whose roots might lie in the past appears to have become taboo. With both Yanick and Caroline, I was struck, as I had been many times before with other teachers, by the feeling of insularity they expressed and experienced: in Yanick's case, an apparently self-imposed insularity (or at least one that he was able to rationalise and justify to himself as a choice), but with Caroline an unfortunate and inevitable fact of life. If Yanick made a virtue out of not seeking out help, Caroline appeared unable to do so, even within a system that has the stated intention of making help accessible. (Performativity, it seems, has very long and powerful tentacles.) Later in the day following my final interview with Caroline, I wrote in my field notes:

> Everyone seems to exist under the yoke of real or imagined surveillance. It discourages collegiality and collaboration, it promotes individual*ism*, whether

personal or institutional. So many people seem afraid of being 'found out', of the consequences of being perceived as weak or deficient in some other's eyes – perhaps, at a deeper level, in 'the Other's' eyes.

If Caroline expressed her emotional reactions and responses to classroom life, it could never be in the professional arena; the tears and anger had to be privatised, hidden away from the professional gaze, finding their expression either in the subject's own private individual space or in the presence of a close friend, parent, partner – or sympathetic researcher. The individual teacher must, in this regard, remain a constituent but affectively detached member of what is a 'collective' (a single school 'staff') in name only. For Yanick, this same circumstance appeared, at least at the start, to be welcomed – offering him the freedom to carry on with his own project unhindered by the distractions of other people's help and opinions.

5

AFFECT, COMMUNICATION AND 'ABSENCE'

Performativity and anti-caring

Archie's bad day

In this chapter I want to explore in a little more depth how psychoanalytically informed perspectives might, in addition to and perhaps as a consequence of developing fuller, more nuanced understandings of the roots and causes of our own feelings, help teachers better to understand and support their students. Staying with Primary One, the structure for the chapter is provided by a specific incident regarding one young learner whom I have pseudonymed Archie[1] – a Year 6 student in one of the few classes I got to know reasonably well, having been allowed to sit in for three half days by Primary One's headteacher Miriam and the class teacher Susan. By the time of the incident, I had already formed something of an opinion about Archie, whose visibility in the class was high despite the fact that his engagement in it and with other students was very low. Though not officially designated as having special needs[2] – a fact which puzzled me at the time – Archie came across very much as a loner, taking no active part in pair or group work regardless of which other children were involved in the activity, and spending a great deal of his time scribbling on paper or in his exercise book, walking about the room for no clear reason, tapping a ruler on the desk, humming or whistling tunelessly, silently staring into space for long periods or putting his head down on the table as if asleep.

Susan was always very patient with him, occasionally quite firm but always attempting to reach out to him with a joke or a word of praise or encouragement; however, she made it clear to me that she worried about having to spend a disproportionate amount of time with him to the detriment (she felt) of other students in the class, and frequently described him as her 'little problem'. She had learned to – or had a policy of being – tolerant of a certain level of what she called unusual behaviour in Archie, only feeling the need to administer some form of punishment when he had what she called 'a bad day'. (Almost exclusively, this would comprise

Archie's withdrawal from the classroom for a while, usually to a rather pleasant room where he could work – or not – alongside other troubled students as part of a nurture group.) A bad day for Archie, which might actually only be half a day, would comprise either an action on Archie's part that would make it very difficult for Susan to carry on teaching the class, or a sequence of slightly less disruptive acts driving her to believe that he was particularly unhappy to be in the classroom and that it would be in his own best interests to be removed to a quieter place where he could occupy his time 'drawing or daydreaming with his head on a desk or, with any luck, actually doing the work he's supposed to be doing!'.

I learned that in the playground Archie sometimes joined in games with other children – in particular, chasing games, which he seemed to be particularly fond of. But even on these occasions he seemed to be an outsider, following different rules from the other children and occasionally becoming overly physical with them. At other times, he would stand or sit away from the other children in a quiet corner of the playground, apparently removed from the social world unravelling chaotically before him, as if occupying a different time and place altogether. He rarely seemed willing to talk to adults: certainly not to me, and only to Susan under considerable duress. When I asked Susan why Archie was not on a special needs register, she told me a little vaguely that he probably should have been, but that his parents had not been supportive about discussing his difficulties and that educational psychologists were 'in very short supply anyway'. The nearest I got to a more detailed explanation from Susan concerned Archie's academic abilities: that is to say, 'Well, actually he's not what you'd call backward. In fact, when the mood takes him he can produce quite good work'. This account of Archie's academic ability was certainly one that chimed with my own observations. Archie may not have been an outstanding student academically, but he could certainly cope well enough, and on one occasion when I was in the classroom he managed to get through almost the whole day quietly getting on with his work, only lapsing into more familiar Archie-like behaviour after the lunch break when he became progressively disruptive – beginning with humming and making repeated click-ing noises with his mouth; moving on to apparently motiveless chuckling and calling out; and finally graduating, with no more than half an hour of the working day left, to walking around the classroom making a nuisance of himself to other children. It became clear to me that although there is more than one category of special needs the school, for whatever reason, seemed to prioritise students with severe learning difficulties rather than those with behavioural and emotional dif-ficulties – who might then easily be categorised as being naughty, silly, annoying or (as I think in Archie's case) eccentric, slightly mad and beyond the school's capacity to deal with properly. The result of Archie not being statemented was that he seemed to occupy a vague hinterland (paralleling that between social and anti-social, learner and non-learner in the classroom) between children receiving specialist care on the one hand and being just another troubled and troublesome child on the other – to be dealt with, as best as possible, from existing material and emotional resources.

The incident that brought Archie particularly closely to my attention and into the pages of this book occurred midway through my second day's full visit to Primary One. Because of a meeting off-site, I had not been in the class this particular morning and therefore had only learned of it second-hand. I recorded it in my fieldnotes as follows:

> Archie's regular class teacher, Susan, has been off sick for a few days, and a supply teacher, Ms Adams, has been taking the class, supported by the Teaching Assistant (Rosa). On the third day of this arrangement, Archie has decided, apparently without warning, that Ms Adams is 'stinky', and he has started refusing to accept her support as she moves about the class, though he seems not to have objected in the same way to the TA's efforts to help him with his work. Any time Ms Adams attempts to sit near him, he shrinks away from her in an exaggerated show of disgust, wafting his hand about in front of his face, grimacing and making a loud 'yuk' sound – increasingly eliciting much mirth from a small section of the class sitting close by, which has apparently had the effect of endorsing and encouraging his behaviour. Delores [the deputy headteacher] was immediately told about what is happening, and she has come to the classroom to remove Archie to the corridor to speak to him about his behaviour, telling him it is disrespectful and unacceptable – only to elicit the sullen response, audible within the classroom, to the effect that Ms Adams is 'stinky' and that it is not his fault.
>
> Ms Adams has clearly been very upset by this behaviour – more so, I think, than Delores, who tends to be of the 'seen and heard it all before' mindset. Ms Adams certainly is not 'stinky', as her colleagues in the staffroom are not slow to reassure her, and no one seems able to understand why Archie should have trumped up such an insult, other than along such lines as 'That's just Archie'; 'He does this sort of thing all the time'; 'We've all fallen foul of Archie at one time or another'; 'He inhabits a different world from the rest of us'; 'He just needs some time out of the classroom'. Given his lack of contrition, Delores has decided to report the matter to Miriam [the headteacher], who yesterday duly called Archie in, with Ms Adams and the TA, to discuss his behaviour and to elicit from him (so she hoped) an apology and a promise not to behave in this way again. Far from apologising, however, Archie has apparently gone on the offensive, telling Miriam with the apparent frustration of the falsely accused: 'It's not my fault, Miss. Most of the teachers are stinky' – apparently suggesting, for good measure, that Miriam is not excluded from this blanket criticism.
>
> Stories of Archie's misdemeanours have leaked into the staff room, where they've been greeted with disgust by some teachers and apparent amusement by others. The result is that a letter has been sent to Archie's parents outlining his 'unacceptable behaviour', and that Archie himself has been sent to the nurture-group room for the rest of the week (this being the remainder of Wednesday, and all day Thursday and Friday) to work away from his regular

> class while he 'thinks about his behaviour' – to be allowed back into class only after a further meeting with Delores, Susan and Ms Adams, and subject to the as-yet-unforthcoming written and spoken apologies and a promise to reform.

The following week, having agreed to the terms of his restoration, Archie was returned without further fuss to his normal classroom:

> I ask Delores how Archie is getting on since he came back to the classroom. 'No complaints so far', she tells me, reaching out very deliberately to touch the coffee table for good luck. Susan is back now in charge of the class. I tell Delores I'd like to carry on sitting in on the class if she and Susan are in agreement. I am given the green light, and will start back in tomorrow.

Though my initial intention had been to observe the whole class – to look at the ways in which the students interacted with Susan, how they sought or weren't bothered about her approval and attention and how she related to them on a personal level – I found myself irresistibly drawn again to observing Archie, almost to the exclusion of the rest of the class. I could detect no obvious change in him, or in Susan's treatment of him. He continued to doodle, to tap his ruler, to wander about the room, to hum and whistle, as if the 'stinky' episode had never happened. I did sense a feeling of mild antipathy, or perhaps it was morbid curiosity, toward him from much of the rest of the class – in particular from a small group of girls who repeatedly cast increasingly pointed and very disdainful glances in his direction when Susan's back was turned. He either did not notice them or chose not to, once again seeming to have occupied a space that was out of time and place with whatever was going on about him. I felt that it would not be long before there was another unacceptable eruption from him, that again he would be sent to the withdrawal room, or, worse, back home – and I wondered why it was that, although his difficulties were looked upon with a maternal eye by his teachers, there seemed little interest in working out what these difficulties actually were – or, for that matter, engaging with the possibility that his behavioural 'choices' as they liked to call them might not have appeared, to Archie himself, as choices at all.

Archie's 'choices': responsibility as (dis)empowerment

We can all, no doubt, understand the school's official response to Archie's behaviour. It is fairly standard practice, after all, and it was all apparently conducted in a very calm and civilised way, offering Archie an opportunity for salvation, forgiveness and a restoration of sorts back within the symbolic order of the school. No one had beaten Archie or shouted at him, and it was clearly understood by all parties (or perhaps mis-understood by some) that missing three days of normal school was unlikely to be a terrible burden for Archie to bear. It was also, at least it initially seemed so, in line with the school's inclusive, sympathetic approach to students identified as having behaviour problems that might or might not be identified as special needs. As with primary schools I had visited in previous studies, teachers at Primary One perceived themselves as – and strove to *be* – caring, sympathetic and understanding of their students' states and needs, including their emotional states and needs. To quote a primary school teacher from an earlier study (Bibby *et al* 2005–2007), in response to a question regarding the extent to which teachers were aware of the impact of children's emotions on their learning:

> That is one of the things I would say has changed over the years. Any good primary teacher is going to be aware, sometimes, that children walk into the class and are not very happy, for some reason or another. It might be that they have had an argument with their mum on the way in to school, it could be for all sorts of reasons, but it is very likely to happen, and most people would pick that up occasionally. I think most people would pick that up sometimes. … And I do think you should be interested in the children, and have some concern over their well-being and their background and what goes on for them out of school.

I felt that, by and large, teachers at Primary One had a similar understanding of and approach to their students' emotional states. I started to wonder, though, if Miriam, Delores and indeed Ms Adams, might have been more capacitated to understand Archie's behaviour, and perhaps have been more reflexive in relation to their own handling of the incident, rather than simply placing the onus on Archie himself to 'change his ways'. (Archie was, after all, still very young and clearly deeply troubled, and I felt concerned that his habitual disaffected behaviour, which I suspected must mask some profound unhappiness, would simply carry on unchecked if it was only addressed symptomatically and periodically, in response to individual eruptions.[3]) What if, for instance, to return to the example of my own not dissimilar experience with a student referenced in Chapter 1, they had tried to understand Archie's behaviour as a particular form of *communication* along the lines suggested by Feldman (1992: 83), whereby Archie had 'unconsciously … sought to re-locate [a] familiar object relationship, in which [he was] the attacked and abused child of an angry, critical [other]'? – or along the lines of Bott Spillius's account [1992: 68] of a form of *transference*, in which 'a patient may have an unconscious phantasy of projecting an experience into the analyst and may act in a way that makes the analyst *feel it*' (my emphasis)? Rather than simply dismissing Archie's behaviour as eccentric or disruptive, or as 'just Archie being Archie', might it not – at least feasibly – have been more helpful all round to wonder whether the negative feelings being experienced in such encounters (in this case, by Archie's teachers) might have been deliberately, if unconsciously, created by the other person in the confrontation – in which case they might be 'read', so to speak, as a mirror of those being experienced by that other person?

The first of these possibilities might suggest an understanding of Archie's behaviour as something of a cry for help and understanding – that is to say, of his deliberately setting up a situation in which he might re-experience having a responsible adult telling him off, inviting his teachers to understand something of what troubled him through forced adoption of the punitive role. The second possibility might suggest that Archie was actually trying to make the supply teacher, and then the headteacher, experience – *feel* – what he himself has been feeling, so that they might understand it – and him – better: in this case, that they might experience or feel what it is like to be shunned, to be looked down on, laughed at, seen and treated as stupid, made to feel dirty, and to express this to them in the only way available to him (that is to say, through affective communication), given that his apparent inability or reluctance or perhaps opportunity to articulate it in words might be part of what was making life so difficult for him in the first place.

I tentatively suggested these possible alternative understandings of Archie's behaviour, and approaches to it, to Susan over lunch on my next visit. I had half expected her to scoff at the idea, suggesting that I was over-thinking things, making excuses for Archie, and, by implication, criticising her. I would have understood that, too, since I have a tendency myself, in spite of my interest, to approach psychoanalytic interpretations with a degree of scepticism and defensiveness – often feeling that too much can be read into what an analysand may say and do in conversation. I also know that it becomes much more complicated and time-consuming dealing with a student like Archie when one abandons tried and trusted approaches to the problem and begins to entertain more complex ones that might necessitate a 'modification of our world view' (Britton 1992: 38). As Bott Spillius herself observed of her own work and her own developing understandings, it took 'some time' to recognise that one of her patients might be getting her to co-experience a negative feeling (in this case, the feeling of being despised), as well as the importance of such a recognition in terms of understanding the patient's experience (Bott Spillius: ibid.).

To my relief, Susan's response to my suggestion was one of interest and curiosity, albeit couched in a reminder of the impact of the pressures of teachers' everyday workloads when dealing with situations such as those involving Archie:

> I'd love – really love – to be able to learn about all these things, I really would. But it's the time thing again, and the pressure. Both together, actually. And I'm guessing that even if you could find the time to learn more about it the chances are you would struggle to put any of it into practice. There's so much pressure to prioritise the SATs results. It's relentless. I used to attend professional development courses in the good old days, and I learned about all sorts of interesting stuff … useful stuff, too … important stuff. But there's not even the time for that any more. It's a terrible thing to admit to, but taking time over something like this, which we all probably know in an ideal world we should do and would probably be better for all concerned … it just starts to feel like a luxury you can't afford.[4]

Susan's response reminds us that, even if teachers have a will to break free from what might be termed standard understandings and practices, there may be all sorts of other constraints obstructing them from doing so, including struggling to find the space for theoretical development. That is one difficulty. Another is that teachers have constantly to be aware of the needs of the many, particularly where there seems to be some conflict between these and the needs of the one. Given that schools are not easy organisations to manage, any more than individual classes are, that teachers are very busy and often very stressed individuals themselves, that rules have to be maintained and followed in order for collective and individual learning to take place, it is quite easy to understand how, when faced with a 'problem child' like Archie, swift action may need to be taken whereas the psychotherapist or psychoanalyst has the luxury – and perhaps the need – to take time. It is easy, too, to see and to understand how the need to sort things out quickly can lead to the proliferation, and the internalisation or embracement, of certain explanatory and justificatory discourses. In Archie's case, though not only in Archie's case (given that his case might be seen as a somewhat extreme one), the dominant discourse is a neoliberal-inflected discourse of 'choice'. 'Archie has been making some bad choices today', Delores told me in the staff room later on in the day his behaviour had come to her attention, and it strikes me again how, in an odd kind of discourse and ideology of 'empowerment', students as young as four or five are routinely told these days that they can make 'good choices' and 'bad choices', and that there will follow inevitable (good or bad) consequences from the choices they make.[5]

All this is understandable. Perhaps it is part of an enforced need to be pragmatic. And yet I can't get away from the thought that, without such changed interpretations of behaviour as that suggested by Bott Spillius, or at least without entertaining the *possibility* of such interpretations, we can never be sure that we have understood the behaviour and experience of a student like Archie, or come up with the best way of helping him and perhaps of re-integrating him into the social and academic life of the classroom and the school. The Bott Spillius analysis, if we can call it that, of Archie's behaviour is not necessarily correct in this case, but it is, at the very least, a possibility worth entertaining. Furthermore, I'd suggest that the very act of entertaining this kind of psychoanalytically informed interpretation of troubling behaviour can have a positive effect on the teacher-adult, subverting our own instinctive, hostile, or perhaps defensive reaction, which often involves personal hurt and unhelpful confrontation or self-blame, while at the same time producing a calmer, more circumspect orientation to the way in which we experience and respond to the other's challenge – potentially leading to a more fruitful and more helpful interaction. In short, moving our response away from the purely affective to a space in which we can interrogate the *affective nature of the exchanges that are taking place* can enable us to adopt a more thoughtful, circumspect and – dare I say it? – more inclusive approach to what is taking place and to what a more appropriate and helpful response might be. While Archie's deviant behaviour was dealt with in a firm but generally forgiving way at Primary One, my experience at other schools suggests that this does not apply to all such students, and that very often, even when emotions are kept in check in the actual verbal exchanges between (adult) teacher and (child) student, emotional wounds are carried away by teachers to continue to fester for substantial periods, while explanations to students as to why they are being punished tend to be corralled within that same discourse of choice, and with reference to standard, 'fairly applied' rules and regulations. In the final analysis, rather than having to engage in any depth with psychoanalytic theory it is the idea of *helping* that may represent a simpler, smaller leap for teachers, that actually is well within the grasp of a responsible and caring adult: one, certainly, that could be made in cases such as Archie's without even a passing knowledge of Kleinian and post-Kleinian analysis. Essentially, it comprises a move away from understanding and responding to a deviant child such as Archie as someone who needs punishment and correction, albeit offered in a relatively humane and understanding way, toward an approach which seeks to work with him to assist him in managing or overcoming whatever it is that is troubling him. We might also say this is a move away from fear (fear of the perceived threat posed by Archie to the symbolic and behavioural order of the school and classroom) toward a different kind of love: one that does not simply care for and about Archie's condition, but that seeks to comprehend it and to help him to overcome it or to live more happily with it. It is the kind of approach that requires what Dennis Atkinson, after Isabelle Stengers, has referred to as 'ecological' (one, that is, which is situated in and determined by the wider social, economic and psychic environment in which actions are carried out and judgments made), infused by 'disobedience' – where disobedience on the teacher's part is seen as a positive, constructive departure from traditional, accepted readings of and reactions to other's behaviours (Atkinson 2017; Stengers 2008). Disobedient students and deviant behaviours, that is to say, may be better served by disobedient teachers and deviant responses! As Stengers argues:

> [W]hat might be termed disobedient subjects … inadvertently, or sometimes directly, put authoritative or normative practices to the test. In doing this they may alter the pedagogical dynamic and the questions asked thus precipitating unanticipated forms of practice.
>
> *(Stengers 2008: 48)*

Forced against the grain: the Marcus problem

It cannot be said too often that such moves are not easy. Some may argue that where fear stalks so menacingly there is little room either for imagination or for love – or that love in public education, as it is often configured and experienced these days, can only manifest itself in helping others to move successfully into a system that may not itself either have or show much love for them. One huge problem for the teachers at Primary One was the extent to which fear was linked to work or to some dubious notion of productivity. I lost count of how many teachers complained to me about the sheer impossibility of their workload – a load made all the greater by an increased emphasis in official (Ofsted) inspections on evidence and quality of written feedback on students' work. When I suggested that perhaps some corners might have to be cut simply in order to survive, I was repeatedly advised that this was not possible because the likely consequences were far too serious. But a quart cannot be squeezed into a pint pot, and it seems to me that something has had to go – something, perhaps, whose absence might not be immediately noticed by an Ofsted inspector. That something, I think (ironically given Ofsted's apparent concerns over a school's safeguarding record), concerns the quality of relationships – including the way in which children's unhappiness is dealt with by teachers and by the school systems they operate within.

This was an issue that was by no means confined to Primary One but that, later on into my study, would produce a harsher manifestation at Secondary Two. This case concerned Peter, a relatively young Head of Year who had become painfully involved in dealing with the deviant behaviour of another student, much older than Archie, called Marcus – a student whom the headteacher at the school had arranged to have permanently excluded. Marcus was not personally known to me, other than by reputation, and my fieldnotes focus on the impact of the exclusion on Peter rather than on Marcus himself:

> Peter has been beating himself up regarding the decision (effectively *his* decision, as he sees it, though he didn't want it to happen) to permanently exclude a student called Marcus, a young man who has been in trouble several times already this term for extorting money from younger students. Peter was telling a group of colleagues with whom I was sitting how exclusion went against everything he believed in, how he resisted it 'with every fibre of his being'. But it had been, he said, a case of prioritising the needs of the many over the needs of the one. To allow Marcus, who had shown no inclination to stop his criminal behaviour in spite of numerous warnings as to what would happen to him if he did not, to stay at the school would have been to restrict the freedom and badly affect the happiness and learning capacity, the enthusiasm for coming to school at all, of a number of other students.
>
> I suggested, as did Peter's colleagues, that the decision to exclude Marcus was a tough and hugely upsetting one, but that it was probably the only acceptable course of action given the circumstances – that it genuinely was a 'last resort', and that if anyone or anything other than Marcus was to blame for his exclusion it was something to do with the system itself: not necessarily or exclusively the school system or the system of this particular school, but a symptom of something wrong in the wider society that neither Peter nor any of his colleagues could do anything immediately to change – that we are all victims of a performativity that both encourages us to cut corners and to take unpalatable decisions regarding individuals in order to protect the many from an external threat.
>
> Later on, I shared with Peter the gist of Archie's experience, suggesting that both his and Marcus's treatment brought to mind, in different ways, Ruti's promotion of psychoanalysis as a way of helping us not only to develop a 'heightened understanding' of ourselves, but to understand others in our lives too, and to develop 'more ethical, generous, and thoughtful relationships

with those we most care about' (Ruti 2009: 143). I wondered whether, if the teachers at Primary One had been allowed and encouraged to develop and put into some kind of practice such heightened understanding of their own and others' subjectivities, they might have approached Archie's plight more empathetically and sympathetically (might even have *seen* it as plight rather than as mere deviance) – just as, perhaps, the headteacher at Secondary Two might have spent more time and energy finding out why it was that Marcus persisted in wrecking his own future with apparent deliberation and with aggression toward his fellow students.

On one level, the rational level perhaps, Peter clearly agrees, nodding at everything I suggest. But he continues to suffer emotionally, and continues to blame himself and his colleagues for, as he puts it, 'allowing things to get this far in the first place' – seeming to confer, retrospectively, a power and control over events that has no obvious basis in the reality of lived experience.

Such was Peter's concern over what had happened that three days after the exclusion he made an appointment with the headteacher in a vain attempt to have the decision to exclude Marcus overturned in favour of something 'less Draconian'. That clearly didn't get him very far and simply drove him deeper into guilt and self-blame. A week or so after the initial decision had been taken, I accepted his invitation to have a drink after work, arrogantly thinking that I might be able to help him through this particular crisis. As we talked, Peter came more heavily down on himself than ever, expanding his concerns over the particular issue to talking about teaching, schooling and education more broadly. The whole system stank, he suggested. He had come into teaching to help and support underprivileged, marginalised and demonised young people, not to kick them out on their backsides. The situation and its resolution, he said, had made him a part of the system – a system that, as with Abigail, he had wanted to stand at the edges of in order to make it work better, rather than at the centre as one of its enforcers. So bad did he feel now that he was considering leaving teaching altogether. It was as if all his previous negative experiences had accumulated in the manner of a huge boil, of which this final one had represented the bursting head – bringing with it, however, not relief but only further pain and anguish.

Peter's case reminds us, if we need reminding, that teachers are not always willingly compliant in the kind of fast-track response to unacceptable behaviour received by Archie and – even more seriously so in terms of its consequences for the student – by Marcus. Many of the teachers at both Primary One and Secondary Two expressed a keen awareness of how the pressures of work, time and surveillance could impact negatively on their relationships with students, as well as sorrow and anger that they should find themselves as reluctant accomplices to the fact. Perhaps I am being unfair, but in the case of Marcus it seemed to be the pressure of surveillance as much as anything that had precipitated his removal from the institution. With an Ofsted inspection looming, and with the very real threat of being found wanting, the stakes were high not just for Marcus but for the school as a whole. What Marcus had done had been harmful to other students, and clearly something equally serious needed to be done about it, but the speed with which he had been expunged from the school role seemed to be all about the threat his presence might pose not just to other students but – perhaps even more importantly when perceived in terms of the school's broader future – to how the school was perceived and judged externally. If this was an understandable response, it still felt like a very troubling one: an example, perhaps, not only of how performativity divides but also how it excludes. While in the scheme of things Marcus appeared as a malfunctioning function, Peter had wanted to *understand* him: *why* he had behaved as he had done, what was it that had driven him to it – and what, if anything, might be done to help him so that he might be happily re-integrated into the system and perhaps even into normal society. Unfortunately from Peter's point of view, and perhaps from Marcus's, the system appeared to be resistant to such re-integration.

'Moments of absence': attachment, detachment and the group

Towards the end of Laurent Cantet's 2001 film *Time Out* ('L'Emploi du Temps'), the central character, Vincent, tells his wife: 'My mind is blank. I look around me, at the people I work with. I see totally unknown faces. Like moments of absence'. Vincent is a man who both hates his work and feels the need to be *in work*. Being in work gives his life some sense of justification, confirming his position within the symbolic order, the Lacanian 'Other'. But this symbolic attachment is not accompanied by an affective one. It is on his return to work, following a lengthy absence during which he presents a false image to the world of continuing to be a hardworking and successful businessman, that he makes this observation to his wife – perhaps more as an invitation to sympathy than by way of explanation of his previous, and by now exposed, duplicity.

These 'moments of absence' experienced by Vincent seem to connect with Ruti's account of the 'states of solitude and noncommunication' (Ruti 2009: 130) evident in Archie. But whereas a state of solitude and noncommunication might have a positive, therapeutic, meditative inflexion, moments of absence seem to signal, instead, a mind-numbing sense of alienation and rejection – a kind of 'difference' that brings with it only trouble and despair. Archie's moments were often, it seemed, more than just moments which, with a little effort, he could quickly snap out of. They were, rather, *periods* of absence, so that Archie seemed to have either come with or developed over time an enduring sense of detachment, of not belonging, and therefore of not really being 'there', where everyone else is – such that it was as if the classroom and his own activity within it had taken on a dreamlike quality: nothing here was real; therefore he could behave unconventionally with impunity. There seemed no sense of linkage between Archie's actions and the feelings of those about him; he was like a ghost. Indeed, perhaps the other children in the class didn't even see him. Perhaps, from time to time, he experienced not just a sense of absence from the lesson and from the classroom, but also a sense of being absent in the eyes and experiences of the other students. How might he cope with such troubling moments, which must be profoundly disturbing for him? Is one obvious way to 'do' something? – to punctuate those periods of absence, those states of solitude and non-communication, when he wakes again into some form of reality, with an activity? Since he could not (so he felt) contribute meaningfully to the development of shared knowledge and understanding, might he not seek to attract attention to himself through 'naughtiness' – through actions which might themselves lead from psychic to physical withdrawal from the classroom: Archie's 'corridor life' as Susan once called it?

This is all speculative. But what is not so speculative, I think, is Archie's isolation and loneliness, his solitariness within the group. As I wrote in my fieldnotes:

> Archie's is a solitariness which reminds me of the sense of isolation experienced and described by Caroline, John and Zoë, who felt that they could not share problems with senior colleagues. This is clearly not exaggeration on their part, or 'paranoia'. It strikes me as a symptom of what can happen to people and institutions as the harsh, cold blade of performativity gets taken up and wielded against the self and against others by those it attacks in the first place. Performativity exhibits like a virus. Starting 'outside' the body it comes to infect it. It is a virus that cannot tolerate 'weakness' – that must seek it out and punish or remove it.

Given the sense of isolation expressed in interview by many teachers like Caroline, John and Zoë, it may seem surprising that Archie's own 'absent presence' did not bring forth more intensive analysis from his teachers, or that it was apparently not considered relevant enough to be included in discussions of his rudeness and disruption or in determining how best to respond to his more invasive behaviour. But perhaps it is the very fact of such isolation *in teachers*, and the circumstances which prompt it and in which it occurs, that acts as an obstacle to such empathy. The fact that we experience something ourselves does not necessarily mean that we see that same experience in others. While it might not be the case that Archie's visible absences were themselves intended as – or were manifestations of – some form of non-verbal communication (though perhaps his ruler-tapping, wandering and whistling were), they did seem to act as a kind of mirror in which his carers might see, if they looked, an exaggerated representation of their own inner, psychic state.

If Archie was an obviously isolated, detached individual within the class group, communicating in what might have seemed bizarre, non-verbal ways to others, there was plenty of evidence from my studies that affective isolation, disengagement and detachment within a physical, organised collective were by no means uncommon among both adults and children. In fact, it seemed to be, to adapt Žižek's account of fear, a 'basic constituent of most people's subjectivity' (Žižek 2009: 34; see also Chapter 3, note 2) – the only differences relating to impact and degree.

Reference has already been made to the sense of aloneness experienced by many teachers in the study, along with a reluctance to share emotional difficulties with colleagues, and of how, within a group or collective supposedly working toward the same broad end, even when at some level there may be a feeling of belonging, individuals can feel that they are effectively working and bearing their problems alone: that is to say, except in cases of true friendship, how they may experience *psychic and affective* detachment in spite of (and perhaps even because of) *organisational and professional* attachment. The encouragement and exacerbation of such relationships by a culture of competition and competitiveness and by the internalisation of the performativity discourse will be considered in more depth in the following chapters, particularly in Chapter 7. At Primary One, it displayed itself most noticeably in relation to the anticipation of an imminent Ofsted inspection, which was predicted to occur – and indeed did occur, though I was not present for it – soon after my first visit to the school.

The fear of an Ofsted inspection – or more precisely, perhaps, the fear of its possible consequences – was one of the greatest and most ubiquitous fears at each of the schools I visited. No matter how well-prepared and well-briefed the teachers were, no matter how carefully the required paperwork had been gathered together, no matter how good the teaching and learning in the school were believed to be, the fear of the damage that a single visiting voice – an errant, rogue, uniformed or even malicious voice, perhaps – could bring about was one that could occupy teachers to distraction. Even when understood or re-cast as part of a collective project of 'saving the school', individuals – like John, quoted in Chapter 3 – would have a very real sense of being under examination personally, with all the psychic – not to mention professional – consequences that this might bring. We have already seen how John reacted to what he perceived as a negative response to a lesson he thought had been outstanding, and no amount of encouragement and comradeship could shift the self-doubt that it had instilled in him. It was clear from his testimony that having someone telling you you're not good enough (by telling you you are 'only good'!), even if you thought you were, and even if you don't have faith in your critic's judgment, can still be a very painful thing to bear and one whose effects can linger within you – like an affective form of post viral syndrome – for a very long time after the event.

For many teachers at both Primary One and Secondary Two, the very thought of 'RI' (popular shorthand for 'Requires Improvement') was enough to deflate the atmosphere in a room. An RI Ofsted judgment resulted in continuing external monitoring and another inspection within two years. For some teachers, it was, to quote Abigail at Secondary Two, 'the start of the slippery slope to academisation'[6] and at the very least meant that 'Ofsted are on your back for the foreseeable future'. If an 'RI school' was deemed not to have improved sufficiently after two years, it would be downgraded to 'inadequate', either being instructed to address 'serious weaknesses' or being put into 'special measures', leading, as Abigail had perhaps recognised, to compulsory academisation – a development which led, almost inevitably, to changed conditions of service and the possibility of becoming wedded to the educational imperatives of business sponsors.

It was clearly in each school's interests to have what they called a 'good Ofsted', and in that regard the effort to bring it about might be regarded as a collective effort. However, this common cause did not always appear to bring people together

in a spirit of comradeship. On the contrary, it seemed just as likely to divide colleagues as to unite them, and for some teachers the fear of 'the inspector' came
to be accompanied by another fear, from inside the institution, that any personal
weaknesses and failings, if discovered by a line manager or member of the senior
leadership team, might result in almost equally unpleasant consequences. Though
both Primary One and Secondary Two presented themselves in their documen-
tation as caring institutions, even in these schools it seemed that an unforgiving,
rather punitive management culture was evolving in relation to staff – as well as in
relation to students – that ran counter to the rhetoric. At either school, an externally produced performativity discourse and culture had, almost inevitably perhaps,
appeared to have infected the higher ends of the staffing structure where teachers
were often much closer to the interface with policy implementation – resulting
not simply in self-policing but, as we shall see later on, in some of performativity's
more brutal practices.

A feature of Archie's punishment at Primary One was that it resulted not from
his feelings but in response to the actions that ensued from those feelings – or, if
we are to follow the post-Kleinian suggestion explored earlier, for his expression of
them: that is to say, the expression itself rather than what the feelings might have
said about his state of being. Meanwhile, the punishment *per se* appeared to hold no
fears for Archie, and we can only speculate as to the extent to which it might have
acted to reinforce his sense of non-belonging and symbolic rejection. For many
of the under-threat teachers, it was a different story. While they feared individual
and group punishment for their actions, or more specifically for the possible (unin-
tended) consequences of their actions (their students' perceived poor performance,
a lesson that did not work as intended) from 'outside', from the inside they feared
punishment too for their state of being – if and when it was betrayed either through
communication or via observable behaviour. Like Archie, many of them talked
about – and could be seen – experiencing moments of absence, some of which
extended into what we might call periods of absence during the time immediately
prior to the Ofsted inspections when they experienced a sense of detachment and
dissociation within the community to which they symbolically and professionally belonged and with which at some level they continued to identify. Susan, an
experienced teacher at Primary One, who had been through an Ofsted inspection
before and knew all about 'the pressures, the pain, and the fallings-out' that it
could bring, felt and looked particularly anxious and preoccupied in the run-up to
their inspection. As Primary One's literacy coordinator, she expressed on a number
of occasions an experience of feeling overwhelmed and isolated by imposed and
internalised responsibility; and even though there was an air of stoicism and ironic
detachment in many of our conversations it was clear that she was very far from
being happy. A week or so before the inspectors finally arrived, she spoke to me at
length about the 'almost intolerable' pressure that she felt she was being put under:

> 'There's only so much you can do, but in the end the buck stops with me'.
> 'Not with [the Head]?'

'Well, yes, I suppose so. ... In a way. But if we flop it won't be her fault. At least, it won't seem that way. ... She won't see it that way. It'll be because I haven't chased things up properly and got everyone singing from the same hymn sheet. I spend so much of my time now chasing up colleagues for marking [exercise books], you wouldn't believe it. And getting my own marking up to date. I'm here at the crack of dawn every day and they have to literally kick me out every evening. Fortunately, I have a very understanding and sympathetic husband. The trouble is, it never goes away. Ofsted is one thing, but [the Head] has introduced ... had to introduce ... our own more rigorous internal systems so that we are always "Ofsted ready" as they say. You have to be these days because you never know when they are about to descend. Heads pick things up on the grapevine, and there's an extent to which you can work things out, but you have to be. ... Unless they've been told otherwise, every school has to be in a state of constant readiness'.

I asked Susan the obvious question: If the internal systems themselves have to be maintained at such a level, why should there be more work involved just because Ofsted might be coming in? Wasn't that the whole point of these snap visits – so that schools wouldn't feel obliged to devote too much time and energy preparing for the inspection and then, once successfully through it, return to more normal practice once again?

> You're right. It shouldn't be necessary. But it is. There's just something about the inspection ... what it does to people. ... The sheer terror it can cause in some people. Even old hacks like me. So even when you know your systems are in place and working pretty well, and even. ... To be honest, I don't really *need* to be doing all this chasing up. ... But that's another thing: you find you start not trusting other people, even colleagues you know who've never let you down. ... But. ... Yep, even when everything is sorted, you just can't stop thinking maybe there's one more thing I could. ... we could do, that would push you up from good to outstanding, or from RI to good. You just don't want to be in the position after the event of looking back and thinking 'God, if only we had done this or that just a little bit better'.

A little later, I asked Susan what it was, given the amount of stress she was under, that kept her in the profession. Her answer reminds me again, somewhat sadly, of Ahmed's notion of the happy object (op. cit.), and of its loss. It is evident from Susan's testimony that, as with Graeme, both teaching itself and the kind of teacher she had once been able to be had become lost happy objects, just as had the joy and rewards of the job itself:

> Well, having a job, for one thing. ... And a relatively secure job at that. And the teaching – though even that isn't as good as you'd like it to be given the amount of your time taken away by other things.[7] But it's not the job I

came into. ... Perhaps I was too idealistic. ... Perhaps not. I just wanted to do good work, you know. ... Help people to live a better life. At times like this, I can't say I get pleasure from coming in to work every day. In fact, most mornings it just fills me with a sense of dread.

Similar feelings – of working alone and under stress, of not enjoying a job that had promised so much in the beginning – were not uncommon among teachers at Primary One, and, if anything, were even more widespread and more deeply felt at Secondary Two. The testimony of Abigail, the deputy headteacher at Secondary Two already cited in previous chapters, serves both to underline the point and to lead us in to the following chapters:

> Abigail is suffering from stress and sleepless nights. She looks tired and unlike her usual confident, gregarious self. She told me today: 'I don't know what I'm doing. I'm running around like a headless chicken, getting everything ready for an inspection that may or may not happen – this week, next week, some time. ... Not never. ... Unfortunately, ... I'm driving myself round the bend getting everyone and everything on track, but most of the time it feels like a dream. Or some kind of game. It's all about winning and losing. And then, when the inspection is over, the game ends and we go back to doing what we've always done. Except we can't, not even if they like what they see. And if they don't [like it]. ... That's the problem. That's what's keeping me awake at night. If we get RI ... it doesn't bear thinking about. So you can't take your eye off the ball. You can't not keep going and you can't stop doing all the other stuff, the marking and stuff, even though you're already working way over capacity. To tell you the truth, it's exhausting. I can quite see why people suffer from burnout or just walk away from it all. Believe me, I've thought about doing it myself often enough'.
>
> I ask her if she has discussed her difficulties with the headteacher or anyone else in the school, knowing pretty much in advance what her answer will be. She smiles at me ironically, as if drawing attention to an outsider's naïvety: 'There's no point in that I'm afraid'. She won't elaborate – I sense, as a result of her code of professionalism. But the message is clear enough. She has already complained to me about what she fears is the emergence at the school of 'a kind of macho culture when it comes to feeling stressed', and I get the distinct feeling once again that struggle here is perceived as weakness – and that weakness is neither sympathised with nor tolerated. A weak link in the chain, and the whole machine comes unstuck: 'The future of the institution is more important than the future of the one(s)!'.

Martin's tale: the anti-ethics of the lifeboat

At the end of my original field note on Archie's solitariness, I had added the words 'reference discussion with Martin for elaboration'. It occurs to me now that the discussion I was referring to, which had been initiated by Martin, also puts a little more flesh on the bones of the observations made by Susan and Abigail.

Martin was a teacher at Primary One. Like most of the other teachers at the school, he was always happy to talk. But unlike many of his colleagues, he did so without fear, displaying, so it seemed, the freedom of someone who knows that whatever he says or does his future career will not be damaged – not least, because he had no plans for a long-term career in the profession anyway, harbouring ambitions to travel the world and to write 'at least one best-selling novel'. It is the freedom too of someone for whom the consequences of an Ofsted inspection are less personally important than the system that demands and shapes them and the manner of their enactment. This is not to say that Martin had no sense of loyalty to his school, or that he did not care about his students: far from it. But if Primary One were to close, or to be put under special measures or academised, Martin would simply seek work – 'even supply work' – at another institution. Though officially subject to the same rules and expectations as his colleagues regarding matters like producing extensive written lesson plans, marking and returning work within a given time frame and insisting on tidy handwriting and careful use of the ruler for underlining, in practice Martin tended to do things his own way and was given considerable (and, it seemed, unique) latitude in doing so – an example, perhaps, of what one of the focus group teachers I spoke to outside of the main study referred to as 'maverick teachers'. 'They just have to look at the results', Martin told me. 'One day the penny might drop and someone in authority might wonder how come my kids do so well when I don't follow the rules that are supposedly necessary for their success'.

On the day we met, Martin wasted no time clarifying why he had asked me to join him. No sooner had we sat down, in a small café just around the corner from Primary One, than he was telling me what a really depressing time it was to be a teacher, and how what teachers were being asked to do was 'just impossible'. He was also 'sick to the teeth' with a system that required young children to be 'battered' every morning of the week with numeracy and literacy work – 'or what passes for it':

> We're also supposed to be fitting in PE, which is a joke, and the science requirements. It's just not possible. Stuff like Art and Music, even geography and history – anything remotely creative or critical – hardly gets a look in any more. And the model of literacy they're promoting is such a limited one: parts of speech, as if no one could function linguistically without being able to define a gerund or recite what a noun, a verb and an adjective is or tell you when and why you should use a subjunctive – let alone what it is; how many adverbs and connectives and this and that in a sentence. If you go down that route they end up just reproducing formulaic drivel. And then they're told they have to write so many words or half a page or whatever every day, because that's how they'll get better at writing. Which is fine if you like writing already and want to get better at it, but not if it's a struggle. And then, if they prove they're good enough, they're given something called

a pen licence. A pen licence! What's that supposed to be? 'Oh, the kids all love it'. – So that's supposed to make it worthwhile. Since when did we do things anyway just because the kids like it?

Martin offered up a rapid-fire inventory of everything that he felt was wrong with education as currently configured, expressing particular concern for the damage he felt it was doing to children, what he saw as the wasteful misdirection of centrally provided resources, and how upset and depressed and angry it made him feel. The time devoted to developing handwriting skills was something that particularly concerned him. It was totally unnecessary, he said, given the rise and ubiquitousness of digital technologies: nothing more than a controlling device. The National Curriculum, and an overemphasis on numeracy and literacy, were destroying creativity and independent thinking, and children were being controlled and constrained at an earlier and earlier age. ('And now we see in the papers that the Education Secretary wants to get children following some sort of spoonfed National Curriculum at the age of two. Two!')

Our discussion covered many issues: the much younger school starting-age in other countries, and whether this had any negative impact on the children's future learning or development; whether a sensible answer to the underachieving poor might be to eliminate poverty; the current obsession, flying in the face of the majority of early reading theory, on phonics, which he believed to be slowing down the reading progress of many students; and the way in which he felt teachers were generally treated and managed in English schools.

It was this last issue that occupied most of the rest of our conversation and that was to develop into a key theme and finding as the research study continued. Although Martin made no secret of the fact that he liked Primary One's headteacher, describing her as 'an old-school head who actually walks around the school and goes into classrooms and knows the children's names',[8] he was 'shocked' at the extent to which she appeared to have adopted and internalised performativity. To my surprise, since I had always thought her to be a caring, sympathetic individual, it was another of the school's senior teachers who bore the brunt of Martin's dissatisfaction. He told me that he had overheard a conversation ('that I probably shouldn't have') between her and another senior teacher, in which they had been quite savagely critical of certain other members of staff, describing one in particular as 'weak', 'pathetic' and 'work-shy'. Martin was familiar with this maligned teacher, whom he felt to be honest and hardworking 'if not the strongest in the classroom', currently going through a very hard time as a result of severe difficulties in private relationships outside school. Martin was saddened that his colleagues should dismiss the teacher in this way, evidently having no sympathy at all for his personal difficulties but rather suggesting that they should be left outside the classroom and not allowed to impact on his performance inside it. It was clear, according to Martin's account, that some senior colleagues would like to 'get shot of' the teacher in question, especially with an Ofsted inspection looming, before he dragged the whole school down with him.

'This', Martin suggested, 'is how performativity works': 'It appeals to the most basic fears and instincts. Survival. We all sink or swim together. Any weak link has to be clinically cut away as a matter of expediency. Forget someone might be struggling with personal problems. There's no room for sentiment. Not in this game. It's like the lifeboat scenario in the Alfred Hitchcock film. Everyone together in a lifeboat waiting to be rescued. Instead of the situation bringing people together, instead of problem-solving their way out of a shared crisis, they turn on one another, only caring about personal survival and striking up alliances with people they normally wouldn't give the time of day to. It's what I call anti-ethics. Anti-ethics and anti-caring. Working together and looking out for each other, in the end that's the only way there's going to be any effective kind of opposition. But you try telling that to some people in senior management'.

I was familiar with the Hitchcock film, and knew that it was not quite as Martin remembered, but his reference to survival and to the way in which performativity can infect a school's soul as well as its practice, pitting people against one another even as they pull together to get the metaphorical boat to safety, rang horribly true. Performativity did not only affect practices; it had a profound effect on social relationships too. If the system really worked so powerfully and effectively against collaboration and collegiality, what hope could there be, I wondered, for the collective opposition to it that Martin craved?

It is with this last question in mind that we enter more deeply the world of Secondary Two.

PART III

Reflexivity, discourse and the affective pull

6

NOT ROCKING THE BOAT

Virtuous pragmatism and the allure of normalcy

Some context

The two chapters that comprise this section require a word of clarification. It would not be difficult to interpret them as being critical of teachers – at least, of those teachers whose testimonies are drawn on for illustration and exemplification. They are not intended to be. The teachers I have referenced and quoted, like all the other school teachers I have encountered in various situations, are doing an excellent job in what are often very trying, sometimes even obstructive, circumstances. In this current chapter, Chapter 6, I am not suggesting that teachers are any different – or indeed *should* be any different – from anybody else in experiencing difficult choices or in arriving at, and justifying, compromises that may involve both affective and 'rational' decision-making processes, or indeed in the matter of self-preservation. Neither, in the chapter that follows this one, am I suggesting that it is wrong for teachers to enjoy and celebrate their students' (and their own) successes, or that they should deny or seek to change such feelings, even when success is measured according to imposed criteria with which they may, in some or all aspects, disagree – or that there are not important practical reasons contributing to anyone's acceptance of or obedience to external diktats, including the potential danger to ourselves and to others of doing otherwise. (It perhaps needs saying in light of the first of these matters that, despite the problems they face, the vast majority of teachers with whom I have had contact during the course of my studies continue to find working with and helping young people a source of great pleasure and satisfaction.) I am simply seeking to invite exploration, through considerations of what I imagine will be familiar situations, of the nature of affect in our professional lives, and of the way in which public policy, which in addition to its own affective dimension may also take advantage of and manipulate affect in others, appeals to affect in order to secure its successful implementation in the practical domain. I will begin this attempt by saying a necessary word or two about the nature and effects of neoliberalism.

Neoliberalism: performativity and individualism

It is not contentious, I think, to suggest that both globally and in the UK neoliberalism has become the dominant political ideology of the day – an 'ideology and a theory of social, political and economic practices' espousing a belief that 'human well-being can best be advanced by the maximization of entrepreneurial freedoms within an institutional framework characterized by private property rights, individual liberty, unencumbered markets, and free trade': a theory in which '[t]he role of the state is to create and preserve an institutional framework appropriate to such practices' (Harvey 2007: 22; see also Davies 2014). Neoliberalism thus understood presents itself as a rational choice – for some, indeed, a rational inevitability. However, I want to suggest that it is an ideology and set of attendant discourses and practices that, far from being inherently rational or 'natural', has to sell itself (in much the same way that any product is sold) through an essentially affective appeal – not least, through the kinds of positively saturated terms in Harvey's summary: terms such as 'freedom' and 'rights', which we have already considered in relation to the selling – and buying – of centrally driven education policy.

The acknowledgment in Harvey's succinct definition that the state has a 'role to create and preserve' the necessary conditions for 'entrepreneurial freedoms' is often identified as the central feature that marks out neoliberalism from classical liberalism: i.e. that makes it 'neo'. As Jeremy Gilbert elaborates:

> Put simply, neoliberalism, from the moment of its inception, advocates a programme of deliberate intervention by government in order to encourage particular types of entrepreneurial, competitive and commercial behaviour in its citizens, ultimately arguing for the management of populations with the aim of cultivating the type of individualistic, competitive, acquisitive and entrepreneurial behaviour which the liberal tradition has historically assumed to be the natural condition of civilised humanity, undistorted by government intervention. This is the key difference between classical liberalism and neoliberalism: the former presumes that, left to their own devices, humans will naturally tend to behave in the desired fashion. By contrast the latter assumes that they must be compelled to do so by a benign but frequently directive state.
>
> *(Gilbert 2016: 12–13; see also McChesney 1999: 7–11)*

Gilbert's gloss helps to explain a characteristic of much central education policy in the UK and elsewhere: that while on the one hand it promotes competition (in the field of UK education, among and between students, teachers and schools), freedom and choice (for example, the freedom for parents to choose from a variety of schools, or for schools themselves to opt out of central control), on the other hand, as Coffield and Williamson (op. cit.) have pointed out, it simultaneously intervenes far more in public education – including in matters of what is actually taught in schools – than at any other time in history. This explains another difference between neoliberalism and classical liberalism – or rather, perhaps, what classical liberalism has evolved into: that neoliberalism, with its emphasis on attending to the running of 'the Market', is far less concerned with individual human welfare than classical liberalism, and far more concerned with managing and stabilising the wider economic system within which we must all live.

In relation to public education, we might say that neoliberalism is centrally concerned with the preparation for individual and national participation in an unchallenged but constantly evolving global free-market – ensuring that a suitably educated citizenry can work with that evolving system in ways that preserve the economic status quo or that render it more advantageous to the perceived overall economic interests of the nation state. In practical terms, neoliberalism attaches a market value to performance and product – a process and set of practices sometimes referred to as 'performativity' (see, for example, Ball 2003, Wilkins *et al* 2012 and the discussion in Chapters 2 and 4 above) embracing or introducing numerical and often summative measures of the 'quality' of such production, such as test and examination scores, inter-institutional 'league tables' or Ofsted grades. Individual freedom and responsibility are stressed in policy rhetoric, in each case attached to the notion that social and financial success, and presumably consequential happiness, is within the grasp of every hardworking individual within the current socio-economic system. Teacher professionalism within the terms of this ideology becomes attached to individual and collective success in meeting targets – mainly related to the numbers of students achieving success in the terms imposed.[1]

Buried within popular neoliberal discourses of freedom and choice – easily internalised, as we have seen in the case of Archie, both in education practice and in teachers' understandings of student behaviour – are two other discourses already referred to: those of responsibility and competition – all having in common a positive affective appeal. As with other affect-laden discourses, the ideas and ideologies which lie at their centre, of freedom and of being able to use our freedom to make choices, however illusory their promise might be in reality, have an enduring and potentially very powerful appeal. Who, for example, has ever wanted to be *not free*? However, as Fisher (in Fisher and Gilbert 2016: 128) has argued, the freedom that neoliberalism offers is of a somewhat limited nature. While neoliberalism promises 'less government' and greater personal and local decision-making, for example, it simultaneously embroils us all in a 'mad, cancerous proliferation' of constricting, government-directed bureaucracy (ibid.). Nor is it just bureaucracy that limits our freedom to choose – we might say, our freedom to access the freedom we have been promised. Despite the notion of 'agency' being touted so loudly within neoliberal rhetoric, agency buried within dominant discourses of responsibility and competition may all too often appear only to exist (and then, only for some) in such matters as choosing what food and clothes to buy, or what school to send one's children to: 'lifestyle choices', that is, within a given system, rather than the choice of a different or radically altered system (or lifestyle) itself. Freedom, in any event, like knowledge and skills, is of little value to someone – and there are very many someones – who does not have the opportunity to do anything with it. As Chomsky (1999: 91) has observed: 'Freedom without opportunity is a devil's gift, and the refusal to provide such opportunities is criminal'.[2]

One particularly important aspect of neoliberal theory and policy in relation to what has been discussed in the preceding chapters is that, except when it comes to nationalism, freedom and choice nearly always refers to the *individual* (or individual family unit) rather than to the collective. This is hardly surprising, given that the nature of the markets into which we are, as individuals, interpellated *demands* individualisation. For most of our lives, we buy as individuals or as families, not as wider collectives, and it is consequently important, in order for neoliberal ideology to thrive, that individual freedom (to make selections within both practical and ideological marketplaces) must be understood and experienced not only as a desired state but as the only natural, feasible state – such that neither its inherent desirability nor its implications for society are called into question. Practising teachers, no less than their students, working as they do in and with social groups on a daily basis, will know that there are problems with the idea of individual freedom: indeed, teachers may often find themselves, quite reasonably and understandably, appealing to the good of the group when challenging or punishing deviant individuals. But they will also be aware that they are working within a school system that demands inter-subjective competitiveness and individualism, a system in which young people are in constant competition with one another for marks and grades, in which collective endeavour is rarely rewarded with any symbolic capital that will be of much use within the professional or higher education marketplace (high grades in public examinations, for example), but rather with medals, certificates and other trinkets: things that may carry the affective attachment stuck to the notion of competition, giving their recipient(s) a positive feeling, but that are unlikely to help them very much to a university place or into a well remunerated job.

Of course, there is bound to be something of an inevitability of the mirroring of a dominant ideological and discursive set of policies, practices and values in the policies, practices and values of the state school system.[3] However, as we shall see in this chapter and the next, the promotion of individualism and competition in the school system brings with it many other problems than the one touched on briefly in the previous paragraph. One of these is its capacity to engender marginalisation and apathy, often through the extreme pressures that it can impose *on* the individual(ised) (but at the same time normalised) teacher and learner. Drawing on Posch's (1994) account, more than twenty years ago now, of the 'challenges which profound social and economic changes are posing for education', John Elliott (2000), in an echo of the argument already made concerning performativity's capacity to impact negatively on social relationships, invites a parallel between individualisation in school (through the school curriculum) and a wider individualisation in British society. Though written at a time before performativity and the centralised control of education in England had taken quite so tight and constricting a hold on schools and teachers, it is worth quoting Elliott at length. Referencing some of central policy's own positively charged rhetoric and terminology, Elliott picks up the theme of 'the loss of "continuity in social relationships" from which people increasingly defect for the sake of short term gains' – the price of which is extremely high:

> [P]eople lose their capacity to trust each other and to exercise 'social responsibility'. In this context, the relationship between teachers and students becomes increasingly instrumental. If pupils cannot discern short-term gains from their experiences in classrooms and schools, more and more of them are likely to 'defect' from engaging with learning. The result of such an outlook is that pupils decreasingly trust teachers to take care of their futures, or to see themselves to be in any way responsible for the well-being of their peers in the way they conduct themselves in classrooms and schools. The challenge for teachers is to create learning situations which provide new conditions for trust to emerge in their relationships with pupils, and a new basis for the latter to exercise their responsibility for each others' well-being. Such situations will need to involve forms of collaborative learning which foster mutual respect and a sense of community, and are valued because they engage and challenge pupils at deeper levels of their personal and social being than simply a desire for short-term satisfaction and gain.
>
> *(Elliott 2000: 253–254)*

The argument here – born out to a considerable extent in the study of young learners referred to in Chapter 3 (Moore 2013; Bibby 2010; see also Holt 1964) – is that current dominant discourses promoting the individual learner within an overarching discourse of performativity leads to pedagogic short-termism on the part of both teacher and learner (and between learners), damaging learning, and learning relationships themselves, in the process. The learner is concerned – if at all – only for their own measurable and externally validated advancement, and is content to settle for the fast return of a word of praise, a commendation, a high test or examination score, rather than focussing on and embracing the pleasures of learning itself or on learning collaborations with peers: in other words, the student has – again, quite understandably – internalised the performativity discourse to become its bearer and perpetuator, as, indeed, may have the student's parents or carers. It seems to me that for all Elliott's very encouraging words of pedagogic possibilities in 2000, the ability and willingness of teachers to create the learning situations and to promote the classroom culture that he advocates have become ever more difficult within a system so intransigent and resistant to challenge and change and so supported by those for whom it is designed as to make it at times seem an almost impossible task.[4]

It might be said that Elliott's proposals for pedagogy and curriculum in relation to student learning and to student-teacher relationships are 'anti-performativity'. However, as we have already seen, it is not only relationships between teachers and their students that may be damaged by and within the performativity discourse.

As I have suggested in previous chapters, relationships between teachers can suffer too – in slightly different ways, perhaps, but in an equally de-humanising way as, within the same discourse and culture of competition and personal, choice-making responsibility, '[s]olidarity, service, love can be found wanting … taking their place within disguised strategies of individual struggle and survival' (Keck 2012: 105). In performativity's decontextualising move (more of which below), just as Archie's behaviour was re-constructed in terms of personal decision-making (his 'good and bad choices'), so too, especially when finding themselves in the 'lifeboat' situation described by Martin (an imminent Ofsted inspection providing one familiar example), can teachers hold colleagues personally and, to all intents and purposes and in spite of rhetorics to the contrary, exclusively responsible for their own 'productivity' in relation to students' measured academic and behavioural 'performance'.

Internalising performativity

If performativity becomes internalised in practice, by what processes does this occur? And what is it that holds it there? In the following section, I want to suggest that schools and teachers internalise the performativity discourse in two separate but connected ways, resulting in its evolution into a revised institutional culture. Each of these ways appeals to and depends upon affect for the successful completion of the process. The first involves a direct affective response on the individual teacher's as well as the collective's part to the discourse itself. In this interaction, language plays a crucial part. The second involves the deliberate adoption, which may come about wholly or in part as a result of the first relationship, of performative structures, practices and systems within the school, typically initiated and orchestrated by the school's headteacher and senior leadership team (aspects, perhaps, of both a molar and a micro *dispositif* as referred to in Chapter 2 above). In effect, this analysis is a development of existing theory relating to 'policy enactment' (Ball *et al* 2012; Singh *et al* 2014), whereby policy is mediated, interpreted, worked on and engaged with by teachers and headteachers, and of 'policy enablement', which is descriptive of the constraints and affordances – we might say, the parameters – within which such enactments can take place.

With reference to the first internalisation, a related discussion was begun in Chapter 2 concerning the way in which certain words or terms become affectively saturated – either positively or negatively – and how such saturation can orient us either to embrace or to reject a concept or policy directive. To develop this in a little more depth, we might consider one such term – *professionalism* – whose contestable nature will, I imagine, be familiar to many readers, and how developments in externally sanctioned meanings of this term work affectively in the service of a broader project of reproducing a performativity culture in schools and classrooms.

Professionalism is one of those slippery terms whose meanings have undergone a number of changes over time, rendering it particularly susceptible to appropriation both by policymakers and by practitioners (see e.g. Hargreaves 2000; Ozga 2000). However, although the precise meaning(s) of the term may have changed or been added to over time it is, always, a word, a concept, even a discourse that remains associated and imbued with positivity. Who does not want to be professional, when the word is used so very often – in the worlds of education, of business, of politics, of entertainment – to indicate approval and respect? Those of us labelled or self-perceiving as professionals may not always agree at the conscious level with what professionalism has come to signify in official discourse, but we still want to *be* professional, and *to be seen as being* professional, even if this is in relation to another's conceptualisation of the term. In short, although the definition of professionalism may change, not only the affective saturation but also, crucially, our affective attachment to the word may remain. To ease such an adjustment, particularly in situations in which, as in the teaching profession in many countries, professionalism has come to be associated more with obedience to externally imposed regulations, procedures and criteria that are fundamentally 'entrepreneurial and business-minded' (Bailey 2015: 164), we may continue to make our own links with previous or alternative versions of professionalism with which we may feel more comfortable. These might include notions of honesty, fairness, sacrifice and the professional's capacity for making wise judgments. It is these reminders – in essence, these remaindered elements – that may continue to circle the revised concept (and its ongoing progression as discourse) like moons around a newly formed planet. As Bailey observes, in discussing how policy more broadly 'subjectivises' individuals and modifies subjectivities in line with its own modifications over time: 'material and epistemological remnants and relics of previous regimes may remain, transform or find a new or more dominant function, rather than disappearing in the shifts from one singularity to another' (Bailey 2015: 77).

It may well be the case that there has never quite been an agreement – including among professionals like teachers – as to what it means to be professional and to act professionally (though a strong case might be made that, despite such variations, professionalism has always tended to be linked to deeds rather than to thoughts). What the discursive development of professionalism achieves, however, is to enable the evolution of professionalism from a term or set of terms that is and has been open to (and has perhaps welcomed) interpretation, contestation and debate, to a term whose meaning(s) seek to become fixed and narrowed by and within official policy and its implied definitions. Whatever professionalism may or may not have meant in the past, or how it was understood and practised by teachers, it seems clear, both from policy statements and from teachers' own usage of the term, (a) that it must now involve hierarchical authority and *accountability* (Evetts 2009); (b) that it attaches itself to notions and prioritisations of individual and collective success in meeting measurable educational 'targets' – that is to say, it is embedded within and supportive of a wider discourse and set of practices of performativity.

Adopting what is essentially a Foucauldian understanding of discourse as a 'technology', that not only delimits meanings but also attempts to construct realities and to shape identities, professionalism itself can thus be seen as having been politically rendered as unproblematic and non-negotiable: what professionalism might mean is no longer a subject for serious discussion, as the meaning becomes crystallised and naturalised as both a good and an essential characteristic of the 'effective teacher' (a similarly evolved concept) in the 'effective school'. Furthermore, the deployment of professionalism in support of neoliberal policy and of its performativity discourse involves not just promoting a particular version of professionalism, but setting up in opposition – either explicitly or implicitly – an *alternative* to professionalism: that is to say, not a different version or versions of professionalism (since the 'truth' of the discourse tells us there can be no other reliable versions), but simply *un*-professionalism or *non*-professionalism. Un-professionalism or non-professionalism must then, like professionalism, be absorbed through language and discourse at the micro level of the school to reinforce, affectively and discursively, the value of the 'aesthetic of existence' (Bailey 2015: 35) that is being promoted. The *discourse* of performativity, thus constituted through a series and also a process of inclusions and exclusions, establishes a structure of relations that organises how we think about teachers' (and other professionals') work – including, of course, how teachers think about their professional work, how they understand their relationships with other teachers, and how they self-identify as successful.

It is this affective aspect of discourse that is central in relation to the extent to which dominant discourses – themselves the bearers of official policy – maintain their dominance as they are recontextualised in school practices, and acquire a level of seeming fixity and resistance to opposition. As individuals, we might become consciously aware of discourse and of the strength of its influence – on ourselves and on others – but this does not necessarily make it any easier for us to resist it or to act outside it. As Hook (2006: 215) observes, discourse also structures and makes use of *desire* 'within the machinery of subjectivity that is not entirely accessible to rational discursive consciousness'. We may need, then, within the psychoanalytically informed reflexive project, to examine through a more affective lens than is perhaps present in Foucault's analysis the ways in which we may be coerced and co-opted into becoming the bearers and disseminators of dominant discourse, wherein an orientation which may have had something to do with rationality at the beginning is no longer subject to conscious, rational interrogation but has been internalised to, so to speak, develop an existence of its own.

This functioning of affect is critical in understanding the responses of many teachers to policy, and particularly their implementation of policy to which they may have been initially (rationally and consciously, but also affectively) oppositional. If we embrace reflexivity in approaching and examining this matter, we need first to understand that affect, *like* discourse, is continuously constructed and evolving; that is to say, it is the product of a process of internalisation, not something which is immanent in terms of its configuration at any given point in time or that has always been there, immutably, inside us. Then, we might think about how affect is produced and how it is made use of as a technology of control (Foucault 1992). One suggestion is that each of these processes operates and is brought about *by* discourse: specifically, by the ways in which discourse works insidiously, both carrying and making use of desire. To continue with the example of professionalism, teachers will almost inevitably, if unconsciously, align their desires in relation to whom and what they want to be as teachers with the desires embedded in the discourse. That is to say, the discourse of professionalism (for example) takes on the function of a Trojan horse, that includes within its terms of acceptance an agreement, however reluctant, to the implementation of certain externally imposed curricula and pedagogies that may be underscored and driven more by perceived (and perhaps misrecognised) national or international market demands than by strictly educational ones. Listening to teachers at Primary One and Secondary Two talking of professionalism and unprofessionalism, a more fixed and limited articulation of professionalism often seemed to involve little more than getting on with the business of preparing students to pass memory-based tests and examinations, 'managing behaviour' and keeping students quiet and on-task in the classroom. As we have already seen, for some teachers some of the behaviours previously associated with being professional – or for that matter unprofessional – may, in the process, have slipped off the professional lexicon. It becomes perfectly acceptable within these discursive parameters, for example, to talk critically about colleagues behind their backs, when those colleagues themselves have been identified as un-professional. Indeed, to do so might even serve to endorse – or to underscore the sense of – the professionalism of those making the criticisms.

The insidious nature and colonising tendency of discourse is not a new phenomenon, of course, nor is its identification a very recent thing. Though using a different terminology, Friedrich Nietzsche wrote, many years ago of discourse's invasively infectious quality and of how it can serve to limit our understandings of and relationships with the world and our self – in his case, focussing on discourses around Christian morality (Nietzsche 1872; Reitter and Wellmon 2015). Of particular relevance to what I have been arguing in this section is Nietzsche's identification and analysis of the triad – initially located within, promulgated by and used as an affective means of discursive infection by the Christian Church – of debt-guilt-blame. Of interest here is the way in which, in Nietzsche's analysis, material doubt (literally, the owing of some money or property or favour to another person or persons) evolved, with the Church's assistance, into a wider, much vaguer feeling of indebted-*ness*, even when no material debt is involved – and of what is known as guilt-without-attachment. Guilt-without-attachment is the feeling, with which I suspect many of us will be familiar, of being guilty, even when one has actually done nothing that might have deliberately caused harm to another, or that others might consider reprehensible – so that, at its worst, we become self-blamers convinced of our own unworthiness, constantly striving to be better people than we (think) we are. There is no room to explore Nietzsche's analysis in any great depth here; however, its relevance to teachers' and students' experiences of formal education will be clear to anyone interested in exploring his work in more detail.[5]

Mimicking performativity: institutional and professional survival

Professional(ism) is just one affectively saturated term whereby, via identification with and the embrace of its positively and affectively saturated content, teachers may find themselves both using the (revised) concept and acting according to its edict. Others in which the term itself has become sufficient to elicit an immediate positive orientation include the already-cited 'aspiration(al)' and 'standards'. However, it is not only through the language and discourse of policy that performativity comes to infect institutions. It is also through the *practical* modelling and mimicking within schools of performativity as instrumentalised in the wider world. This modelling of performativity may arise initially from pragmatism (for example, 'in order to be sure to meet the demands of an Ofsted inspection and have staff appropriately prepared for it, we must model inspection practices ourselves through equally rigorous internal monitoring'), whereby it is a deliberate, thought-through choice, but it can very easily embed itself more enduringly in institutional culture as naturalised, almost unconscious mimicking, so that it continues to thrive even when the specific pragmatic decision is less pressing. (Such an embedding is made all the more likely, of course, when, to pursue this particular example, Ofsted inspectors are no longer required to give advance warning of an inspection but can effectively turn up at the drop of a hat – something which, as we have seen, impels schools to be in a state of constant 'Ofsted-readiness'). There are echoes of this phenomenon in the next chapter, relating to teacher response to public examination results, but the following extracts from my research diary serve as initial examples of how this works in practice:

> I have already discovered that there are many ways in which dominant discourses are internalised locally, often largely as a result of pragmatism though with clear affective (and practical) consequences. I've witnessed the isolating effects these can have – of how they can produce a not always healthy culture of internal competition and, conversely, work against collaboration. I have been told by Marie, one of the beginning teachers at Secondary Two, that because of a reduction in the number of visits by Ofsted inspectors (presumably, an economic decision), inspectors are focussing more and more attention on the 'visible evidence' of students' work and progress and of teachers' teaching – in particular, students' exercise books. One result of this, it seems, and I have heard the same story from Martin at Primary One, is that teachers are in turn focussing their own attention increasingly on students' exercise books, making sure not only that there is plenty of writing in them (both students' and teachers') but that their appearance is neat and tidy too. Martin tells me that at Primary One teachers are also spending a significant amount of time enforcing the 'correct use of the ruler' for underlining purposes, and that they are devoting 'an inordinate amount of time' to developing students' handwriting skills. Looking at Primary One students' books, they are certainly, in the main, impressively neat and well presented; however,

reading what the children have actually written I do wonder, in line with Martin's analysis, if presentation has become more important than thinking, experimentation and expression – a feeling not dispelled by the teachers' dutiful on-text comments concerning the neatness and general presentation of each student's work.

★ ★ ★

James, the young history teacher at Secondary Two, who has become good friends with John (they're both attending the same Masters course at the university) has just told me about a visit he's had from one of the Senior Leadership Team [SLT]: 'They've introduced a system here which they are using at most schools these days, which is called the learning walk. Basically, one of SLT wanders around the school dropping in on lessons for a few minutes and making a snap judgement about the quality of your teaching, so that any weakness can be picked up and sorted out before Ofsted come dropping by. You're just under this huge pressure all the time. When will someone drop in? Am I good enough? Do I actually trust someone else's judgment more than my own that I am [good enough]? What are the consequences if I don't come up to scratch in a particular lesson?. … It's meant to raise standards of teaching, but I think it just makes us less confident, more anxious. It makes us focus our attention more on the inspection itself – you know? – and what hoops you have to jump through, more than on, you know, the quality of the actual learning that's taking place. If you want me to teach differently – better, whatever that is – give me some decent professional development, or a curriculum that isn't just painting by numbers and trying to get kids to memorise and regurgitate stuff'.

This learning walk, which Abigail (one of the deputy heads) and Mary (the head-teacher) have already told me about in far more positive terms, is one of a number of what I call Ofsted Preparation Practices that have been introduced at Secondary Two. One is the 'Mocksted' – a kind of lighter-touch mock Ofsted inspection calling in external expertise. Another is the spot-check of exercise books, whereby nominated senior members of staff can demand to see the exercise books of specified students without notice – meaning that every students' book, including the marking, has to be kept completely up-to-date at all times. No one is exempt from this process: the Senior Leadership Team, too, are likely to have another member of the team or a Head of Department ask for a selection of exercise books, and if the comments of Simonetta (the Head of Modern Foreign Languages) are anything to go by, it can place everyone under a considerable degree of stress:

It's a bit of a tyranny, actually. I can see why it has to be done. But I do think we could concentrate on monitoring people who we know are already not cutting it, rather than just having this random, blanket coverage. I mean, my books are always up-to-date, and I don't need anyone checking up on me. But it always, always feels like an intrusion, and that it's not only my up-to-dateness that's being judged but the quality of what I'm doing. You feel like a child yourself sometimes. I must say, I do find it a tad insulting. In the end, it's really a trust thing, isn't it. … We need to be trusted. … I do, anyway.

★   ★   ★

John told me a story he had heard about a practice at a nearby school, that apparently Mary [the headteacher] thinks is a good idea. It seems that after the annual GCSE (public examination) results come out statistical comparisons and analyses are carried out by SLT whereby departmental results are compared with those of other departments: a process described by John and others in one apparently well-known term: 'residuals'. This is done by student as far as possible, so that it's possible to compare the grades achieved by the same students in science, maths, English and so on. However, it appears that at the neighbouring school – 'and not only there' – the headteacher is using residuals as a way of retrospectively assessing and passing rather public judgment on the quality of teaching – not just in each subject, but by individual subject teacher.[6] John tells me 'there is some kind of event' at this school, at which '"high performing" teachers receive special praise and "lower achieving" teachers are effectively told to pull their socks up'. I agree with John that, if the story is true, this seems a horrendous, simplistic and ultimately rather pointless and potentially very divisive practice: one that plays on fear, and appears to run counter to the school's published ethos in its various brochures and policy statements of being caring and inclusive (though perhaps this is not intended to apply to the teaching staff!). It appears to take little or no account of the contexts within which teaching and learning take place, or of the make-up of whole classes, or of the differing skills required in different subject areas, or of the relative difficulty of exam papers either between subject areas or from year to year. I ask some of the other teachers at Secondary Two what they think of it, and whether they see it as an acceptable approach to so-called performance management. John and many of his colleagues share my concern, horrified at the prospect that Mary might take it on at Secondary Two and describing it as typical of what John calls a 'new management culture that's invading everywhere'. James says that he's heard that at another nearby school there has been an upsurge in teachers initiating grievance procedures 'exactly because of this sort of thing' and because they are afraid or think it would be a waste of time sharing the pressure they are feeling with senior colleagues at the school. Many of the others, though they disagree with the idea in principle, tell me that in relation to some of these practices there is no option, that it's all part of getting Ofsted-ready, and that if it helps the school to maintain or improve its position in the local and national league tables of public examination results it is probably worthwhile.

I tell some of them that from my own point of view it all seems part of a wider policy direction that simultaneously demands responsibility and blame and seeks to out-source these away from the centre ground of policy to schools and to individual teachers within schools – and certainly not to the wider socio-economic systems that politicians promote and perpetuate. I suggest that, as with specific policy initiatives such as 'Every Child Matters' and 'No Child Left Behind', responsibility for success and failure are effectively removed from the learner (not a bad thing in itself), from parents and from central government, and shifted very firmly on to the teacher (if the child 'fails' or is 'left behind', it has nothing to do with socio-economic circumstances, themselves constructed as natural and largely unchangeable; it is the teacher's responsibility to push them forward to success regardless) – and along with the responsibility goes the blame and the guilt when things do not work out perfectly in an imperfect, unhelpful world. As usual, I am listened to politely, some agreeing with me, some not. But I know how hard they all work. And perhaps engaging with these thoughts is simply, for many of them, a bridge too far.

★　★　★

It's easy to be critical of some of these internal performativity practices, especially when one is not facing the pressures of performativity personally or in quite the same way. They can seem very divisive, creating unnecessary amounts of additional stress and pitting teacher against teacher in what at times bears resemblance to a talent show. But there is an understandable logic to them as well. National performance measures might be crude and misleading. However, they exist. They can be opposed but they cannot be ignored, and they can have a profound impact on the lives of teachers, students and schools. One way to ensure – as far as is possible – good 'performance outcomes' within a flawed performativity model might well be to replicate it internally in order to avoid being caught unawares. The problem is that although such practices might be introduced and carried out on these largely pragmatic terms, they may bring with them, buried away but waiting to burst forth like a virus out of the portal offered by practice, the infectiousness of the performativity discourse itself: to return to an earlier point, the modelling may be replaced or attended by mimicry.

Belonging and desire: the allure of normalcy

The question of individualism and conformity touched on briefly in the first section of this chapter offers a useful starting-point for approaching the issue with which the previous section ended, relating to what Ruti (2009: 11) terms the 'complex – and at times profoundly antagonistic – relationship between the demands of social conformity and our desire to attain a measure of individual uniqueness'. While an exploration of the pragmatic and the discursive are helpful in understanding how discourse infects and changes practice, philosophical orientations and social relations, there is more to social and perceptual shaping, as Foucault (1994) has pointed out, than discourse alone; and there is also more to the modifications we may make to our practice than pragmatism alone. I want to suggest that in addition to some of the other physical-contingent affordances and constraints that Foucault references, something called desire plays a key role in these processes, perhaps even *the* key role: one that concerns our relation more broadly to the symbolic order – the Lacanian 'Other' – and to what we may experience as a psychic and at times a physical need for belonging.

To digress very slightly, though I hope interestingly and helpfully, there is a fascinating exchange in the second (2011) film adaptation of Stieg Larsson's novel *The Girl with the Dragon Tattoo*. The central character, a journalist called Mikael Blomkvist, has been discovered in the grounds of the home belonging to a man, Martin, whom he is pretty convinced of being a serial killer – a man with whom, in the course of his investigations, he has had a considerable amount of not unpleasant social interaction. When Martin spots Blomkvist and invites him into the house – not, as in the novel, at gun-point, but for a drink – Blomkvist accepts the invitation, despite knowing that in so doing he must be placing his life in considerable danger. Once inside the house, Blomkvist is, of course – to the evident amusement of his would-be assassin – at Martin' mercy. Soon after, as Blomkvist finds himself strung up in a basement room waiting to be tortured and killed, his captor chides him: not for allowing his stubbornness and curiosity to get the better of him (again, as in the novel), but for allowing his servitude to the Symbolic Order (a servitude rejected with continuous delight by Martin himself) to take precedence over what we might call Blomkvist's affective wisdom. 'Let me ask you something', Martin begins:

> Why don't people trust their instincts? They sense something is wrong, someone is walking too close behind them. You knew something was wrong, but you came back into the house. Did I force you? Did I drag you? No. All I had to do was offer you a drink. It's hard to believe that a fear of offending can be stronger than the fear of pain. But you know what? It is.

This is a fiction, of course, and watching the scene unfold we may find ourselves also chiding Blomkvist for his idiocy in accepting so dangerous an invitation, or equally vehemently criticising the film for inviting *us* to accept that such an invitation would be accepted by a smart and reasonable man. However, in the more mundane world which most of us inhabit, I suspect there are few who would claim never to have acted out of politeness rather than – perhaps even in opposition to – wisdom, even though it might knowingly be at some personal cost.

Another, more naturalistic film, *Rosetta*, by the Dardenne brothers – referenced in greater detail by Lauren Berlant (2011: 161–189) – explores this same phenomenon in ways that we might more directly and easily relate to. In this film, an impoverished young woman (Rosetta), living literally and psychically on the margins of normal society, is so driven by her desire to work – to become a 'normal earner' in the socio-symbolic order – that she is prepared to betray her only friend and lose his love in order to achieve that end, effectively getting him sacked so that she is able to inherit his job. Sharing cramped living conditions with her ailing and difficult mother in a caravan park, Rosetta rejects welfare and charity and refuses to slip into her mother's trap of making the best of things and of turning their caravan home into anything that might suggest permanence. Her determination to be – and to be seen and acknowledged as – the 'good worker', earning regular money, having a 'legitimate place in the world' as Berlant puts it (ibid.: 164), and her despair at her condition, bring with them great psychic and physical costs, including regular psychosomatic stomach cramps. In her pursuit of a better life that is hardly any better at all, and to confirm her place in the socio-symbolic order of capitalist society, Rosetta will allow neither love nor friendship to get in her way, ending up inheriting the harsh dog-eat-dog values and mentality of the very system that has let her down. It is not simply money – not money *per se* – that draws Rosetta on (such would be a pragmatic choice, born of necessity), nor is it a wish to make herself more attractive and likeable (that 'imaginary identification' referred to in earlier chapters). It is, rather, *desire*, whose seat is in the affective domain: desire to be symbolically included, to be recognised, to be present, to be deemed to belong in the normal, normalising world of regular paid employment: of getting up in the morning, of going to work, and of coming home again at the end of the day. In the end, this is what drives Rosetta: the desire to be seen and to be able to see herself as normal, however conscious she may be of the ab-normality of her away-from-work life. To re-cite Keck's observation (op. cit.) in relation to education: love and solidarity are 'found wanting' in Rosetta's ultimately successful pursuit of work – not so much taking their place in 'strategies of individual struggle and survival' as never having been able to engage in such struggle in the first place. If normalcy is alluring for Rosetta, it is understandably so, its power unsurprising. As Berlant (ibid., 163–164) says: 'The ongoing prospect of low-waged and unin-teresting labor is for Rosetta nearly utopian. … [W]hen the world exists between the routinized rut and the ominous cracks, she chooses the rut' – and perhaps it is this desire for normalcy that makes it so hard for Rosetta to adopt or even to wish to adopt a critical stance toward that other normalcy, the normalcy of the very system itself in which the normalcy of a steady job, a home, enduring relationships is produced and sustained. Rosetta is not simply drawn by normalcy; she embraces it and accepts it as kin.

We must always be careful not to confuse the world of film with our lived reality, however close to reality it strives to be, and Rosetta's circumstances, even just from an economic perspective, are very different from those of any of the teachers in my own studies. However, the desire to fit in, to be accepted, justified, legitimated, though it may be felt far more strongly by some than by others (and by some not at all), and the affective – and material – consequences of not doing so, whether imagined or actual, can be profound. As we shall see, the desire – likely to be experienced as a need – to fit in, not just for pragmatic reasons (the fear, for example, of being rewarded with a poor reference or being passed over for promotion) but for affective ones is just as likely to be experienced by those in far more comfortable and advantaged circumstances than Rosetta. Indeed, normalcy may have some degree of allure for us all, even for those willing and able to resist it. While for Rosetta – and those millions like Rosetta – in her dire circumstances, acceptance of the allure might have brought a degree of happiness and certainly of physical and emotional comfort, for those of us enjoying more privileged lives it might have, instead, a profoundly conservatising and restrictive influence on how we perceive ourselves professionally and how we set about our business.

If the desire for a symbolic mandate experienced by Rosetta, and the pull toward symbolic identification, may affect us all in some way and to some degree or another (for example, in our possible acceptance of a mandated definition of professionalism), there is, however, something else in the affective domain that can impel us equally powerfully – perhaps even more so – toward 'fitting in' (that is to say, toward conformity in our actions and expressed opinions) and toward normalcy in relation to how we feel about ourselves. Just as the Other attracts us to conformity, so does the 'other other': that is, our relationships with other people; how we would wish to be seen – and liked, loved even – by them. This second pull concerns that other identification discussed in Chapters 2 and 3 (and, briefly, regarding Blomkvist and Martin, above): 'imaginary identification'.[7] As with symbolic identification, normalcy not only pulls us in, powered by the fear we may have of not fitting in, of being 'left outside' as it were (a fear evident in the cited testimony of James); it also offers us a means of escape: not from discourse itself but from the uncomfortableness and pain of resistance and refusal. What I want to suggest is that while succumbing to normalcy's allure is not something to be ashamed of, neither is it something to be ignored. In fact, any chance of resisting the allure depends on our recognition of its existence and its nature. In the examples that follow, it is just such a recognition that seems to be lacking.

'Virtuous pragmatism': the (necessary?) justification of retreat

To pursue the matter – and the power – of imaginary identification in a little more detail, I want to turn, briefly, to two cases I have explored elsewhere (e.g. Moore 2004, 2006). In doing so, I will reintroduce the notion of *virtuous pragmatism* as one strategy whereby we can justify to ourselves acts of compliance with which we may otherwise feel very uncomfortable in order that we can remain likeable to ourselves as well as to other people. We may experience these justificatory acts not as choices but as necessary evils undertaken for the sake of survival. The cases are of Bill, the deputy headteacher already referred to in Chapter 3, and Edward, a young geography teacher at the same school. (I should add, perhaps, that I am not recommending virtuous pragmatism as a psychic strategy – merely drawing attention to its existence as a fairly widespread coping mechanism.)

I met Edward some years ago during the course of a study investigating the ways in which teachers professionally self-identify (Halpin, Moore *et al*, op. cit.). Like other teachers at his school, and in common with many I was to meet later at Secondary Two, Edward told me that he had decided to abandon group work, which was a technique he had been very actively encouraged to use during the course of his pre-service education and training, on the basis that 'it doesn't work'. I can still recall my surprise at this rather blanket dismissal of a well-tried pedagogic technique (one that I had often used myself and had witnessed many times working extremely effectively), being more than a little astonished that group work should be reified in this way and linked to some kind of unspoken universal Law. I had initially thought that what Edward had meant was that it did not work for him or that he felt he lacked the skills to make it work effectively. However, further discussion revealed this not to be the case. Group work, it seemed, had been heavily discouraged by Edward's Head of Department, and there had been a strong steer toward more teacher-led approaches on the part of the school's headteacher. However, he had presented his decision in interview as one undertaken autonomously and for reasons reached as a result of his own experience and analysis:

> No. I think that group work *per se* just doesn't really work. Not in terms of getting everything done and in time. There's just too much to get across these days. So … sometimes you just have to be pragmatic and accept that something that might sound good in theory just doesn't work in practice. In the end, it's a learning issue: what's best for the kids. You do what's necessary.

Edward's references to 'amount' and 'get across' suggested that whatever pragmatic decision he might have made regarding his teaching and his students' learning had to be undertaken within a wider situation and culture in which there was a finite but extensive knowledge-based curriculum to be covered and that the most logical way to cover this was through a largely transmissive, 'traditionalist' approach. But (not unlike James, referenced earlier) Edward had also told me that he believed in 'far more democratic classrooms' than he had experienced as a school student himself, and I wondered how he could square what, to me, had appeared as contradictory pedagogical and philosophical orientations. The clue to Edward's apparent resolution of these positions had lain, I decided, in his reference to the 'necessity' of changing his stance, and in his reference to having learned, 'from experience', that something he still might feel to be good in theory simply did not translate into practice. In short, Edward was presenting his pragmatic move as a virtuous rather than a retrograde one, summoning a reified 'necessity' in order to justify both virtuosity and the move itself.

Edward's pragmatic approach to his modified pedagogy – and to his explanation of it in ways that denied the possibility of retreat from a previously held set of beliefs – was further illustrated in his explanation of why he had his students sitting in rows in opposition to his previous practice of sitting them in small groups around tables, and the promotion within his classroom of the greater democracy he had previously spoken of. Observing that he saw himself as 'neither "progressive" nor "traditional"', and that the rearrangement of the classroom was not directly linked to his abandonment of group work, he went on to say:

> I try to look back on each of those approaches and use parts of them both. … I would say I am a happy medium of traditional and progressive. … Traditional – you can see the chairs in rows; but progressive in the sense that I'm … keen on allowing students to speak for themselves.

Though sitting his students in rows may have originated – at least partly – in Edward's perceived need to re-think classroom management in the context of externally imposed constraints, it was clear from his testimony that he had come to see – or perhaps to find – a *value* in this different approach, arguing that, contrary to what one might expect, the physical isolation and compulsory order-ing of his students had not compromised his agenda for developing democratic processes and practices within his classroom, or for promoting student voice: on the contrary, he suggested that the increased amount of teacher control effected by the arrangement provided a better context and climate for the development of 'academic conversations' which, he felt, most of his students had hitherto been unused to and had consequently been rather poor at. When I asked Edward if he felt any remorse or regret at having abandoned group work, given that he had once believed in its importance and still recognised it as appropriate 'for a different kind of education – one that, yes, I probably would prefer if I'm to be honest – in a different kind of world', he was able to express broad comfort with the new non-binary pedagogic identity he had fashioned for himself, declaring himself 'shamelessly' as a pragmatist, suggesting that in the modern world this was 'probably the best thing to be' and criticising some of his (generally older) colleagues in other departments for being 'far too dogmatic and locked into old ideas'. He also observed, 'in passing', that it had made life more comfortable for him within the Social Science Faculty anyway:

> You don't want to be seen as the only one not towing the party line. Not that I'm saying I don't believe in the party line. Maybe I should say 'the only one not prepared to change with the times'. But … I think it's much better – as a department and faculty – if we're all on the same page. I actually used to get some flak from some of the old stagers because of the way I was going about things in my lessons. I think there was quite a bit of jealousy in there, you know. … Kids were always saying they wanted me to be their teacher and stuff. But they realise now I'm not this crazy ideological guy who won't fit in. … I can change.

When I wrote about Edward in the past, I suggested (Moore 2004) that

> while it could be argued that Edward was simply seeking a justification for an action which he initially (and perhaps still) found undesirable in his own or others' eyes, inserting an indefensible resort to traditionalism into an acceptable discourse of democracy, his undisguised enthusiasm for the change tended to argue against such an interpretation.

Having looked again at our data from the study, I am not sure that this analysis is entirely justified, and provides a useful example of what can happen when we bring an affective, psycho-social lens to our reading of data as opposed to a more straightforwardly sociological one. It is quite feasible, for example, that Edward *had to be – had to feel* – enthusiastic for the changes in his developing pedagogic identity, having constructed them as coming from within rather than as a result of surrender to some other's more powerful ideology, in order for his fantasy pragmatic identity to be accepted by (and acceptable to) himself as well as appealing to other people. If we understand identity itself in terms of fantasy, we might, then, agree with Ruti's suggestion that such fantasies can serve to 'alleviate anxiety and fend off the threat of fragmentation because they enable the subject to consider itself *as more unified and complete than it actually is*' (Ruti 2009: 97, emphasis added).

Edward's rational explanation of his change may then be understood as an example of using articulated argument in support of a move that may be any-thing but rational – as a way, perhaps, of sustaining happiness and comfort. Just as his change of heart enabled him to become 'normalised' within the depart-ment, perhaps within the school as a whole, so his rationalised justification of it enabled him to accept what in reality must have been a difficult change (effec-tively, a change of pedagogic identity) in a way that resurrected a sense (fantasy) of identity that had been in danger of fragmentation, back to one of perceived wholeness. This new identity was apparently accepted much more readily among the flock of Edward's colleagues – or so he believed, which in the end was all that mattered – thereby adding to the comfort that the justificatory process had already brought about.

Another teacher at the same school as Edward – Bill, a deputy headteacher – had brought with him into teaching a powerful opposition to setting and streaming stu-dents according to notions of ability, and to the imposition of school uniform. His view on setting and streaming was that it worked oppositionally to a comprehensive ideal that he very strongly believed in. As he put it, it 'reproduced' the differentials of a previous two-tier grammar school/secondary modern school system within the comprehensive classroom. His objection to school uniform, meanwhile, had its roots in a strong belief in the power of education to encourage and enable students to express themselves as individuals within a system which inevitably required of them a high degree of conformity. Uniform smacked to Bill of corporatism; it sent out the wrong message to students and their parents about the fundamental purposes of education.

For much of his teaching life, most of it spent in the same school where he had risen through the ranks from a class English teacher, Bill's views had been reflected in and by the school he worked in. Indeed, he revealed in interview that he had chosen to work – and to remain working – in this school precisely because it had reflected his educational values. Times had changed, however. Central govern-ment had become increasingly involved in state education, putting in place systems and practices in which schools now found themselves competing for students in a quasi-marketplace in which parents had some choice in relation to where to educate their children – often using published 'league tables' of public examination successes on which to base their decision. As Bill explained:

> We have to compete with other schools now. Our results are never going to be as good as [another secondary school, about three quarters of a mile away] because of our relative catchment areas, so we make the best of the figures, value-added and all that, and play up the non-academic achievements stuff, but we still have to find other ways of selling ourselves to prospective parents. Anti mixed ability propaganda is everywhere these days. Theres' no evidence whatsoever that streaming and setting do anyone any favours, but parents have been made to believe they do, and it kind of plugs in to a perceived wisdom about slow learners dragging down brighter ones. So ability setting becomes a selling point, and mixed ability is yesterday's mistake. So now the Head has decided to introduce setting, even though I for one actually don't think it's a good idea. In fact many of us … well, maybe a few of us: perhaps we're in a minority nowadays. … I'm very worried it will do more harm than good, especially to our most vulnerable learners. The same goes for uniform. We must be the only school for miles now that doesn't have one. That used to be a selling point – but uniform has been so popularised, as if it's some kind of marker of discipline and academic achievement, that not having it makes you less marketable. So, once again, the Head is introducing uniform from next September, which again I don't like. But it seems that the kids, most of them anyway, and their parents have bought into the idea. So I can see it was a democratic decision.

It was clear from Bill's testimony that his attitude toward each of these developments remained touched by ambivalence. While the decision to adopt school uniform, had, he said, been taken very democratically, involving teachers, parents and pupils, he had openly opposed it at the time, arguing that the existence of school uniform was likely to create even more problems – including more staff-pupil conflicts – than it would solve, though, as he explained in a later conversation, his vocal (as opposed to his philosophical) opposition had weakened very quickly. While he had expressed his opposition when the school uniform proposal had first been mooted, for example, he would confess now, in interview, that 'I haven't really argued against it much, even though possibly I should have done. … I actually could have done a lot more to put the counter-argument across'. Even though Bill's view was based to a considerable degree on his own experience of having moved many years ago from a uniform-school to a non-uniform-school, he had, by the time of my second interview with him six months later, come to accept – if somewhat tentatively – that 'probably, overall, [introducing uniform] was the right thing'. His subsequent, elaborate defence of his position, however, suggested a continuing lack of comfort with this personal shift of view as, indeed, with his shifting ground over mixed-ability teaching. It also prompted questions as to how far these shifts of attitude had been genuinely brought about by a moral imperative that prioritised democratic processes, or how far they had simply been *legitimated* by such an imperative in order to make them less uncomfortable:

> I think [on reflection] we had to go for uniform because of the rivalry, the competitiveness – and parents overtly wanted it. … In the end it was a matter of necessity really. I think probably overall it was the right thing. You know, I think it was because of a sense of identity. We made the uniform friendly. Most of the parents like it. Some of the kids don't, but most of them do. … I think it's very hard to know in the long run. You know, our intake has gone up, and we are much more popular. That might be one of the reasons. … I think it might lead to an improvement in exam results, and a good Ofsted report – you know – because those things do have an effect, quite a large effect, out there. But I'm still not. … Again, I suppose it's like the mixed-ability thing: I'm willing to go along with whatever we agree democratically. But I was not one of the people necessarily in favour.

Bill's self-conscious and slightly reluctant change of view was typical of the pragmatic responses of many of the classroom teachers I spoke to during the course of this particular study. While its apologetic, somewhat unconvincing nature speaks of half-hearted acceptance rather than full-blown allegiance to an item of policy change, it seeks to justify what has clearly been an uncomfortable, enforced change of approach within the terms of a pre-existing, comfortable and highly valued one – in this case, that same allegiance to 'democracy' as expressed more obliquely by Edward (in relation both to his positioning as a member of staff and to the reorganisation of his classroom), as well as in James's testimony introduced in Chapter 3, along with a direct appeal to 'necessity' – immediately undermining the power of 'choice'. This, then, is more than simply pragmatism: it is also retrospective justification (an agreement, perhaps, to 'consent without consent') – one strengthened by Bill's suggestion that his acceptance of these particular changes was something of a temporary settlement, flagged by the parenthetical but significant 'I think probably. … But I'm still not …'. Both the acceptance of change and its justification certainly appeared to have provided Bill with some degree of practical and affective comfort that allowed him to carry on with the principal task of teaching to the best of his ability within the pulls and constraints of (from his perspective) a not always sympathetic system. As such, it is reminiscent of Abigail's and Mary's ambivalence about exam systems and league tables. In either case, a philosophical/ethical opposition to one thing is trumped, so to speak, by a pragmatic acceptance of another. To paraphrase Bill: I don't like it for some reasons, but for other, more important reasons I must accept it. As suggested in Chapter 3, this can be more than just a matter of making oneself more comfortable about a change of position or philosophy; it can also be linked to a 'longing for belonging'. Bill, for example, would talk about how his initial opposition to the proposed changes had made him feel very awkward: like a 'troublemaker' or an 'awkward customer', even a 'dinosaur' (as he had overheard one colleague put it to another in relation to another opposer), and it is perhaps not too fanciful to suggest that his subsequent acceptance of the initially unacceptable, and its justification through reference to another concept laden with positive affect – that of democracy – had as much to do with Bill's desire to be liked and to remain popular with his colleagues as it had to do with any authentically ethical stance. Bill was keen to explain in interview that he was a 'natural democrat at heart', but also described himself as 'a pretty reasonable bloke' who '[liked] to get on with with everybody regardless of their educational views'; as a 'middle-of-the road sort of socialist'; and (exactly as with James) of 'not liking to rock the boat'. Importantly for Bill's psyche, and for his sense of identity, his pragmatic, provisional acceptance of an abhorrent policy could be understood and experienced, as with Edward, not as weak but as virtuous. Furthermore, not only had it ensured that, to use his words, he was able to continue 'to live with himself'; it also meant that he would continue to be seen as an untroubling, collegial colleague by his peers.

Bill and Edward were by no means alone or even in a significant minority when it came to balancing the libidinal economy in this way. Data from all the studies on which I have drawn provide numerous examples of virtuous pragmatism and of retrospective justification. One of the maths teachers, Stuart, at Secondary Two, for example, told me:

> Sure, it's a lousy system. No question. But I don't have a choice [other than to follow the curriculum and exam criteria as laid down]. In the end I need to be able to look my colleagues and my students in the eye knowing that I've done everything I can to get the best results – and that's for the school *and* for the students. I don't want any colleague or any child looking me in the eye at the end of the day and thinking 'Who the hell does he think he is that he should have the right to do things his way knowing what the consequences are going to be for all of the rest of us?'

At the same school, Mary, the headteacher, said:

> We are results-driven yes: we have to get the results. We don't do anyone any favours – ourselves, our students, our parents – any favours by not getting them. Like it or not, and most of us probably don't like it very much, but … that's our job now. I can't let this school close. I can't let the children down, let their parents down, the local community. We've all worked very hard together to build it up from where it was when I first arrived. It used to be a school that, to be honest, none of the local middle-class families wanted to send their kids to, to now a place that's genuinely inclusive and comprehensive. … Do I lie awake at night worrying about results and Ofsted inspections? You can bet your life I do. To a large extent it's what I get paid for.

Like Bill, both Stuart and Mary explained their pursuit of initially unpalatable policies through reference to allegiance to a wider community, to not letting others down, to not putting their own feelings first. There are clear, rationally explicable reasons within their justifications, and their decisions are understandable and 'make sense' given the circumstances within which they work. The point, however, lies in the justification itself: in its *need* on the part of the individual subject, in its 'content' and in its wider political necessity in relation to the implementation of an unliked policy and a regrettable set of external circumstances. If the decision to implement the unlikeable is driven by circumstance and the material consequences of resistance, the acceptance of the move, however reluctantly experienced, is driven by and made possible by affect (we might say, by desire), as one negatively saturated discourse is trumped by others that are positively saturated – that is to say, the (connected) discourses of togetherness, of self-sacrifice, of the care of others and of democracy. One of the more remarkable findings to emerge from my studies is the way in which these discourses continue to flourish and circulate, even within realities in which, for the most part, individual survival and group fragmentation are the order of the day.

7

THE LOSS AND RETURN OF THE HAPPY OBJECT

Fear and anxiety: a judgment looms

The previous chapter explored in a little more detail the affective pull of discourse: how it can infect institutions so that it becomes instrumental in the development of (or perhaps transforms itself into) an institutional culture and set of practices, and how it can in turn infect individual subjectivities within the institution. In this process, wider discourses – most notably here, that of performativity, located within an ideology and a politics of neoliberalism – are subjectively and institutionally internalised via the mimicry of both language and practice. I have suggested that we may be rendered more susceptible to such internalisations through our desire to be liked, to be symbolically validated, and to have a sense that we 'belong' – that is to say, that we are sufficiently 'normal' in others' eyes to be accepted by whichever group we contingently identify with.[1]

In this chapter, as a prelude to the final chapter which will consider possibilities for group reflexivity and group, I want to explore what might be termed *mass affective experience* by focussing on two events that took place at Secondary Two during my time there, to each of which I have already alluded: an Ofsted inspection (and the lead-up to it), and the day – 'Results Day' – when teachers came into school during the summer holiday to receive and begin to make sense of the implications of the public examination results of their Year 11 (16-year-old) students. My aim in doing this is twofold. First, I want to further illustrate the ways in which centralised, rationalis(ed) policy relies on affect in order for its successful implementation in practice. I will suggest that, paradoxically in this process, a collectively met challenge can result in the spreading of an intensified affective response (fear, panic, love, joy) at the same time as cementing divisions, and emphasising competitiveness and difference between members of the group (a phenomenon reflected in the widespread cynicism expressed by teachers in the main study, regarding the concept of the school as a 'community'). At such times, when there can occur a further dis-integration of social relations, we may also experience an apparent disintegration of the familiar world about us – including the way in which systems and practices once seen as adequate are suddenly perceived as wanting. Identifying teaching – and the positive, affectively rewarding experiences that teaching can give us – as 'happy objects' (Ahmed 2010a, 2010b), I will argue that specific, short-lived events such as Results Day and an Ofsted inspection can bring about both a sense of loss of the happy object and (potentially) a return of it. This return might be either fleeting or more durable, but it can never take on the character of permanence; for until there is radical change, there will always be another inspection, and there will always be the annual examination results day. My second aim is to indicate how unchallenged affective responses of this kind can act as a hindrance to reflexivity – a more complex version, that is, of the similar barriers encountered by the beginning teachers Yanick and Caroline described in Chapter 4.

In her book *The Cultural Politics of Emotion* (2004) Sara Ahmed challenges traditional distinctions between fear and anxiety, in which the former is typically understood in terms of a subject's relation to a specified (concrete or abstract) object. Some fears may be perceived or understood as rational (i.e. posing potentially a very real physical threat to the person, as in fear of snakes in certain parts of the world), others less so (e.g. fear of the dark even when in a secure environment, or fear of spiders in countries like England where spiders are generally quite harmless). Anxiety, on the other hand, is often understood more as on ongoing condition which may or may not be related to a specific object, often experienced as a rather vague, albeit very troubling feeling concerning the possible short- or long-term consequences of something bad that is happening, that may or may not be beyond our control. Ahmed's suggestion that 'we fear the object that approaches us' and that 'fear involves an *anticipation* of hurt or injury' (2014: 65) immediately blurs the classic distinction between fear and anxiety, seeming to suggest that certain forms of what we understand in everyday life as anxiety can be described as a particular kind of fear. As Ahmed continues (ibid.):

> Fear projects us from the present into a future. But the feeling of fear presses us into that future as an intense bodily experience of the present. One sweats, one's heart races, one's whole body becomes a space of unpleasant intensity, an impression that overwhelms us and pushes us back with the force of its negation, which may sometimes involve flight, and other times may involve paralysis.

Ahmed does not go as far as rejecting distinctions between anxiety and fear altogether, but proposes a distinctive quality to anxiety that marks it out from what we might understand as fear. This is the quality of anxiety to, so to speak, originate in and move out of the human subject to 'attach' itself to an object – indeed, to any number of objects: a state of mind – in effect, almost a subject identity – that has a degree of longevity about it and that has an existence independent of any object(s) to which it might attach itself. In Ahmed's words again:

> One becomes anxious as a mode of attachment to objects. … Anxiety becomes *an approach to objects* rather than, as with fear, being *produced by an object's approach.*
>
> *(ibid.: 66)*

Whether or not we need to draw such distinctions, whether they are valid, and/ or whether this is all just a matter of semantics are moot points. The discussion, however, is useful, I think, in the point it makes about negative feelings in the present that are brought about by projections into possible (whether likely or improbable) futures. This feature makes possible (for 'fear' in Ahmed's analysis) a 'role … in the conservation of power' whereby, in the political/cultural field, for example, 'narratives of crisis work to secure social norms in the present' (ibid. 64). In an echo of Žižek (op. cit. 2009), Ahmed offers the example of the political narrative of the invisible, international terrorist, which simultaneously renders mundane and distracts us from such concerns as social and financial inequalities in the national status quo. In the case of an impending Ofsted inspection, it might be difficult to decide whether teachers experience fear, caused by the approach of the object (i.e. of the inspection), or anxiety caused by their own approach *to* the inspection, which may itself be produced in part by their previous experience of similar inspections and by their existing knowledge of the possible negative impact of an inspection. It is the 'known' element of the future event, however – for example, the negative impact of an unsuccessful Ofsted inspection – that is likely to render the teacher anxious rather than afraid. Equally, it is the circumstance of not being sure when, or even if, the inspection will take place that may make possible its capacity to engender fear.

Whether we think of it as anxiety or fear or both, the anticipation of the future event (the object) of an Ofsted inspection, and its potential or likely negative consequences, clearly impacted, often in very painful ways, on several of the teachers, and indeed many of the students, at both Secondary Two and Primary One. Negative feelings were often related to (potential) loss: loss of respect, loss of affirmation and validation, loss of one's job, loss of the possibility of a bright future, even loss of one's school. In short, it was not so much the future event itself that caused pain – the encounter with the object *per se* – as the possible consequences, the 'hurt or injury' (op. cit.) that might result from the encounter: What might happen in the future if an Ofsted inspection or a school's exam results go badly? This is not to say that such fears and anxieties are groundless; on the contrary, they may have a basis in one's existing experience of the world. Teachers know all too well what the consequences of a poor Ofsted inspection can be. Indeed, many of them will already have experienced them first hand.

Before turning to some of Secondary Two's teachers' own accounts of their experience leading up to an Ofsted inspection – and of the relief and pleasure experienced after it – I want to pick up briefly on Ahmed's observation concerning the ways in which fear and anxiety can be politically deployed and manipulated, and can act as a distraction in the interests of 'the conservation of power': how (constructed) 'narratives of crisis work to secure social norms in the present' (ibid. 64). The argument here is a familiar one in the field of 'bio-politics' (Foucault 2010; see also Chapter 3, note 2 above): the State promotes fearful, anxious subjective orientations in relation to a dangerous, threatening future, drawing our attention and energies away from matters of current social conditions and social organisation and systems, which thus continue to remain stable. How possible – and useful – is it to think of school inspection regimes of the kind currently in operation in England as existing not simply (perhaps not at all) in order to ensure 'high standards', to respond to a perceived national education crisis, to help all children experience a good quality of education regardless of where they live and study, but rather as a means of exercising control and of sustaining existing relations and power within existing *inequitable* systems? What if, despite its claims to the contrary, the inspection process, whether those most centrally involved in its form and implementation are conscious of it or not, actually exists to create fear and anxiety, with an objective of exercising control over teacher and student conduct and absorbing energies that might have the potential, otherwise, to be deployed subversively?

Whatever else might be said of it, the expectation of an Ofsted inspection certainly did nothing to boost the confidence, pleasure in work and social bonds among teachers at Secondary Two. To return to Ahmed (ibid.), many, indeed, seemed 'overwhelmed' for much of the time, both by the prospect of the inspection itself and by the amount of additional preparation deemed necessary in advance of it. Pushed back 'with the force of … negation', the looming judgment of the inspectors sometimes involved 'flight' (literally, in the sense of an even greater physical withdrawal from normal social interaction with colleagues, and metaphorically in the kind of 'absence in presence' described in previous chapters), and sometimes, even in the midst of busyness, a 'paralysis' of the kind articulated by one staff member who said very loudly in the almost empty staff room one morning: 'This is ridiculous. What are we doing? We're never going to be good enough. They'll have already made their minds up. We might as well just put our heads on the block and wait for the axe to fall'. Nor did more recent noises from Ofsted about rewarding 'innovative practice' or expecting to find 'creativity' in teachers' practice do anything to ease the pressure: a pressure still exacerbated by an unwavering conviction that in the end it is results that count and that if results are not deemed good enough then neither is the teacher or the school. (During my informal discussions with teachers, away from the main research data, the suggestion that Ofsted was apparently broadening its view of what constituted good or effective teaching, to include evidence of innovation and creativity, was greeted with almost universal derision – partly because teachers did not believe what they were being told, and partly because the expectation on Ofsted's part to find evidence of innovation and creativity, and of a 'broad and rich curriculum' appeared to be demanding of teachers yet more than was being demanded already. For a powerful response to Ofsted's apparent change of tack, see Hanson 2017.)

The kind of distraction – and distractedness – referred to by Ahmed in the face of future-inflected crisis, whether real or imagined, has its parallel in Lauren Berlant's notion of 'impasse'. *Impasse* of one kind has already been referred to, in discussions with Yanick in Chapter 4: the *impasse*, that is, arising out of a kind of stand-off between a beginning teacher and his class, in which he refused to teach them until they sat silently and in which they, in turn, steadfastly refused to comply with his condition. Berlant, however, introduces us to another kind of *impasse*: the *impasse* that we may all experience on a habitual basis as we, so to speak, tread water at certain times in our lives, keeping ourselves afloat until rescue arrives (or doesn't!) – that is to say:

> a stretch of time in which one moves around with a sense that the world is at once intensely present and enigmatic, such that the activity of living demands both a wandering absorptive awareness and a hypervigilance that collects material that might help to clarify things, [and] maintain one's sea legs.
>
> *(Berlant 2011: 4)*

Berlant begins on what will, by now, be familiar ground, carrying echoes of Britzman's 'cacophony of calls' (Britzman 1991: 223) in its considerations of 'different styles of managing simultaneous, incoherent narratives of what's going on and what seems possible and blocked in personal/collective life' (Berlant 2011: 4). Caught – frozen, perhaps – in the midst of this set of 'simultaneous, incoherent narratives', we may experience *impasse* not so much as a conflict of wills as a condition. For Berlant, *impasse* of this kind designates 'a time of dithering from which someone or some situation cannot move forward' but rather circles within the present in a desperate search for answers and explanations that might restore the equilibrium needed for genuine progress.

Impasse thus understood is not necessarily a bad thing: in relation to reflexivity, it may simply be to acknowledge how human experience and learning often works – that there are periods in our lives when we are engaged in looking around for answers to a felt sense of confusion; that these may even be necessary prerequisites for future development, that without the experience of *impasse* there can be no release from *impasse*, no moving away into new places of thinking and understanding. A problem for teachers, however, is that even as they 'seek clarification' while 'maintaining their sea legs', certain (perhaps unhelpful) voices may be cutting stridently through the confusion, instructing them, under pain of punishment, what to do and how to do it – simply adding to the confusion and to a sense of being overwhelmed by competing directives.

From fragile togetherness to personal survival

Extracts from various teachers' accounts of their pre-Ofsted experience speak of anxiety, uncertainty, confusion and a sense of being stuck in an extended moment during which all thoughts of innovation and imaginative pedagogy can become submerged beneath a tsunami of preparations in meeting the demands of externally imposed judgmentalism. Though this kind of situation may have existed for as long as Ofsted has been in existence, the relatively recent change of notice for standard school inspections in England, from around two to six weeks previously to no more than a day or two, or even 'same-day', had clearly impacted even more powerfully on teachers' anxiety levels and sense (and fear) of being punitively and perpetually judged, even at schools like Secondary Two where the headteacher was sufficiently well-connected to be able to predict with a reasonable degree of reliability roughly when an inspection was likely to occur.

The headteacher at Secondary Two spoke to me herself of 'running around like a headless chicken' during this time, while John, the English teacher, expressed a sense of futility – believing, in line with many other voices in the staffroom, that the judgment to which he and others would be subjected could never be a fair one:

> The idea that you can just drop by for a day or two and judge on the basis of typicality is just plain crazy … and wrong. There's no sense of context … what you call contingency.[2] We all have good days and bad days. Whole schools have good and bad days. That's life – but just not as Ofsted knows it apparently.

Even for Abigail, the systems that she and the other senior leaders had put in place, and the work they had done ensuring high-quality teaching across the school, was suddenly a cause for concern and self-doubt:

> You start to doubt yourself. All the systems, all the hard work. … Have you really done enough? Are you working as hard as everyone else? Are you going to be as good as you think … thought you were?

Others, like Zoë, became quite angry during this time, wondering why everyone was being forced to stop what they were doing to put out a blaze that should never have been their business in the first place:

> We shouldn't have to be doing this. I'm really cross with [the senior leader-ship team] now. The whole point of the new system [of inspectors carrying out inspections at very little notice] is that they take us as they find us. As long as the paperwork's all in order, and the stats are acceptable. What's the point of everything else we've been made to do to get Ofsted-ready if now we're having to do something else? We are meant to be always Ofsted-ready. Aren't we? What they are forcing us to do is to be Ofsted-ready-ready.

It was no different, either, at Primary One where, just as at Secondary Two, the headteacher, Miriam, had been able to predict with some confidence roughly when the next Ofsted visitation would take place. One of the school's longest serving teachers, Ruth, had told me:

> They tend to visit in local clusters, so we have some pretty good idea. They were down the road at [a neighbouring primary school] last week. So we know they'll be here any day now. They're on my shoulder, all the time. You can't let your guard down. 11.30. 12. If there's been no call, you can relax a bit. Tomorrow's OK. They might be in the day after. We got the Head's email ten days ago: make sure your books are all marked and up-to-date, records are watertight, etc.

Even in the periods of relative relaxation, Ruth said that Ofsted-readiness was high on the school's list of priorities, its performativity culture modelled in just the same way as at Secondary Two:

> The pressure is constant: learning walks, checking on the up-to-dateness of wall displays and marking, the regular what [SLT] call 'pop-ins'.

Like Simonetta at Secondary Two, Ruth resented what she saw as the blanket, heavy-handed approach to book-checking and unannounced SLT visits, feeling that it spoke of a general lack of trust on the headteacher's part, even in those members of staff who were highly experienced and known to be competent. Rather than uniting the staff, the very existence of Ofsted appeared to create a disconnect between classroom teachers and SLT, leading Ruth to describe the Ofsted modelling activities, as well as the school's Performance Management practice, as 'unsupportive' and inauthentic – the latter too easily descending into 'game playing' in which some of her colleagues had learned how to massage their data to ensure a positive evaluation. For Ruth, this same perceived division and lack of support had seeped into the Ofsted inspections themselves, in particular when an Ofsted inspector came to observe her class:

> To be honest, it's not so much the inspector sitting there in the classroom watching and judging: it's the accompanying [Senior] Management person – the roll of the eyes, the 'I'll see you later' look.

If some of these classroom teachers appeared to be suffering independently – an anxiety not shared by the school's senior leaders but imposed by them – the testimony of the headteacher Miriam suggested otherwise, highlighting the pervasiveness of the pressures produced by Ofsted from the top down. Miriam may have been ambivalent about Ofsted, suggesting to me that she felt it had contributed to teaching generally getting better, but she was in no doubt that there could be a better, more humane and more just way of going about inspection and regulation:

The anxiety beforehand is relentless. And the day itself is the most nerve-wracking experience you can imagine. As a member of SLT you sit there in front of inspectors, terrified you're going to say the wrong thing, make one small mistake when you're questioned about the data, and it's not just the inspection result that can suffer but your own credibility – your reputation. I mean, your professional reputation is on the line. But it's not just from the outside. It comes from inside, from yourself too, maybe even stronger: Am I good enough? What if I do everything I'm asked to do [to raise the Ofsted grade] and it's still not good enough? Should I be doing this job? I always think I'm up to it, but what if I'm not?

It is true that not everyone at Secondary Two was as negatively affected as Abigail. For some – though in truth not many – Ofsted represented a not unwelcome *challenge*, a chance for external validation, for confirmation that they were, indeed, doing a good job even if the school as a whole was not. Whether they were anxious or excited, however, the weight of anticipation hung over the school, increasing in intensity with each passing day. For some it was almost unbearable. 'It's like waiting for death', said John's friend James:

Just not knowing when it's going to strike, knowing it could be any time – this week, next week. … And [the senior leaders] never let us stop. Like they seem incapable of drawing a line, saying 'Well, that's it. We've done all we can do. The data looks good, and that can't lie. All we can do now is wait and get on with normal teaching while we do'.

In this state of permanent imminence, cracks began to appear (or in some cases to widen) in relationships, as the disintegration of familiar procedures and practices brought with it a parallel disintegration from a whole-staff challenge to one of individual survival. As any lingering camaraderie faded, so doubt and suspicion of colleagues grew – both on the part of those feeling personally comfortable about the prospect of being inspected and for those continuing to face it with anxiety. Typically, this came down to a concern not just for the implications for the whole school of a 'bad Ofsted', but for the internal repercussions of being given a poor grade in the event of an inspector coming in to one's individual classroom – even though, by now, Ofsted grades were no longer officially supposed to be awarded or shared. Comments like the following from Secondary Two teachers were common at this time:

'I just need to make sure I get through it and out the other side in one piece.'
'I have a set of best lessons up my sleeve if they do come in to any of my lessons.'

'I'm cool about my own performance. You can always lose it on the day, that's true, if you let the nerves kick in. But I'm not sure about some colleagues, to be honest.'

But comments comprising more overt, specific criticisms of other teachers, often those in other departments, were also not uncommon:

> 'God help us if they decide to visit certain people who shall remain nameless in [another] department'
>
> 'You can do everything you can to make sure you are not going to let yourself or anyone else down on the day, but unfortunately that doesn't necessarily apply to everyone, and I could tell you the names if I was unprofessional about it of at least a dozen so-called colleagues who really aren't bothered about their own career or the fate of the rest of us'.

I discovered that such antagonisms had developed over time, along with a growing sense of internal competitiveness in which teachers talked openly of wanting to make sure that, at the very least, their subject discipline fared better than others – but that at the beginning it had been somewhat different. I was told by several respondents that there had been a special 'Ofsted staff meeting' at the start of the term in which the inspection was expected, followed by a lunch-time social event. In their presentations to colleagues, the Head and her senior leadership team had praised staff for their efforts to date, and had emphasised the importance of teamwork and togetherness as the only appropriate way of facing the impending challenge successfully. Peppered with reminders of the implications should the dreaded Requires Improvement judgment be forthcoming, the speeches had been generally upbeat, confident and inspiring. Lines of communication had been clarified; staff had been told whom they could or should approach should they have any concerns. Every effort had been made to create a happy, optimistic mood, even as teachers had been reminded of what had brought them into teaching in the first place: of their responsibility to their students, of the love and enthusiasm they had for their subject specialism, of their determination to make a difference and to ensure that every student deserved to be given an opportunity to succeed.

The move from such a discourse of camaraderie and mutual support to a culture of individual survival, and its partial move back again – which might also, in Ahmed's terms again, be understood as the loss and return of the 'happy object' of teaching-as-experienced – can be traced partly though teachers' testimonies in the uneasy run-up to the inspection, and partly through their accounts of what occurred once the inspection – in the event, a very successful one – had come and gone.

John would tell me after the inspection was over that, 'with the benefit of hindsight the cracks were already there, in the so-called social event after the start-of-term speeches'. Rather than mixing together as encouraged, he said that subject groups had instantly 'coagulated' while Mary and her senior leadership team had set up occupation of one corner of the room 'apparently for their sole use'. It had not taken long, it seems, for these cracks to widen as, in spite of the confidence the headteacher had professed to have in her staff, the random book-checks and learning walks had been ratcheted up to create, as John put it, 'a culture of criticism and distrust' in which 'any semblance of this supposed "togetherness" turned out to prove. ... What should we say?: "fragile" I think is the word'.

John's reading of events was endorsed independently by Margo and Zoë, both of whom shared examples of some members of staff vitriolically criticising others behind their backs in the manner described by Martin at Primary One. While Margo talked of a rapid decline into 'collegial disintegration', Zoë spoke more specifically of how, as people came increasingly to understand the extent to which their own futures might be determined and shaped by the performances of others, a pre-emptive resentment kicked in among (in particular) some of the more confident, more experienced members of staff:

> So much bitchiness, you wouldn't believe. Some colleagues have genuine problems, outside I mean. They obviously need support. But what an unforgiving place this has become. What an unforgiving profession. No sympathy. Just 'Get your act together' sort of thing. 'You can worry about other things once Ofsted is finished'. Like people can just put their lives on hold ... and their feelings on hold, just like that. There's a guy in the [subject name] department. I won't say him by name. He's obviously close to having a complete breakdown. But no one in [the senior leadership team] wants to know. You hear them talking about him, no attempt to keep it private. It's like 'Oh everybody knows about him, so we don't need to keep quiet about it'. As far as they're concerned, he's just making excuses: using his private life to make excuses for problems he's having with a couple of his [subject] classes – one of which, I should add, has a lot of our most difficult Year 10s in it. Funny thing is, they were all very understanding when he started to talk about his problems last term. All that duty of care stuff came tripping off everyone's tongue, you know. Apparently, that particular duty no longer applies when the inspector comes calling.

This unforgiving, potentially punitive spirit – or 'atmosphere', or 'mood', or 'culture' as it was variously named by teachers – seemed to offer a graphic example not simply of internal(ised) manifestations of an externally imposed discourse of performativity but a clue, too, as to how – and why – centralised policy like this can come to infect and transform schools and teachers rather than simply being mediated or enacted by them and how it can divide a staff and individualise experience and activity rather than bringing it closer together. If a school is anticipating a high-stakes inspection and if it has a good idea of what the inspection will involve – what its manner and its criteria will be – why would the headteacher and senior leadership team *not* model the inspection in its own practices? Whether the modelling, and all that it brings with it, 'stays put' as mimicry after the inspection is over is an important question. For John, among others, the answer was worryingly clear:

> 'One of the clever things about Ofsted changing from four to six weeks' notice, which was probably the average, to this short-notice see-you-tomorrow kind

of drop-by is that it changes the whole culture of a school. Before, you could prepare for an inspection and then get back to normal working relations after they'd gone'.

'Working relations with colleagues?'

'Yeah, and with students. But … now everyone has to be kept in a high state of readiness – you know, Ofsted-ready they're calling it here – all the time, except if you're lucky for a period after the inspection is done, so it does get worse, yeah, when there's word an inspection might be imminent, and this Head here is pretty good at that, you know, pretty well-connected by all accounts so she hears stuff on the grapevine. … So it's worse when we think they're about to come: you know, everyone on battle stations as I like to call it. But it never goes away. … It can't do really, because you just would never have time to get ready if you only had a day or two, or even less. I've heard in some cases, they'll phone the school the same day from the café across the road, and they might like to say "Oh, we don't want schools preparing for the inspection and doing anything different from normal", but we're human beings in the end, believe it or not! … But the point is, we are now doing everything the way the government wants us to rather than the way *we* want to – and the two things are not always the same thing, as you know. . . '.

'And that's the performativity way?'

'Of course. Not just the paperwork and getting students doing well in SATs and GCSEs, which we would be doing anyway, but almost without knowing it we're buying into that whole culture'.

'"Doing" performativity'.

'Yes. And in some cases starting to believe in it … if that's the right word. It starts off as a matter of expediency but it ends up as a changed culture. And it's fear that does that, for sure'.

'Fear of the consequences of *not* doing it. . . '.

'Exactly. All sorts of consequences'.

John's words, which provide an interesting counter-point (not to say a potential contradiction) to his own and his friend James's previously cited testimonies concerning 'necessity' and institutional democracy, echo Fisher's observation (also cited above) that, more generally in life, 'we are in a condition of indefinite postponement. Our status is never fully ratified; it is always up for review' (Fisher and Gilbert 2016: 128), and indicate the ease with which an immediate, localised fear can evolve into a more enduring anxiety as, in this case, the inspection process and the performativity discourse which it reflects and represents create, fuel and take advantage of an enduring need for validation and reassurance. But his account also reminded me of Caroline at Primary One: of her negative sense of self, her feelings of never being good enough, and of the way in which external voices and practices that focus negatively on 'performance', on what, in Bernstein's (2000) terms, is 'absent', rather than on 'competence' (valuing and building on what is *present*)[3] become internalised and adopted so that we turn unforgivingly, punitively and with an exaggerated and perhaps unrealistic set of expectations upon ourselves – losing touch, in the process, of teaching's happy object, as the pleasures and rewards and positive feelings of our work disappear in a distracting fog of anxiety and self-doubt.

The brief return of the happy object: celebration and contagion

What draws us into the performativity discourse – or grants it some measure of control over our thinking and practice? And what holds it inside us (or us within it) so that it becomes an institutional(ised) and perhaps personal(ised) culture?

In the previous sections, discussion focussed on the impact of one element of a particular Foucauldian *dispositif* (Foucault 1994: op. cit.) – an Ofsted inspection – both on practice and on personal and social relations, including its capacity to fragment a school staff and to create or expand divisions between subjects. In such a time, it seemed difficult for many teachers to experience love, either for what they were doing or for their students and colleagues – driven, rather, into what Martin, at Primary One, had called the lifeboat mentality. I want to devote the majority of the rest of this chapter to a further exploration of the internalisation of performativity and its effects on our sense of being and on social relationships, but this time within a different context: that is to say, when teachers, though still locked within the performativity discourse, can experience collectively, albeit briefly, something more like a positive affective response. These are times when the lost happy object of teaching returns, joyfully but fleetingly, to remind us not only of affect's capacity (and the manipulation of affect's capacity) to bring about individual and collective anxiety and obedience, but also to engender shared delight – even if, in the process, it might also be drawing us a little further into compliant orientations and practices.

I was not able to be present at Secondary Two either on the day of the Ofsted inspection itself or on the day when its positive result was celebrated at a whole-school staff meeting. However, I did have the good fortune to be around at another event when, as I imagine was the case with the Ofsted result, an individually experienced set of fears and anxieties came to be replaced, on the receipt of good news, by a collective, contagious experience of happiness, validation and relief. This was the occasion which I have referred to as Results Day, when schools in England receive and process the 16+ examination results of their students, knowing that the results from all schools in the country will be subject to centralised statistical analysis which will be publically broadcast and that, as with the results of an Ofsted inspection, the impact both on student recruitment and on the school's immediate and longer-term future can be critically positive or negative.[4]

In the course of the main studies I have drawn on, and the more recent school visits and discussions I have undertaken outside of these main studies, I have been fortunate to have been present at two secondary-school GCSE Results Days (including the one I will be describing in more detail below) and two primary-school SAT Results Days, all providing rich illustrative evidence of the extreme pressure that such events can place on teachers as well as the powerful sense of individual and shared relief and victory that can follow. One of the most striking stories I had already come across during the course of my research came not from Secondary Two itself but from another secondary school in the vicinity. It came from Harvey, a friend of John's who was Head of English at that neighbouring school and who had expressed an interest in talking to me after school one day. Harvey told me how his annual summer holiday was always ruined by the uncertainty of the day in mid-August when the GCSE results were published. Even on a beach in some remote part of the world, he would be unable, he said, to drive that uncertainty from his head. Unable, too, to wait until the light of day and the annual pilgrimage into school to find out how the students in his subject area had performed, he would wait up until midnight the evening before so that he could access the results online as soon as they became available. Sometimes, he could not access them straight away, forcing him to wait up until 1am or later – knowing that he would be unable to sleep unless and until he had seen them, and without knowing whether his own, his English colleagues and his students' fates would be a cause for celebration or despair.

I had asked Harvey if he thought this level of anxiety was a common phenomenon, and if it had increased over the years. He had told me that he knew of 'many, many other teachers' – in particular, Heads of Department and members of Senior Management Teams – who were likewise affected. The anxiety had always been there to an extent, he had said, because 'teachers always want their students to do well because they care about them', but it had grown into something far more powerful within a growing 'punitive accountability culture' in public education in England over recent years, as the stakes had got higher and as teachers had been held more and more accountable for students' performance shortcomings:

> It isn't just the pressure from inside the school, from SLT, or concerns about what results can do to your career. It's the parents too. Gone are the days when if a student underperformed the direction of travel was from the school or the teacher to the pupil and the home – you know, 'Jill or Johnny has let themselves down'. Now, it's parents coming in and demanding 'Why haven't you taught my child properly?' I'm all in favour of parental involvement, but increasingly what we're getting is so-called empowered parents effectively being conscripted by central government to put yet more pressure on already hard-pressed teachers.

Harvey had shared several other stories with me, including how his school had been kept open all night on the eve of an Ofsted inspection so that teachers could come in to make final preparations and how some teachers in his department would deliberately avoid sharing what they felt to be good resources with colleagues for fear of undermining the academic edge they might give to their own students. Such examples were not isolated or uncommon, either. Felicity, a young Secondary Two English teacher whom I spoke to briefly toward the end of the current study, told me about conflicts between English and maths teachers related to what she called 'nabbing kids for interventions' – that is to say, competing with one another for the right to withdraw certain students identified as 'grade borderline' from regular classes for additional coaching:

> It's crazy really. Everyone's so desperate to make sure their and their department's results will be the best possible, they'll fight with people in the other department to stake a claim for the borderliners. Even though everyone knows it's the school as a whole that gets judged [according to GCSE results or Ofsted reports] you just end up fighting your own corner. It can get really nasty as times.

I had witnessed similar pressures to those expressed by Harvey and the other secondary-school teachers at Primary One, and would do so again in my more recent school visits in relation to Year 6 SATs, sat by students at the end of the Spring term with results coming into schools early in July. Ruth, at Primary One, spoke of the pressures on both teachers and children of 'intermediate' testing, whereby children were mock-tested once a month between January and May, comparing it to the stress of an imminent Ofsted inspection. Her account of the 'gut-wrenching days' immediately before the publication of the results, and of the powerful feelings of guilt and self-blame that can follow – or even precede – it echoed Harvey's account of his suffering:

> In spite of everything, all the efforts you've put in with individual children, weaknesses you've picked up in the intermediates, you still can't help worrying, and it's on a very personal level, more even than what the results might mean to the school: what it means to individual children, what it says about your own teaching. Is it my fault that so and so did not do better? You get particularly concerned about the borderliners [the ones who hover between two grades]. Was there something I missed? Something more I could have done?

As with some of the teachers at Secondary Two, Ruth felt that the Senior Leadership Team, and the headteacher in particular, were less supportive at these times, and more punitive and prone to over-reaction, to paranoia and to 'pressing the alarm button'. She talked of the school's 'Pupil Progress Meetings' in the Spring Term, of the pressure this puts on classroom teachers, and how it impacted on family life when there was even less opportunity than normal to spend quality time with partners and offspring. 'My husband keeps telling me "You don't have to do this"', she said, 'when yet again I'm bringing home piles of work':

> I know what he means. He means it's not in my contract, it's not reasonable. But he works in a different world. I tell him I *do* have to do it – nothing to do with contracts; all to do with pressure and knowing what the consequences are if you don't put in all the extra unpaid hours. [The government]'ve got

you over a barrel. They know we'll put in the extra hours, and they'll still blame us and punish us if the stats don't look good.

Results Day at Secondary Two

The stories of externally imposed pressure and stress from various teachers at Primary One and Secondary Two and elsewhere provide some further context for the brief account of Results Day at Secondary Two. In exploring this event, I will effectively be presenting what I take to be an example of what Bailey (2015: 146), in his elaboration of the relationship between affect and policy, calls an 'affective form of governmentality'. This is the process, akin to that of mimicry discussed earlier, whereby workers are expected and encouraged 'to become '"active subjects" in the coordination of various functions of production, instead of being subjected to it as simple command' (Lazzarato 1996: 135): that is to say, to become the bearers and perpetuators, or, to use a currently popular expression, to assume 'ownership of' a policy directive, rather than simply obeying it. As Bailey continues, in relation to what he calls 'technologies of performance', in which such policy-bearers are convened together in an act of systemic ratification and celebration:

> [I]t is … important to recognise that these technologies of performance are not simply repressive and negative; they can also be rewarding, both materially and emotionally. One can feel proud of one's performance, fulfilled in the knowledge that results were better than last year and that one is contributing to the success of the school.
>
> *(ibid.: 146)*

What follows is a brief account of Results Day at Secondary Two, drawn from my fieldnotes at the time.

★   ★   ★

It is a pleasant August morning in the middle of the long summer vacation, which in England runs from around July 20th through to the first week in September. In spite of it being holiday time, the school is packed with teachers, all of whom have taken their holidays early so that they can be here on this day. The reason for this unseasonal busy-ness is that this is the day on which, like every other school in the country, Secondary Two is receiving notification of the public examination results achieved by its students at 16 plus: in England, the GCSE (General Certificate of Secondary Education) examinations. These are high-stakes exams for the school's students, for whom they may mean the difference between having to leave school or being allowed to continue with their studies, or between future academic or future non-academic study – ultimately, concerning the kinds of jobs that might be available (or unavailable) to them once they have left the world of formal education. But they are high stakes for the teachers, too, and for the school.

Staffroom discussions and more formal interviews with teachers during the course of my previous visits have already revealed high levels of anxiety as teacher after teacher has talked of feeling forced into desperate, cut-throat competition with other local schools, under the constant threat, real or imagined, of inspection- or market-initiated closure. There is even an unofficial, but widely known about, league table of secondary schools within the borough: one in which Secondary Two's previous results, I am advised, have placed it in the 'top four' once student intake has been factored in in terms of 'value added'.[5] Some teachers have told me how this pressure has led them to do things that they do not believe in, including things that may even, they feel, work against the children's best interests. As one of my regular informants, a young English teacher, John, put it to me in interview a few weeks back:

> I [majored in] English and Drama when I was at school and uni[versity], and when I joined the profession – in fact, basically *why* I joined the profession – I had all these dreams about how I was going to get the kids to develop a love of reading ... develop their own creative writing, find their own voice, encourage them to develop their natural curiosity – all that stuff. ... But in this world you just can't do that, not if you want to keep your job and make sure the kids leave with decent qualifications. ... Well, you have to get them good exam results if you can, and if that means teaching them formulaic ways of writing, and saying the right things – you know, even if they may be the wrong things! – things about what somebody else decides is worthwhile literature, that's what we have to do. ... It's crap for the kids, whatever way you look at it. You can say it helps get them good results, which might or might not open some doors for them later in life – but what kind of quality of life does it actually promote? And what kind of people are we trying to reproduce anyway?

John has not been alone in expressing such concerns. Many teachers at Secondary Two have shared serious criticisms of and doubts about the pressures their students are being put under, not just to perform but to perform what teachers themselves often see as meaningless activities – and about the pressures and anxieties placed upon students both by high-stakes public examination achievements and by the sit-down Standard Attainment Tests (SATs) that the students are all now required to take at ages 11 and 14. In interview and discussion, I have struggled to find a single teacher who has a good word to say either about the SATs or about the construction of league tables and the uses to which they are put[6] – uses which seem to provide little useful information about what students actually are or are not doing and capable of doing, and which seem to me to decontextualise teaching and learning in a way that invites misleading cause-effect relationships between teacher and student performance. Nor have I found a teacher – any teacher – who has not expressed, to one degree or another, another kind of anxiety, not so much about the possible positive and negative impact of testing (and of teaching *to* testing) on their students, but about what perceived failure in terms of the results might mean to their school's future and to their own careers.

The anxiety – and, for most, subsequent relief – that I have witnessed at Secondary Two this August morning comes, therefore, as no surprise. What strikes me with particular force, however, is the dramatic emergence of something I have never witnessed at the school before: something that can only describe as collective joy.

The apparent and immediate cause of this joy is, of course, the examination results themselves. To a considerable extent, it is a joy that is quite clearly and obviously related *to* fear, in that it speaks of relief: the relief at a fear, at least for now, not materialised, of a nightmare giving way to the familiar security of the waking world. It turns out that the exam results have, to quote one of the deputy heads, been 'quite brilliant', rising from 37% of students achieving a top-3 grade in at least 5 GCSE subjects the previous year (which had been a shade below the then national average) to 'a whopping 51% this year'.[7] Despite its recent positive Ofsted report, I know that several members of staff, acknowledging the school's rather chequered past, still fear the threat of enforced academisation, and I'm thinking that in these circumstances such relief – a relief that quickly sweeps like a contagious blessing through the school – is only to be expected. Indeed, following the pessimistic predictions that various respondents have previously shared with me and with one another in staff-room conversations, it is very understandable. What is harder to make sense of is the sheer intensity of mutual congratulation, of joy verging on tears at particular students' higher-than-expected scores, of smiling, laughing teachers hugging one another as if being re-united with long-lost family members, and of a togetherness and camaraderie that I have never seen in the staffroom before and that was conspicuously absent in the days leading up to the school's Ofsted inspection. What has happened to all those condemnations of government policy, too – those ubiquitous opinions about the negative nature and impact of the GCSE examinations? Are these really the same teachers, celebrating successes in the examinations, who have previously had nothing good to say about them – people like John, Zoë, Margo and Abigail? And what about those students who have not done well? – the ones who have *failed* to achieve five or more grade A-Cs? Where are the tears and sympathy for them from these normally very caring and inclusive teachers?

A little later in the day, I sit in a corner of the staffroom jotting thoughts down in my research diary as I wait for the headteacher to finish giving a short speech telling the staff who are still present how proud she is of them and how they must all be proud of themselves and of one another:

> Something interesting is happening today, that I think speaks volumes of the nature of affect and of its role in the implementation of unpopular educational policy, and that serves as a reminder that fear alone can only take policy implementation so far. Today, that which was worthless seems (perhaps for the day, perhaps for longer?) to have achieved value; that which was despised has been warmly embraced. The students may generally have achieved very

well in relation to something many of Secondary Two's teachers do not normally have much faith in – but they *have achieved*, and achievement itself has great currency. From the teachers' point of view, it can subsequently act as 'evidence' – not just for Ofsted inspectors, but in answer to the perpetual, never quite completed quest for a symbolic mandate: 'What do I have to do, to be, to deserve the title of, teacher?' ('teacher' always preceded by a silent 'good') – and it is clear that many of the teachers in school today are revelling not only in the joy of their students' success within a system which, in less emotional times, most of them criticise, but in their own successes too within that same system. For some, in fact, it seems that their own revealed 'performance' is every bit as much a source of happiness and satisfaction as the successes of their students.

Later still, I add:

> Equally interesting is my own affective reaction to all of this. This is not my school. These are not my students. I am here as the 'objective' observer. But I can't help getting caught up in the euphoria myself. I, too, am 'feeling the love', finding myself celebrating along with the teachers – unable to wipe a permanent happy smile from my face. In short, I'm glad that, broadly speaking, the students, the teachers and the school have done well. I know not everyone here is happy. But for a while that seems less important, as do the possible fates of neighbouring schools, as does the fact that, inescapably, this celebration serves as a confirmation of a system that I, also, find repugnant.

★   ★   ★

If Results Day at Secondary Two exemplified the power of affect in determining our actions, including its potential primacy over decisions taken more 'rationally' or on the basis of an espoused philosophy, it also provides a further insight into how education policy, including elements of it that might be unpopular or that might run counter to our beliefs, speaks to and relies upon affect for its implementation, acceptance and stabilisation in practice. In answer to a previous question, the joy experienced and expressed so vividly by the teachers on Results Day might have had a temporariness about it; however, it seemed highly likely that it would sustain itself as *memory* (Gibbs 2001) – such that teachers would be likely to want to experience the feeling again at some future date rather than experiencing the despair that, presumably, was being experienced at the same time by other teachers elsewhere. In this way, a positive experience can produce or reinforce a *desire*, which itself is likely to trump – or at least to call into serious question – any reservations that one might have concerning the fairness and validity of the *system*.

But there is another side to this too; for while my attention had been drawn initially to the outpouring of joy I had witnessed, assuming this to be a universal expression of feeling at the school, it became apparent as the day wore on that it was not only teachers at other schools who might be experiencing an equal and opposite reaction of despair; it was also something that was affecting a small number of teachers at Secondary Two, some of whom, by lunchtime, had become conspicuous by their absence. In an examination system there will always be winners and losers, both between and within schools, and I soon discovered that not all subject departments at Secondary Two and not all teachers had achieved (so it was generally understood) as well as they had been expected to. Indeed, it was quite upsetting to overhear a small group of teachers from one of the school's faculties enthusiastically celebrating the successes of 'their students' in direct comparison with the results of many of the same students in another discipline. I suspected from previous conversations that the culture of the school was unlikely to engender much sympathy for these other teachers, who were more likely to be constructed as weak links, but I could not help feeling sorry for them. Just as love of the other can produce or reinforce, in moments of success such as those I had witnessed, a love of oneself, I could only begin to guess how it must have felt for those who had 'failed' – for those whose love had not been sufficient to achieve for their loved others that which love had demanded of them. Yet again, I thought of Caroline at Primary One, and her concern – or belief – that she could never be good enough: of how briefly, on Results Day, so many *could* feel 'good enough' while others might continue to find themselves wanting, and of the guilt that so many teachers had told me they carried with them on an almost daily basis. Neither could I stop myself thinking about some of the *children* I had spent time with on an earlier project (see Moore 2013) – of how they had been driven to provide answers to questions by a desire to win or secure the love or respect of a teacher at all costs rather than by any desire for learning itself.

Once again, it must be said that none of this was altogether surprising, and certainly not in any way reprehensible. Like it or not, within most education systems, as currently configured, young people will end up having to take examinations in which some skills, knowledge and expertise are externally valued more highly than others, in which they will be awarded grades that will be higher or lower than those of other young people, and in which, for most, those grades will determine not just the nature of the work available to them after leaving education but also, since academic value continues to have the capacity to be translated into economic value, the amount of income they can expect to earn. To encourage students to succeed as best as they can within this system is perfectly natural, particularly if we factor in the desire that brings teachers to this 'impossible profession' in the first place. Teacher 'effectiveness', too, is subject to external scrutiny and also, to a considerable extent, judged according to the results of their students. It is not, then, so odd that they should feel happy when their effectiveness is, so to speak, proven. It is also understandable – and some might argue laudable – that teachers should inspire in their students a belief that they can, *every one of them*, go on to succeed within the wider social system if they succeed first in school, where success is measured in examination results and where good results are achievable through hard work, even though this is an economic impossibility – even though, as Raymond Williams (1958) pointed out more than half a century ago, some will be *required to fail.*[8]

To accuse teachers of complicity in perpetuating not just an inequitable and unjust system but also a false belief in the fairness and justice of that system is, therefore, grossly unfair, not to say a misleading oversimplification: teachers do what they can do, not always what they would like to do, and to succeed within the system that exists, for all its failings, might well be seen as being more beneficial than to refute it through acts of failure within it. A central problem here, which is precisely that confronting the resistant teacher, concerns the tension between what we may 'know' about social systems and structures, including any inherent failings and inequities within them, and how we allow or encourage ourselves and others to experience those systems and structures – including how our 'affected selves' may embrace things that our more rational selves might find repugnant, and how affect can take primacy within such tensions, especially so when affect has the empathetic support of dominant rhetorics, ideologies and discourses. We might have no difficulty trying to help our students do as best as they can within a system we cannot wholeheartedly support or believe in, and no great difficulty justifying such an endeavour. But should we also be encouraging our students to understand and engage with a system's weaknesses, and with its dominant discourses' inherent dishonesty? Or should we (*must* we, for success-within-the system to be possible) allow and encourage our students to believe in a bright future that we know, for a great many of them, will never materialise? As Berlant suggests, 'a kind of love' (the love that will have brought many teachers into the profession in the first place and that may sustain them through it) can also produce or become characterised by a relation of what she calls *cruel optimism* – an optimism, that is, which engenders hope (in ourselves, and in those others we may have influence over) that is ultimately doomed to failure and disappointment. Perhaps it is the case here that the teacher's love itself contributes, albeit unwittingly and in act of *cruel irony*, to the continuing existence of an inequitable status quo as it re-focusses itself on helping students succeed within somebody else's notion of achievement and success: and perhaps it is the teacher's moments of joy, every bit as much as the moments of despair, that can act as a block to his or her *reflexive* endeavours, as affect itself, produced within us, renders itself resistant and hostile – if not entirely impervious – to critical examination.

More of these conundrums in the following chapter I want to round this one off by referencing a passage by Gilles Deleuze that I came across soon after my experience of Results Day at Secondary Two, describing what he calls the submerged irrationality (in translation, the 'nuttiness') of current dominant socio-economic systems and the way in which this irrationality is concealed through and by our active usage of such systems at the surface level of everyday life and practice. Though Deleuze speaks specifically of capitalism, the possibility of transferring his analysis to education and to what seemed to be occurring at Secondary Two is compelling. Deleuze writes:

> Everything about capitalism is rational, except capital or capitalism. A stock-market is a perfectly rational mechanism, you can understand it, learn

how it works; capitalists know how to use it; and yet what a delirium, it's nuts. … So then what is rational in a society? Once interests have been defined within the confines of a society, the rational is the way in which people pursue those interests and attempt to realize them. But underneath that, you find desires, investments of desire that are not to be confused with investments of interest, and on which those interests depend for their determination and very distribution: an enormous flow, all kinds of libidinal-unconscious flows that constitute the delirium of this society.

(Deleuze 2004a: 262–263)

It feels now as if what I was witnessing on Results Day (that great joy and sense of victory-against-the-odds, of the arrival of a happy and just ending), both in the teachers and in myself, was a brief surfacing of similar underlying 'libidinal-unconscious flows'. Fear on this day had been banished, however temporarily: partly (of course) by sheer relief, but partly, too, because love[9] had made what was to become, for a little while, its intensified annual appearance as ecstasy – filling the teachers with love for their students (whom they had always, of course, loved, though as feeling rather than as emotion) and, at least in those on whom success had smiled, an all-too-rarely-experienced love for themselves. To transpose Deleuze's account of Capitalism, we might say:

Everything about the exam system [or about public education, in its current guise] is rational, *except exams and the exam system [or public education]*. You can understand the system, learn how it works. Some students, parents, and of course all teachers, know how to use it. But actually it's nuts – and only because of its use is its nuttiness not recognised. It may be addressed rationally or as if it is itself rational (even experienced thus), but it is only the *use* of the system that is rational, not the system itself. And underneath that rationality there lie something else: 'investments of desire' (the desire for validation/recognition, the desire to have 'worth', to love and to be loved), that make us accept the system despite our protests, that make the system work because we work it, because underneath its rationality and our rational rejection of it something else, something more powerful than rationality, binds us to it. Of course, there are investments of interest, too, as we have seen: the system serves the material and hierarchical interests of those who organise and design and construct it, who demand the system's perpetuation, as well as those enmeshed within the system, who accept its potential for future financial and hierarchical reward or whose future careers might depend on its success. But these investments of interest cannot be served without the investments of desire. Though the examination system may, at one level, be understood as unfair and repugnant, at another level it serves a function; it offers a space in which relief, love and approval *can* be experienced and enjoyed.[10]

PART IV

Resistance and refusal: towards a reflexivity of the group

8

REFLEXIVITY AND THE GROUP

Validating affect, challenging hegemony

Is there something wrong with me? I don't know. Maybe there is. I feel I'm constantly being made to do things I don't think are right. But you're powerless [to resist], aren't you? There's just no support. It feels like everyone else is going one way and you're going t'other. I know there are some people here who think I'm just a throwback, living in the past. But I'm not wrong, am I? Am I? We shouldn't be making kids feel as if they're no good, and under pressure all the time – should we? Isn't learning supposed to be fun? Apparently not any more. ... You can feel so isolated at times, and I find I can very easily start to get paranoid.

(Ruth, class teacher, Primary One)

Reflexivity and the group

In this concluding chapter, I want to re-focus on the role of language in social organisation and control. This discussion will take us back to the two aspects of reflexivity explored in Part I. The first these is aimed broadly at developing new relationships with the self and with others through a changed relationship with our own biography and a critical re-engagement with our feelings. The second is more concerned with developing understandings of how the structural, organisational and political contexts within which we act and experience life work upon us. Each of these reflexive approaches demands an exposure of – and a confrontation of sorts with – our affective self. In the case of the latter approach ('Reflexivity 2'), this includes developing understandings of how orientations and acts of refusal and resistance are made more difficult by policy's discursive-rhetorical appeal to our affective core – an appeal that may, as it were, bypass any ideological and philosophical barriers to resistance that we may have set up. An additional problem for each reflexive endeavour relates to the fact that reflexivity is still, typically and essentially, undertaken (if at all) alone, as a work of the self on the self – even though at times we may use others as sounding-boards or sympathetic ears. This is a feature which, I have suggested, mirrors the feelings of isolation-within-the group (often intensified by the very fact of *being* a nominal member of the group) expressed by many of the teachers in my studies. Promoting the idea of group reflexivity as a way of overcoming this particular impediment, I will be arguing for the development of a certain kind of group, away from those in which the overriding pressure is to conform, to belong, to fit in (though those pressures may continue to exist and to demand a response), toward one in which the overriding motivation is to connect, to share, to challenge and to create a new sense of collective belonging. Essential to both reflexive approaches is the matter of 'getting affect out in the open', at the same time, as I have suggested elsewhere, as 'validating affect' (see also Moore 2013) – so that we do not demonise affect or trivialise it or exclude it from our considerations as irrelevant, but rather recognise and comprehend its power, in the process empowering ourselves as social actors.

If getting affect out into the open, which involves giving it the status and the stage for serious, honest discussion, is one key element of group reflexivity (as indeed it is, in a different way, of individual reflexivity), a second element is that of getting to grips with and taking a critical stance in relation to dominant discourses and the linguistic strategies they deploy in order to entice or impel us into their membership. This element is not dissimilar to Michel Foucault's notion of 'critique'. Critique in Foucault's elaboration is 'not a matter of saying that things are not right as they are', but rather of 'pointing out on what kinds of assumptions, what kinds of familiar, unchallenged, unconsidered modes of thought the practices that we accept rest' – in order to show 'that things are not as self-evident as one believed, to see that what is accepted as self-evident will no longer be accepted as such' (Foucault 1988: 154, 155). As McChesney says, referencing Chomsky's analysis of the importance of resistance, and of the nature of consent and its alternative, *dis*sent: '[I]f you act like there is no possibility of change for the better, you guarantee that there will be no change for the better' (McChesney 1999: 16).

Foucault offers critique as an indispensable prerequisite for genuine self-empowerment, at the same time acknowledging the limits within which any individual or group of individuals can expect to achieve change through active resistance: 'criticism' (and radical criticism), Foucault argues, 'is absolutely indispensable for any transformation' (ibid.: 155). It is a matter of 'flushing out' the thought, often unarticulated and 'hidden', that is always present within us, affecting and 'animating' our everyday behaviour – and then 'trying to change it' (ibid.). Critique can thus be seen as a deliberate practice which involves 'making facile gestures difficult' (ibid.). As with the confronting of affect, it is a matter of 'making conflicts more visible, of making them more essential than mere confrontations of interests or mere institutional immobility' (ibid.: 156). Critique does not necessarily result in obvious change in, for example, our surface relationships in the wider society; nor does critical awareness always translate easily into radical action, even when that awareness is shared by a group. In fact, critique itself does not require, demand or expect direct action by way of justification – precisely because it concerns the establishment of a necessary precursor to such action:

> A reform is never only the result of a process in which there is conflict, confrontation, struggle, resistance. … To say to oneself at the outset: what reform will I be able to carry out? That is not, I believe, an aim for the intellectual to pursue. His role, since he works specifically in the realm of thought, is to see how far the liberation of thought can make those transformations urgent enough for people to want to carry them out and difficult enough to carry out for them to be profoundly rooted in reality.
>
> *(Foucault 1988: 155)*

The actively resistant teachers I have identified in earlier pages might be seen as intellectuals in this way – charging themselves with the key role and purpose of keeping alive a challenge to dominant processes and discourses (to *dispositifs*), that at the same time generates and keeps alive alternative ways of thinking, doing and speaking without necessarily implementing (or attempting to implement) radical change to practice that is too often constrained by externally imposed rules and criteria. As with the organisation of reflexive groups, even this is no easy task, for it involves a serious discursive-linguistic battle which seeks not only to challenge hegemonised views of the world but also to question, to usurp and to undermine the language through which hegemonies achieve and hold on to their status. One major front in this battle concerns what might be referred to as a war against propaganda[1] – both that which is overt and that which is more insidious. It is this latter kind that is perhaps understood as most in need of – and most resistant to – Foucault's 'flushing out' in the reflexive process.

The discursive battleground

Summarising Lacan's conceptualisation regarding the subject's relation to – and construction within – the symbolic order of signification, Ruti advises:

> [A]lthough [Lacan] consistently accentuates the subject's relative helplessness vis-à-vis the larger systems of signification that envelop it, he at the same time suggests that it is only by virtue of its membership in the symbolic order that the subject possesses the capacity to make meaning in the first place.
>
> *(Ruti 2009: 96)*

Language, in short, both empowers and emprisons. It gives us the means to engage – critically, if we should so choose – in discussion and debate, but it also tends to establish the parameters within which we are able to communicate, to experience and to think: that is to say, it has a liberating potential alongside a controlling and repressive function. Even as we challenge dominant discourses, and the specific language which feeds and sustains them, we may find ourselves doing so within those discourses' own frames of reference, constrained by the very language with which they seek to determine our thoughts, words and deeds.

Ruti suggests that the way to use language counter-discursively, even when operating (as to an extent we must) within dominant discourses, is to use it poetically. Speaking, writing and thinking poetically involves the strategic creation of new language and linguistic forms, new metaphors, new ways of dressing and expressing oppositional thought, that refuse simply to borrow the linguistic clothes of the dominant ideologies whose authority we may seek to challenge. As has often been observed, the political Right has been very good at this (much better, certainly, in England than the political Left) – in particular in creating and popularising slogans which seek to ossify meanings and to place them beyond critique: the 'standards' in 'raising standards'; 'the 'hard' in 'hardworking'; the 'people' in 'the people have spoken'; and of course 'democracy', in all manner of platitudes. (For related and alternative accounts of poetic language, its nature and its possibilities, see Kristeva 1984; Brik 1964.)

As with reflexivity generally, using language poetically – effectively, (re)claiming it for our own purposes – is not an easy matter, particularly when we factor in the power of affect; nor is it yet entirely clear how such a venture might be undertaken. As Mark Fisher (Fisher and Gilbert 2016) has observed, and as we have seen to an extent in the linguistic and conceptual manoeuvres of Bill and others, dominant discourses have a way of thriving even in inhospitable circumstances in which they may appear to have been rejected. Fisher's analysis of what he calls 'capitalist realism' (whereby capitalism is perceived as just the way things are, rather than as constructed and therefore replaceable) draws on his own experience of working in Further Education. In an account that will resonate with the experiences of many readers, and which contains loud echoes of considerations of pragmatism discussed in Chapters 1, 3 and 6 above, he writes:

> There was an acceptance amongst managers of the inevitability that education would increasingly be modelled on business. Some managers would typically introduce new procedures by explicitly saying that they didn't themselves think they were a good idea, but what could you do? This was how things were to be done now, and the easiest option all round would be for us to go through the motions. We didn't have to believe it, we only had to act as if we believed it.
>
> *(Fisher and Gilbert 2016: 126)*

What Fisher suggests next is of particular relevance in relation to the accounts of teachers explored in the earlier chapters, but also in relation to the role and power of language in the dissemination of dominant ideologies:

> The idea that our 'inner beliefs' mattered more than what we were publicly professing at work was crucial to capitalist realism. We could have left-wing convictions, and a left-wing self-image, provided these didn't impinge on

work in any significant way! This was ideology in the old Althusserian sense – we were required to use a certain language and engage in particular ritualised behaviours, but none of this mattered because we didn't 'really' believe in any of it. But of course the very privileging of 'inner' subjective states over the public was an ideological move.

(ibid.)

Fisher's description of the privileging of the 'inner self' over the effects of the acceptance of socially unjust policy on those we teach and work with speaks of a kind of faux resistance: that is to say, a resistance which has not been preceded, as active resistance must be, by *refusal*. It therefore exists only symbolically and discursively, avoiding confrontation with affect in favour of a retreat into some form of rationalism. It is the kind of resistance that facilitates – perhaps even, at some level, welcomes – the internalisation of powerful ideologies and discourses. A function of the 'positive discourses' (such as those around 'democracy') in situations where teachers may find themselves compelled to embrace that which is initially or even enduringly repugnant seems to be to enable a voiced denial, in the process of which one moral imperative is relegated in favour of another. The decision may involve an assertion that what is being done is being done reluctantly rather than complicitly: when all's said and done, one way to live with the decision to be 'only obeying orders' is to convince oneself that, in some way, such obedience is in the interests of the greater good rather than (in an act of self-deprecation) out of personal hypocrisy or treachery. In this way, the role of the positive discourse becomes one of support for, rather than resistance to, the negative discourse.

There is another challenge for poetic language, however, that is not directly concerned with the resistance it encounters from dominant discourses and ideologies: one that may seem to come from within rather than from without, but that is equally subject to the force of affect. Poetic language may be subversive and (to quote Atkinson 2017) 'disobedient', but we should not overlook the fact that poetic language is still language, and subversive discourse is still discourse – in either case, subject to the affordances and constraints that language and discourse inescapably bring. In an account of some of his own poetic language around the concepts of 'desiring-machines' and 'schizo-analysis', fashioned in collaboration with Félix Guattari, Gilles Deleuze makes the following cautionary observation:

Neither Guattari nor myself are very attached to the pursuit or even the coherence of what we write. … [W]e are not among those authors who think of what they write as a whole must be coherent; if we change, fine, so there's no point in talking to us about the past. … When a term is introduced and has the least bit success, as has been the case for 'desiring-machine' or 'schizo-analysis', either one circulates it, which is already rather pernicious, a sort of co-optation, or one renounces it and seeks out other terms to upset the order. There are words that Félix and I now feel it urgent not to use:

'schizo-analysis', 'desiring-machine' – it's awful, if we use them, we're caught in a trap.

(Deleuze 2004b: 278)

Deleuze's apparent dismissal of some of the terminology that he and Guattari had previously produced, along with his embracing of the provisionality of written texts, may come as a surprise to some (and indeed as something of a relief to others!). What Deleuze seems to be saying is that poetic or creative language offers us no better than a temporary, albeit important and necessary, pin with which to fasten, for a time, our current evolving understandings of the world – and perhaps of our selves in the world – rather than (as the language of custom and officialdom may seek to do) a more permanent nail with which to give it some measure of fixity. If we allow it to, language which at first enables our thinking and moves it forward along unpredicted paths may come to inhibit it, in just the same way that the language of dominant discourses and ideologies tries to do. Even when we seek to create new language as a way of moving beyond inhibition, as a way of subverting dominant discourses and linguistic givens, we must not allow that new language to limit our further thinking and development. Rather, we need to repeatedly reject our own subversive language once it has achieved its purpose, rather in the manner of a rocket's booster engine being ejected in order for the rocket to be able to make further progress. Just as the rejection of existing language, meanings and metaphors enables us to think differently, so it is the rejection of our own subversive language that enables us to make further progress in terms of our thinking, opening up the way for us to come up with yet newer language – and newer conceptualisations – which act as another temporary pin.

I don't believe Deleuze is suggesting that we should not enjoy our moments of pleasure when, for example, we take some control of the discursive reins, when we discover new language or new metaphors through which to experience and understand things differently. On the contrary, we may feed off such moments and such achievements: they may excite us; they may make us feel empowered; they may give us the resolution and momentum that is required of resistant think-ing; they may even enhance our sense of self-worth. However, once enjoyed and celebrated, they must be left behind and moved on from – just as (one might say) we should move on from the temporary pleasure and uplift of our students' positive examination or SATs results. Above all – and to ease this reluctant rejec-tion, perhaps – we may need to recognise the role and nature of affect in these transactions: in particular, of how the more conservatising influence of affect might encourage us to 'hold what we have' or to bask in the pleasure of an answer having been achieved. Once we allow ourselves to become enduringly self-congratula-tory, or to believe that a war has been won, or to trap ourselves in linguistic and discursive prisons of our own making or, as Deleuze (2004b) puts it, in the 'sacred texts' of other oppositional thinkers, we run the risk of becoming trapped in our own subversions, rendering ourselves vulnerable again to the invasive intentions of conservatism.

Language and fantasy

Of all the teachers I spoke to at any length at Primary One and Secondary Two, John at Secondary Two was the one who had taken on the idea of challenging discourse most seriously, perhaps as a result of the reading and discussion he had undertaken on his Masters degree course. He had decided ('for the first time') that he wanted to write, and perhaps to publish – not just *about* education (academic papers, and perhaps a book), but also *for* education (materials and manuals appropriate to his philosophical approach to education and specifically to teaching and learning) – both to bolster and to disseminate his increasingly critical orientation:

> What the [Masters] course has done, apart from giving me some theory to support my ideas and help me make sense of them to myself, if that makes any sense, is that it's given me a critical language. I know not everyone is happy about this, even on the course. It sometimes looks like it's just about being … you know, clever-clever. … But it's kind of empowering having this language and knowing that most politicians and policy makers probably don't have it, and will struggle with it. It's a bit like being able to speak openly about stuff in a very critical way but in a kind of coded way too, so you can start to feel a bit more like you're playing at home to use the football metaphor, instead of always having to play away. … You've got more chance to set the agenda, and through taking control a bit more of the language you have more control of the discourse and more space to move around inside it. And then you can start to share the language with colleagues, who are actually more interested than you might expect in the ideas that lie behind it. Like the one I'm thinking about particularly is cultural capital, which really starts to make you challenge ideas you might have about natural ability, and in a much more useful and appropriate way, I think, than policy drives like 'Every Child Matters'.

John's observation about language – including his emphasis on the *power* of language, which he now appears to see as a two-way process – offers a useful way into thinking more about using language poetically and engaging with greater confidence in the discursive arena of policy construction, enactment and subversion. Language not only establishes what is said – and how it is said – allowing, simultaneously, opportunities for establishing new agendas and new ways of saying; it is also a necessary tool in the construction both of 'realities' and of possibilities, of understanding what is and what might be.

In an argument that has obvious implications for the possibility both of radical agency and of critical reflexivity, Mari Ruti continues her own discussion of language to describe two kinds of 'fantasy', each in tension with the other in much the same way as concerns the tension(s) within language between affordances and constraints. The first kinds of fantasy, with echoes of Bourdieu's notion of 'habitus' (Moore 2012b), are 'unconscious fantasies that curb our existential options' and that may manifest themselves as 'delusions that derail us from the concrete realities of our lives' (Ruti 2009: 100). These are fantasies that may tell us that the contingent and the arbitrary are the natural and the normal, that impel us to conformity and acceptance of (imposed) limitations as regards our choices, and that perhaps encourage us to believe that, with reference to the more significant areas of our lives, we simply have no choice – that, as in 'Capitalist Realism' (op. cit.), 'what will be will be'. To return to an abiding theme, fantasies of this kind also serve to undermine reflexivity – or at least to place obstacles in the way of our approach to it. Fantasies of normality can be traced, perhaps, in Yanick's acceptance of children's intrinsic naughtiness and in the teacher's role as disciplinarian, in Caroline's acceptance of the 'politics' embedded within partnership models of initial teacher education and training, and in Bill's acceptance of competition and the inevitability of having to conform to market forces – acceptance, in each case, establishing limitations both on available actions and on engagement with possibility.

The second kind of fantasies are 'imaginative and creative fantasies that allow us to observe the world from novel angles' – fantasies that are both the motivation for and the fruit of reflexivity. As with Foucault's critique, fantasies of this kind can be 'a means of disclosing previously unknown realms of meaning' (ibid.). The trick is to recognise or unmask our restrictive fantasies for what they are and what they do for – and to – us, and then to allow freer rein to our imaginative and creative fantasies as we sidestep the symbolic order's more hegemonic tendencies. This is a move which necessitates recognition that it is not only the individual subject that is fractured, multifaceted, caught up in a state of tension, but also the Other (the symbolic order of language, discourse and custom) – that there is a 'lack' in the Other that 'by necessity renders it porous and alterable' (ibid.: 106) and that 'keeps it from ever becoming a closed totality that could convincingly legitimate the ideology that it espouses' (ibid.: 105).

The difficulty is that our fantasies, whether of the unconscious or of the creative kind, can serve to blind us not only to the inconsistencies and fissures within our own subjectivity, but also (ibid.: 106) 'to screen the inconsistency of the Other' – so that rather than encouraging and helping us to challenge a naturalised status quo they may simply (to hark back to Bill's response) serve to find us a comfortable place within an Order which not only remains unchallenged but is effectively internalised and endorsed. I suggest that restrictive fantasies, supported discursively and affectively, can only be exposed and challenged, perhaps moved on from, through reflexivity – a move which, as has already been argued, depends on critical engagement with the 'normal' as embedded in discourse and in the wider *dispositif*:

[T]o the extent that fantasies function as a support of cultural adaptation, they conceal the divisions and antagonisms of the collective field, thereby solidifying the subject's ideological investment in, and attachment to, dominant social structures; they seal the gap of the Other so as to provide a seamless ideological support for the subject's experience of collective reality, for its ability to envision the world as dependable and meaningful. ... *On this account, the most efficient means of defending against the Other's hegemonic desire is to gain access to symbolic resources of signification that permit one to articulate nonhegemonic configurations of desire. This is a matter of pitting the Other against itself, as it were – of fighting the repressive dimensions of the symbolic order with the resources of meaning-production that this very order makes available.*

(ibid.: 106, emphasis added)

Ruti's argument may be seen as a version of the notion of a discursive battleground: of the importance of 'taking on' the symbolic order, of seeking to wrest control of it as far as we are able, and of inserting our own symbolic constructions into the Other – drawing on, playing with and developing the resources (essentially, the language, however understood) that it already places at our disposal. Sociologists, philosophers and public psychoanalysts such as Foucault, Butler, Deleuze and Lacan have adopted precisely this ploy, in creating and inserting into the symbolic order a raft of new vocabulary and innovative metaphors by way of drawing their readership away from the language and terminology we are more accustomed to, compelling us to think differently and in different words about ourselves, about others, about society and about language itself. Though any individual can contribute to this process, the validation and *circulation* of challenging thoughts newly expressed is crucial if truly effective critique of – or opposition to – dominant discourses is to take place. Naturally, a further difficulty occurs when critique and its language fails to permeate the boundaries of, say, Academia or of certain introspective political movements, where it may simply circulate endlessly within a small and somewhat limited membership and never reach sufficient numbers for it to be able to take root and manifest itself in practice and debate. Unfortunately, in public education, this has tended to be the case. Even when discursive subversion does make its way inside the school, as in Secondary Two where it may be said to have done so in a small way in the shape of John and James as bearers of a counter-discourse, little will be achieved, even at the most local of levels (the individual school, itself dominated by hegemonic discourse and ideology) if it cannot be disseminated and shared – and if potential disseminators like John feel too fearful or are simply too busy to elaborate their thinking with colleagues, or if their colleagues are likewise kept too busy and distracted by performativity's ever-tightening grip to listen. Not so long ago, there existed many CPD courses in the UK that encouraged the promotion of alternative understandings, the challenging of dogma and orthodoxies, the sharing of different languages through which to encourage fresh and critical thinking. Masters courses, too, which did the same, were made easily available to practising teachers. (When I undertook my own Masters Degree in the mid-1980s, I was financially supported, like every other participant, many of whom had been given year-long paid sabbaticals, by my Local Education Authority – which not only paid my fees but also allowed me a generous period of study-leave in which to write up my dissertation.) Times have changed. But they can change back again if only politicians in sufficient numbers and with sufficient clout can be persuaded that they should do so. Of course, such persuasion might demand their own reconsideration of what it means to be a professional teacher and indeed what the purposes of mass education are. It might also require a major shift in some nations in the way education policy is understood, constructed and disseminated: away from its increasingly didactic, monologic nature and its propagandised implementation, back toward a more collaborative, thoughtful, dialogic approach which recognises and values the knowledge, the experience and the wisdom of those charged with putting policy – a policy that will itself have been co-constructed – into practice in their classrooms.

Structure, agency and 'care of the self'

Osler and Starkey (2005) describe as a 'crisis in democracy' the feeling of powerlessness we may experience as individuals (or even as small groups) to affect or to change things that we know to be wrong in the world. Such feelings – exacerbated perhaps by an overwhelming tide of policy rhetoric that can make us feel deviant or out of touch unless we also absorb and accept it – can engender and contribute to an abiding, potentially debilitating feeling of impotence and even self-deprecation: one certainly that does not encourage either reflexivity or resistance. We might also convince ourselves that, even if we were to act oppositionally, it would ultimately be in vain. As McChesney argues:

> In our demoralized times, a few may go a step further [than experiencing a sense of resignation,] and conclude that we are enmeshed in [a] regressive system because, alas, humanity is *incapable* of creating a more humane, egalitarian, and democratic social order.
>
> *(McChesney 1999: 15, emphasis added)*

In my own studies, John was not the only teacher to express a feeling, despite his resistance, both of powerlessness to effect change and of being an outsider whenever he adopted an oppositional stance to the status quo – even in the absence of any specific acts of ostracisation on the part of his colleagues. It is easy to state the obvious: that the way to stop feeling impotent is to stop feeling impotent. But even when rationalised and broken down into steps (along lines that John, in another conversation, suggested), it is not so easy. In a discussion concerning the nature of refusal (refusal to accept, to buy into and to have one's actions overly determined by dominant discourses and ideologies) and active resistance (taking steps in one's practice and observable behaviour to oppose orthodoxies with which one is in fundamental and philosophical disagreement), John highlighted both a feeling of powerlessness and that feeling of isolation-within-the-group illustrated in earlier chapters in discussion with other respondents:

> 'Like you have suggested, I guess the first step is to challenge orthodoxy. That's refusal, right? Kind of challenge the permanence or intransigence or whatever of the symbolic world of customs, language, ideologies and so on. All those things that provide the kind of framework we experience

and conduct our lives inside. Then there's a second step, which is maybe more about agency … or possibility … because agency is also part of refusal. It's more about speaking out and sharing, and not being afraid to do it. … Having the strength and confidence'.

'And that surely is the hard part?'

'Definitely. Though in my case I have to say it's been made easier by having someone who shares my views and feelings around to talk to. Talking to James always makes me feel sane again. … It also gives me the confidence to try and carry on doing the things I believe in. … As much as the curriculum and the exam system will let me'.

The affective experience of isolation within the group is identified by John as one obstacle to be overcome in sustaining refusal and contemplating forms of more active resistance, though it appears that, with the aid of his friend James and the discussions they have enjoyed with other students (many of them from overseas) on their Masters programme, he has already thought more seriously about possible avenues of resistance – albeit bringing its own additional set of problems:

> The competition drives you to conformity. Kids having to compete with one another for exam grades, teachers judged all the time on their performance in relation to other teachers, schools judged against each other in league tables. The results are everything, and if the results are about kids remembering mainly fairly useless facts, and showing off some basic mastery of skills they most probably will never use, that's what you have to focus on or you – and they – go under. I think that's why it's so hard to talk about other things – like learning, which it's funny I know to think about learning as other things when you're discussing education. … It feels like you are betraying your colleagues, letting them down. I've even been accused by one senior colleague of letting the kids down because I was spending too long on something: a bit of Dickens, actually, which I thought at the time 'Wow, these kids are actually getting into Dickens', which you would have thought might be considered to be a good thing even by people like [the current Education Secretary]. So it's so much easier to talk about this stuff outside of school, which is why the Masters has been so great, and meeting people from other countries who are actually as horrified as you are by what's going on here – and the irony being that they come here thinking they're going to learn from some kind of exemplary system … which is a bit of a joke.

John's identification of a culture and discourse of competition and competitiveness as working against refusal and resistance – in effect, against being critically reflexive, either individually or with others – is in a small way counter-balanced by his observation that such resistance-to-resistance can be countered more effectively when not undertaken alone: in his case with James, a likeminded colleague whom he feels he can trust. As Gilbert has argued, a 'competitive individualist ideology' is 'at the core of neoliberalism' (Fisher and Gilbert 2016: 137): its insidious invasion and occupation of individual and collective subjectivities is essential if neoliberal ideology and policy is to be sustained. Schools, teachers and school students, like most of us, find ourselves pressed into 'a corrosive ethic of competitive self-interest which both legitimises inequality and damages community' (Littler 2016: 75) – an effect we have already seen played out in the run-up to an Ofsted inspection at Secondary Two, at Results Day, and in competition's never-ending, overbearing presence even in the spaces between formal inspections.

In revisiting John's testimony, questions of individual and collective agency inevitably resurface, including matters concerning the limits and expectations of what can be achieved by the resistant self. A helpful way of exploring these issues a little further is offered by Michel Foucault's conceptualisation, linked to 'technologies' of the self, of 'care of the self' (Foucault 1990).

Like many of Foucault's terms, care of the self – a concept derived from classical philosophy – needs some explaining. As Foucault (2000a, 2000c) points out, it is certainly not to be confused with self-ishness, with feathering one's own nest, with embracing neoliberalised self-sufficient subjectivity, or with narcissism or 'self-attachment or self-fascination' (Foucault 2000c: 269). Nor is it to be confused with self-knowledge (Foucault, ibid.). Effectively, care of the self is another articulation of the kind of radical reflexivity discussed in Chapter 2, involving a '"losing-finding" of the self' (Blacker 1998: 363), in which we examine ourselves critically, including what can be achieved within the discursive and material constraints of our lives, in an ongoing struggle to 'become what we are not'. It comprises an ongoing, personal interrogation of the 'ways in which one can exercise some kind of influence on the self one is becoming [via a continuing search] for a way of getting outside of existing governmentality' (Devine and Irwin 2005: 325, 326). To return directly to Foucault, care of the self requires 'technologies' of the self which, as with psychoanalytically informed reflexivity, 'permit individuals to effect by their own means, or with the help of others, a certain number of operations on their own bodies and souls, thoughts, conduct, and way of being, so as to transform themselves in order to attain a certain state of happiness, purity, wisdom, perfection, or immortality' (Foucault 2000a: 225). 'Care' thus understood 'describes a sort of work, and activity; it implies attention, knowledge, technique' (Foucault 2000c: 269).

We might say that care of the self takes account of the power of material and linguistic-discursive structures but without encouraging us to embrace or to accede to determinism. It recognises that all human relations are infected by and embedded within relations of power but attributes a measure of power to the individual to positively 'fashion an identity' (Ball 2017) – so that we are able, at least to an extent, to construct our subjectivities in a social world that may be limiting but that also, as with language, contains possibilities for resistance, opposition, creativity and subversion – if we can only enable ourselves to seek them out. Seen thus, care of the self may be understood and undertaken as a(nother) practice of freedom (Foucault 2000b). Discourse, infused with power and affect, might attempt to affect and shape who we are, how we perceive ourselves, the world and our place and connection in the world, but it cannot totally subjectify us. Foucault's suggestion is that we can work dialogically and critically within discourse, and with the other material and non-material elements of *dispositif*, as a way of empowering ourselves that, while it may not in itself equip us to change larger systems and sanctioned practices, or to overthrow and replace ideologies and discourse that we find repugnant, can at least offer us ways of maintaining resistant orientations more comfortably and positively, even within situations and circumstances in which resistance may be demonised and ridiculed.[2]

An understanding of our circumstances – those that have shaped us and those that continue to contain and affect us – is an essential aspect of this process, for, as Foucault puts it:

> [T]his work done at the limits of ourselves must, on the one hand, open up a realm of historical inquiry and, on the other, put itself to the test of reality, of contemporary reality, both to grasp the points where change is possible and desirable, and to determine the precise form this change should take.
>
> *(Foucault and Rabinow 1991: 46)*

Of particular relevance to the argument being put forward in this final chapter, Ball (2017), in his recent work *Foucault and Education*, cites care of the self in developing his account of another concept we have considered, that of refusal. Ball takes as his starting-point Pignatelli (2002), who identifies two kinds of refusal linked to two concomitant forms of risk. The first kind of refusal has two aspects: a disengagement or renunciation of our 'intelligible' self, coupled with a willingness to test and transgress the limits of what we are able to be, 'what it would mean to exceed or go beyond oneself' (Pignatelli 2002: 166) and, at the same time, a renunciation of the comforts of a transcendental self and of the belief that we can know ourselves entirely 'authentically' (i.e. as anything other than ideologically and discursively constructed).

The second refusal is essentially the refusal we have already considered: that is to say, a refusal to be colonised by or to accept dominant discourses and ideologies themselves, even as we acknowledge the impossibility of ever freeing ourselves entirely from them – including, centrally, those categories, parameters and norms by and within which we are represented and encouraged to understand our selves.[3]

The risk attached to the first kind of refusal is similar to the one raised in Chapter 2 regarding the potential dangers of reflexivity – that it can challenge our very sense of identity, of completeness, of closure, resulting in confusion and despair rather than in empowerment. An additional risk, also raised in relation to reflexivity, is that it can lead to self-blame rather than self-liberation, particularly if reflexivity takes place within and is tainted and restricted by the very ideologies and discourses it might seek to challenge. In such a situation, the danger, as Nikolas Rose puts it, is that through reflexivity we may simply become complicit in ways that are not obvious to us in our own repression – that is to say 'through the unceasing reflexive gaze of our own psychologically educated self-scrutiny' (Rose 1989: 208). The risk attached to the *second* refusal – the refusal of the discourse that seeks to infest and absorb us – is the one expressed by a number of teachers in my studies, in relation to loss of popularity with colleagues – who may perceive resistance and refusal as troublesome, bizarre, or 'eccentric, if not outrageous' (Zembylas 2003: 112).

Getting 'outside governmentality', which is effectively moving away from the centre of dominant discourses, is also easier said than done. As Devine and Irwin (op. cit.: 326) remind us: 'the self has only the tools of its own time (including its own past) and place (however imagined) with which to think itself out of that time and place'. In her critique of Judith Butler's ongoing discussions about structure and agency, Amy Allen goes further, to ask: Is critical reflexivity possible, or is it just an impossible dream, its existence merely illusion – even, perhaps, one of 'power's clever ruses' (Allen 2008: 2) – that makes us think we are in some way unmasking and subverting power relations when we are actually supporting and perpetuating them through our very acts of perceived opposition? Devine and Irwin are, like Allen (and presumably like most of us), reluctant to accept the more deterministic take on agency, preferring to argue that the very notions of structure and agency may need to be re-thought and re-defined and that, although the power of discourse and ideology are not to be understated or underestimated, agency to some degree *can* be achieved – perhaps through a process of what Foucault calls 'conscientisation' which involves 'the honest appraisal of governmental techniques and an understanding (*as far as we are able*) to make these techniques visible to ourselves' (Devine and Irwin, ibid. emphasis added). Allen suggests that critique is not necessarily futile, any more than 'autonomy is impossible' (Allen 2008: 173). It does, however, require considerable courage and effort, whether undertaken by the individual subject individually subject-ivised or, with greater promise of affecting the wider system, through the development of what Mark Fisher has termed a 'new (collective) political subject' (Fisher 2009: 53).

Refusal, resistance and solidarity: group subjects and group reflexivity

While care of the self may help us to develop as individuals, and while we may accept the limited role for the intellectual that Foucault suggests, it is not the intention or the expectation that this will result either in subjective isolation(ism) or in a rejection of more active social interventions. In this section, while acknowledging the value of individual reflexivity and critique, I want to underline what to many will be an obvious point – that refusal, as well as active resistance, is likely to be made easier and to be potentially more effective when it involves us in memberships of likeminded, reflexively disposed groups. I have already argued that there is a problem for many teachers in that, as one of the effects of performativity, they may feel isolated, notwithstanding positive surface relations, within the group or groups of teachers with whom they work. Individual reflexivity might help us come to terms with and manage this situation *as individuals* – but it is unlikely to make the problem itself, or the conditions from and within which the problem emerges, go away. It may, in short, impose quite serious limitations on what might be achieved through reflexive activity.

The example of Bill, introduced in Chapter 3, suggested a particular set of difficulties that may hinder acts of refusal (to 'accept' the discourse) and active resistance (taking steps to subvert it) when the individual subject is, so to speak, acting alone. Bill's fear of isolation within the (largely uncritical) group resulted not so much in an individual 'care of the self' as in a retreat from the discomfort of disagreement and a voluntary return to the discursive fold: as Amanda Anderson (2006: 173) puts it, perhaps a little unkindly, such potential refusers/resisters have failed – or perhaps have chosen to fail – to cultivate (for it does not come without sustained effort) the 'effort of refusing the comfort of a claimed collective identity'. A problem for Bill was that, although wanting to feel a sense of belonging to the group, he was working within local (school) and wider (societal) systems that encourage us to think and operate as individuals in competition with one another while at the same time encouraging us to conform as individuals to wider political and social conventions and directives. As has already been suggested, policies and ideologies of neoliberalism, embedded within an economics of free-market capitalism and sold via discourses of personal 'freedom', 'choice' and 'responsibility', has no truck with the collective or with solidarity – which is why it is so suspicious of and antagonistic toward trades unions. The only group neoliberalism is interested in seems to be the fantasy group – the 'nation' (often, the mysterious 'one nation'), occupied by 'the [monolithic] public' whose unsung heroes are 'hardworking people': fantasy collectives, in essence, whose popularisation instantly and repeatedly demonises those who would dare to challenge their authenticity.

Within the same neoliberal philosophy and politics that promotes and celebrates individualism (and, as Foucault puts it, 'individualization') and competition, it is not surprising that schools, involved as they are in the business of preparing young people for life (or more specifically these days, for economic life and social and financial survival), should follow suit. School students in most countries, England included, are still pitted against one another in public tests and examinations, and continue to sit, by and large, in rows behind tables facing a teacher whose own, often more substantial desk is situated at the front of the class. Collective enterprise might be allowed or encouraged from time to time, but it is seldom if ever validated by the award of a meaningful, useable grade or mark. Boys may be separated from girls on registers, 'more able' and 'less able' students may find themselves allocated different classrooms, different teachers, and even different syllabuses, while more generally students are likely to find themselves learning alongside other students by virtue of their chronological age. Schools, too, as we have seen, are often pitted against one another, competing for students and popularity within centralised inspection régimes and through the national publication of 'league tables' based on numbers of students doing well – or not so well – in public examinations. Teachers within schools may also find themselves in competition with other teachers, either within or across departments, or for contested internal promotions. Except on special occasions, such as Results Day, when individual and collective fates collide, teachers, even though working with and alongside other teachers, may often experience working life as a lonely, even secretive affair.

It is not just performativity's pressure of competition that divides schools and teachers; it is also the amount of work generated by performativity politics, as 'accountability' compels teachers to become the personal producers and guardians of 'performance indicators' and 'evidence of excellence'. One of the greatest surprises in store for me when re-visiting schools after several years away was how empty and quiet the staff rooms were. It seemed that teachers had so much work and were under so much pressure to keep up with detailed assessments of student progress and the bureaucratic demands of the job, that during break-times many of them felt compelled to remain in an empty classroom marking or catching up on paperwork.

Even when groups of resistant, likeminded people do get together, actual resistance may not necessarily follow. In *The Politics of Our Selves*, Amy Allen (2008) rehearses an account by the social historian Joan Jacobs Brumberg of the apparently contradictory behaviour of some of the young women in one of her university classes with whom she had been critically exploring, among other things, media manipulations of perceptions of femininity and female beauty. These young women, Brumberg observed, were very aware of the way they were encouraged and manipulated by profiteers to conform to a certain stereotype of female attractiveness, and could be vociferously and unequivocally critical of it. However, despite their awareness of what was being done to them they continued to conform to those same stereotypes – not least, in worrying about the shape, size and general appearance of their bodies. Why is it, Allen asks (echoing Brumberg's similar question), not only that young women should behave in this way, but that they do not collectively militate to challenge or seek to change the criteria against which they are being judged and to which they feel, in spite of themselves, obliged to conform? Why, when they have taken the first step of achieving some form of 'autonomy in the sense of critical reflection: the capacity to reflect critically upon the state of oneself', can they not subsequently 'on this basis … chart paths for future transformation'? (Allen ibid.: 2). Both Allen and Brumberg are drawn toward the same conclusion: that in the end it is the power of individual survival, produced and/or emphasised within a socio-economic system which pits individual against individual in all manner of ways, that wins out against or inhibits collective action:

> If I challenge the stereotype myself, if I refuse to conform to the favoured image, it will simply leave me spurned or ignored or seen as strange. Many, many others would need to take a stand with me; but there are too many of us living disparate lives; I/we, as permanently minoritised resisters, will always be swimming against the tide.[4]

We might say that Brumberg's students have achieved the first goal of reflexivity: that of refusal. That is to say, they have not been colonised by a dominant discourse to the extent that they 'believe in it' and become its bearers. However, they have not taken the further step of some form of individual or collective resistance – conforming, as they do, to the discourse's physical requirements despite their intellectual rejection of it. While their refusal might be seen as having some therapeutic value, it might equally lead to a loss of self-worth and self-image of another kind: that is to say, 'I know that what I am doing is playing into the wrong hands, and it is not in the best interests of women in general. So what kind of person – what kind of woman am I, that I conform in this way and perpetuate this stereotyping by not actively opposing it?' The irony pinpointed by Brumberg and Allen is that *mass resistance and refusal* (the only kind likely to change things) are undermined by the superior firepower of *mass identification*. Only when the object of the identification is changed can collective action begin to emerge. When push comes to shove, it is desire – the desire to be loved, to be accepted as normal (a perceived prerequisite here for love to ensue) – and fear (fear of not being loved or accepted as normal, or of losing the love and acceptance one may feel one already has) that appears to win the day for affect against the counter-discourses and counter-ideologies that these young women embrace at the level of consciousness and rationality.

In addition to illustrating the point that groups can be either subversive/supportive or conforming/exclusionary, Brumberg's account offers a graphic example of how very difficult group opposition and resistance can be to countenance, to initiate or to sustain, especially in a world in which we may have been brought up to be suspicious and mistrustful of one another's intentions and reliability. How much more difficult, then, when opportunities for physical, communicative interaction are also seriously reduced by the pressures of personal and institutional survival. Even if teachers in a school are able to find a way of working together reflexively and critically ('care of the selves', perhaps) at the intra-institutional level, there will remain very substantial barriers to the kinds of inter-institutional co-operation between groups that may be necessary to mount an effective (national/global) challenge to restrictive ideologies or to achieve an openness about felt experience that is both validated and transferrable across sites.

This is not to say that teachers should give up on reflexivity, refusal and resistance, either intra- or inter-institutionally. Nor is it to deny that they can and already do operate effectively in many ways in groups and as individual members of groups. One of the more interesting findings to emerge from my most recent discussions with teachers has been the emergence of localised, in-school acts of resistance and refusal in secondary schools, such as abandoning formal lesson observations in favour of collaborative planning-teaching-assessment activities, reducing the amount of homework students are expected to complete, and reorganising the school day to create time during normal school hours for teachers to work together on planning and evaluation. While these initiatives cannot ignore mandated requirements or risk failing to meet mandated targets, and while they address strictly educational issues rather than affective ones, from what I have understood they have had a positive effect not only in terms of the quality of teaching and learning but in relation to promoting collegiality, mutual understanding and job satisfaction.

Rather than giving in to the imposed constraints on and objections to collaborative group activity, as neoliberalism would like us to do, I want to argue for collaborations not just of the practical kind but that are consciously and deliberately reflexive: a kind that acknowledges the restrictions, constraints and objections within which it must operate, and also the dangers and constraints that group resistance can visit upon itself, but that enables its members, at the very least, to become more comfortable – and more open – about the impact of affect on their experiences of working life and about voicing and managing the tensions they may feel when they are at odds with central policy directives. Such a call is preceded and informed by a belief that without sharing problems, feelings, 'truths', as well as ideas, we may always remain, as individuals and as collectives, locked into a space from which eventual transformative action and more immediate therapeutic benefits remain forever out of reach.

Unlike the fantasy group of neoliberalism, or the kind of group described by Foucault as an 'organic bond uniting hierarchized individuals' (2013: xiv), the group I am proposing is more akin to what Guattari (1972) has called the 'group subject' (*groupe-sujet*): a group he contrasts with what he calls the 'subject[ed] group' (*groupe assujetti*).[5] The subject[ed] group (also referred to as the 'dependent group') – which might include a teaching staff, a whole school, or even an education system including its dominant rationales, ideologies and policies – takes its direction, its purposes and its limitations from another superordinate group or groups, either declining or not being able seriously to critique or to counter such determinations as it perpetuates and reproduces them.[6] To quote Bogue's summary (1989: 86): 'Such a group constructs a group fantasy around an "institutional object" that is never called into question thereby granting the individual a parasitic immortality' – or, as Guattari himself elaborates: the group contributes to the *naturalisation* of the structure within which it is located, through the collective adoption, articulation and circulation of signifiers that serve to 'crystallize the structure as a whole', hindering its possibilities for effecting change (to itself or to its circumstances), and restricting 'to the utmost its possibilities for dialogue with anything that might tend to bring its "rules of the game" into question'. The 'group phantasy', as Guattari calls it, thus 'produces all the conditions for degenerating into what we have called a *dependent group*' (Guattari 2015: 109, emphasis added).

As we have seen in the testimonies and reports of Secondary Two and Primary One, this 'crystallisation' of a system in and through the adoption and usage of dominant discourse and its signifiers was a common occurrence, and one which certainly eased the adoption of pragmatic responses to unpopular policy. As Guattari notes (1972: 164), the very purpose of officially circulated signifiers is to 'close off and forbid the emergence of every subjective group process' – the *recognition* of which practice becomes an essential first step in the formation of the second kind of group posited by Guattari. (Another necessary step is to acknowledge the way that *affect* works in and upon us, including the way it operates through the signifiers of discourse.) The importance of this recognition and, then, knowledge about how power works and how it establishes and perpetuates itself through discourse and language, is endorsed in Foucault's account of the importance of developing, along with a critical understanding of one's self, a critical understanding of a system or one of its institutions, before being able to mount an effective challenge to its practices or underpinning rationales, or to maintaining our personal conviction that challenge is necessary:

> [I]nsofar as power is a procedure of individualization, the individual is only the effect of power. And it is on the basis of this network of power, functioning in its differences of potential, in its discrepancies, that something like the individual, the group, the community and the institution appear. *In other words, before tackling institutions, we have to deal with the relations of force in these tactical arrangements that permeate institutions.*
>
> *(Foucault 2006: 15, emphasis added)*

In contrast to the subject[ed] group, which works together to fulfil another's demands, the group subject has, in a sense, a common subjectivity and sense of purpose regarding a specific issue or set of issues, rendering it truly reflexive in both senses of the word: that is to say, it is constructively and honestly critical both of itself and of the structures within which it is located. The group subject thus

> opens itself to its finitude, calls into question its goals, and attempts to articulate new significations and form new modes of interaction. *The group-subject continues to produce fantasies, but these function as 'transitional fantasies'* [Guattari 1972: 169] around which the group coalesces, but which the group eventually transcends through its self-directed actions. ... The group-subject reinforces neither vertical hierarchies of command nor conventional horizontal distributions of roles, but establishes unorthodox, transverse relations between various levels of a group or institution. The task of the group-subject is 'to modify the different coefficients of unconscious transversality at different levels of an institution' and to bring about 'a structural redefinition of the role of each person and a reorientation of the whole [1972: 80]'.
>
> *(Bogue 1989: 86)*

Though the group subject *is* a group, it is a group that accepts the possibility of change – in the system(s) within which it exists, within its own collective subjectivity, and within each individual subject of which it is comprised. It is the kind of group that some may find themselves in if, for example, they take part in a campaign of some kind or perhaps join a political party that promotes fundamental societal change. Some might argue that such groups exist in and through social media now, too.[7] However, such groups can only genuinely be described as group subjects when they are characterised by inclusion (in relation to 'membership'), by collective reflexivity, and by self-conscious empowerment. They are certainly not to be confused with the kind of group that describes itself as innovative and empowering but that in reality submits to and collaborates with a fundamentally conservative and conservatising system.[8] In terms of public education, the group subject suggests pedagogies and curricula that are eminently possible but currently some way from realisation in most countries. In an echo of Smyth *et al*'s (1999) conceptualisation of 'collaborative' and 'socially critical' school cultures, they demand flatter, more democratic management structures, co-learning between teachers and students, more genuinely democratic schools and classrooms, and curriculum development that includes informed discussion between what politicians and policy makers like to call 'key stakeholders' – including, *inter alia*, representatives of teachers, students, parents, faith and community groups and, if the group is to free itself from the gravitational pull of orthodoxy, of sympathetic and flexible examination boards and politicians.

Group resistance and the power of affect

If the formation of 'group subjects', if active resistance itself, appears a daunting business, it is worth noting a recent event in English educational history which illustrates what can be achieved, albeit in a relatively small way, through collective action that overrides, as it were, affective diffidence: of how initial refusal can develop into consequent action; of the affective as well as the discursive and educational gains that can come about as a result; of the importance of forging alliances that cross constructed symbolic and professional boundaries; and also of the dangers and illusions of apparent success, and the limitations that may be imposed on acts of resistance by our affective engagements with and attachments to the very policy we have found the strength to oppose.

I am not suggesting that what follows is an example of a full-blown group subject as envisaged by Guattari. It remains incorporated and validated, for example, within a wider system, largely on that system's own terms to the extent that it must behave and speak in certain prescribed ways, through certain prescribed channels and through acceptance of certain ratified structures and practices (for example, an existing public examination system and its modus operandi), in order to be granted a formal hearing. Inevitably, this very incorporation persists as a fundamental weakness in relation to the nature and extent of any subsequent achievement. However, it might qualify as a nascent or fledgling group subject of a certain kind, or perhaps as an 'in-between' one – one that is flatter, more inclusive and more democratic in its composition and operation, and one that has demonstrated a willingness and a capacity to work oppositionally to a particular element of a centrally disseminated policy that benefits, itself, from the advantage of its own hegemonic approval.

The example concerns recent developments in the History curriculum and history teaching in English state schools: specifically, events arising from a recent review of the English National Curriculum in which the then UK Secretary of State for Education, Michael Gove, sought to revise the school History curriculum in a way that would remove or dilute many of the empathetic, critical, global and source-focussed elements that history teachers (and indeed not only history teachers) had argued for, fought for and won during the previous five decades.[9]

Gove's stated intention, for which he made no apology, was effectively to take the History curriculum back to where it had been before these changes had been made, to an essentially facts- and memory-based programme that would chronologically take young learners through British (rather than global) history, highlighting the achievements of and events surrounding selected British (mainly English, mainly male, and almost exclusively white) historical figures. As Richard Evans (2013) was to observe in the *Guardian* newspaper, this attempted imposition 'met with near-universal derision from the entire historical profession' (2). Classroom teachers and school headteachers, academics, examination boards and even some celebrity historians acted together not just to make their very emotive opposition known to the Secretary of State, but to argue so strongly and cogently and with such unity against the proposals as to effectively enforce what some commentators saw as a rare policy U-turn. As Evans continued:

> The new draft [following the collective resistance of historians] is less pre-scriptive than the old, leaving teachers more scope to use their own initiative and imagination. ... Social, economic and cultural history re-enter the syl-labus alongside political history, which monopolised the earlier draft, [and] where Gove originally wanted children just to learn facts and dates, the new curriculum includes a focus on analytical skills and historical understanding.
>
> *(ibid.: 2)*

Evans was to conclude:

> The new curriculum has abandoned Gove's original intention of using history teaching in our schools to impart a patriotic sense of national identity through the uncritical worship of great men and women from the British past. Gone is the triumphalist celebration of victories such as the Spanish Armada or the Battle of Waterloo. ... The new history curriculum represents a victory for the opponents of Gove's tub-thumping English nationalism all along the line.
>
> *(ibid.)*

There is little possibility, it has to be said, that this apparent victory will have removed the fears that many history teachers can still expect to experience as they go about their business of teaching. The revised curriculum might well be more like the kind of curriculum they would wish to be teaching; but the structures within which they must work – the hierarchies, the inspection regimes, the unequal power relations between 'teacher' and 'taught', between learners and examiners, between teachers and politicians – will continue to work oppositionally to the kinds of democratic, anti-hierarchical transversality identified by Guattari, or the wider development of autonomous, iconoclastic group subjects or of their continuation beyond successes relating to single issues. Although one fear – that of doing harm to our students through our enforced complicity with misguided curricula and attendant pedagogies – might have, to a degree, been assuaged, the fears of students under-performing in externally imposed national examinations will remain, regardless of curriculum content itself. The pleasures and pains of constructed success and failure – our students' and our own – will, at least until they can somehow be stopped, continue to be driven by an imposed obsession with easily measurable, potentially misleading 'outputs'. There is another issue, however, concerning this perceived victory: one that is summarised in the following observations by Simon, a university-based history specialist I came into contact with at Secondary Two via my meetings with the beginning teachers there. It is an observation which I think identifies a missing emphasis in Guattari's analysis: that is to say, to return to a central theme, the impact of *affect* on our engagements with public policy, and the importance of drawing on psychoanalytic theory not as a way of pathologising difference or ascribing responsibility and blame, but of helping us to understand and to fight against affect's apparent complicity. I had asked Simon for his take on what I had understood as the history specialists' victory:

> I suppose you could call it a victory of sorts, but I'm very sceptical about it. I think what [the government] did was to put out something so outrageous, that went far further than they expected to have an easy passage, knowing it would be resisted. So they would then come back with a less extreme set of proposals that would be seen [by its opponents] as a victory, and accepted and celebrated as such. The so-called victory is that the extreme version has been abandoned – for now, but it will come back because this is the way [this government] always does things. But actually you could look at it as a small victory for the government anyway. By accepting a temporary compromise, they managed to get through some of the changes they wanted accepted – mostly, those to do with how we understand and work with knowledge. Effectively, what they've got out of it is an accepted rejection of the more interactive, constructivist understandings of historical knowledge that history teachers have been arguing for and developing for years, in favour of a more reified version of knowledge – which is exactly what they publically claim they haven't done!

Regardless of what would appear to be a very serious objection, it is worth pausing to consider what it was that drove so many interested parties to resist the attempted imposition of the revised History curriculum and to unite in that opposition: indeed, to consider also the effect that unity and collaboration themselves can have on how individuals perceive and work with resistant feelings. If fear does continue to stalk the lives of classroom teachers, we need to acknowledge the existence and potential power of another feeling: that of anger. Certainly, in informal discussions with History teachers at Secondary Two it appeared that it was a sense of anger and outrage as much as anything else that prompted (or more accurately, perhaps, that enabled) this collective act of resistance – but that it was only the security involved in undertaking widespread, collective action that was able to turn individual anger into individual and collective resistance, albeit a resistance involving emailing, petitioning and letter-writing rather than the somewhat more daunting (and ultimately unnecessary in this case) activity of professional or contractual disobedience. John himself expressed this rather nicely in an interview given prior to the challenge to Gove's proposed History curriculum, in a discussion concerning the negative effects of competition between schools and teachers and the actual and potential role of teacher trades unions:

> Collegiality is good. You want to be collegial and feel part of … like, you're all basically on the same side. And not just in your own school, but between schools. I mean, how good would it be to do some collaborative fieldwork, say, with other schools, maybe along the lines of some kind of local history project. It would be good for the kids, surely … and for creating togetherness in the neighbourhood − especially when you consider the different social and ethnic make-up of the different schools in the area. But it always feels like the other schools are the enemy. And you even get it here, inside the school. You know, the History department fighting for its share of resources and to show how much better it is than the other departments − 'Look at our results', and all that − and every other department doing the same. It's classic divide and rule. It's really getting to be like 1984. You know, you'd shop your own colleagues in other departments if you thought it was going to get you off the hook or make you look better. So you get suspicious and paranoid and when things come along that you don't like you just hate them and fantasise about leaving but you don't really do anything except just bury it all away and get more and more unhappy. … Until someone or some group does something about that and gets everyone back working together again, singing from the same sheet, there's never ever going to be an effective resistance to what [this government] keeps doing to us.

A little while after the History curriculum rebellion, I sought out John's friend James for his account of what had happened, and of how the whole experience had made him and his History teacher colleagues feel:

> It's actually made me feel a lot more empowered … generally. And happier, too. It makes you realise how much better things would be … how much happier you would be coming to work knowing you were actually going to be able to teach things you believed in … believed were important … and interesting. … The feeling we all got after the change was overturned, it was like almost euphoric. I've been in touch with several colleagues too, since − people I wouldn't normally find the time to talk to − through the [History] association, and there's still a real buzz about. … Like History has just been invented as a subject, and we're all in at the start. It's not true, of course. And there's still a lot − a massive amount actually − that's wrong with [the curriculum] in my opinion. But there's a real feel-good factor about, that like maybe if we carry on we can change some of the other things as well. I

just hope we can manage to sustain that, and don't get bogged down again by all the marking and the bureaucracy. That's a real killer. Well, you know all about that.

Speaking to James, it felt as if he and his colleagues, perhaps even his subject, had reached a fork in the road. In one direction lay a kind of resting-on-the-laurels, brought about, perhaps, by a partial mis-recognition of what had taken place, in which a feel-good factor deflected attention from what should have been a continuing battle to change that other 'massive amount' that was still seen to be wrong with the curriculum. Taking such a route, James and his colleagues might become the victims of one of power's 'clever ruses' (Allen, op. cit.) – making us think we are in some way unmasking and subverting power while our oppositional acts actually serve, in the broader picture, to perpetuate and support it. In the other direction lay a further utilisation of the powerful feelings and the group connectedness prompted by and further developed in the course of the oppositional stance – a utilisation that, even if it might not feel it had the power or had the inclination to push for desired reforms of its own, might continue to consolidate its own developing status as a group subject, setting its own agendas, critically, constructively and reflexively examining its own identities, and re-establishing itself as a more critical, influential voice in wider policy theory and implementation.

I felt that this latter option was going to prove particularly difficult to sustain once the sheer volume of work and the affective exhaustion of dealing with performativity had returned to prominence in the lives of James and his teacher colleagues – particularly within a culture in which reflection on the role of one's feelings and of affect is so marginalised; and it is this point – and at this point – that the concept of the more localised reflexive group returns: one that might comprise relatively small groups of teachers within or across subject areas and/or institutions, who meet regularly and informally to share refusals, resistances, feelings and ideas, in which the focus might be on the quotidian rather than on single high-profile issues. Such groups would embrace dissidence rather than apologising for it and would be constructive and positive rather than simply oppositional, recognising and celebrating the group's therapeutic possibilities in addition to its intellectual ones.

What such groups might achieve, what they might prioritise and how they might go about things is a matter for the group itself; otherwise, it cannot truly be deemed anything approaching a group subject. I would humbly suggest, however, that the discussions and sharings, whatever else they set out to do, would be utilised as a forum for talking about how affect operates both in relation to how we experience life at – and connected to – work, and in relation to the role it can play in guiding us to (often reluctant) conformity away from our most treasured practices. The benefits of *group* reflexivity in relation to the first of these agenda items are, principally, twofold. First, group reflexivity can help us as individuals to move more quickly and effectively to resolutions of obstructive tensions and *impasses* that might arise when we feel locked in battle either with a class (or perhaps a colleague) or with some key aspect of imposed policy. Several heads are certainly better than one in this regard, and the group becomes an increasingly helpful and support network as new knowledge and understandings are produced and shared. Second, the very validation of affect that group reflexivity brings enables us more confidently and regularly, both with others and on our own, to add a reflexive dimension to our reflective armoury and to free ourselves from inappropriate feelings of guilt or weakness or oddness in exploring our feelings – in particular, those that might be described, to begin with, as negative. The benefits of group reflexivity in relation to the second item, that of affect-oriented social and political analysis, including considerations of how policy attempts to work on us affectively to ensure its effective recontextualisation into practice, are similar to those related to the first but bring also the dimension of shared ideas and the preservation of cherished but threatened practices and ideals.

I'm aware that I have made much of affect's own inbuilt resistance to reflexivity (we might say, its success in concealing its identity from our conscious selves), and this certainly presents a conundrum. How do we get beyond those positive and negative feelings that affect generates in us, apparently without our control, in order to persuade ourselves to address affect's nature and workings critically and rationally? Perhaps the example of the History curriculum battle provides an inkling as to how this might be achieved: that, just as in the case of Results Day, it suggests a need to create spaces – maybe formal spaces – away from the immediate affective experience in order to analyse it, and what it might tell us about ourselves and others, retrospectively, on terms that are not entirely its own – along with a determination to avoid falling into the trap of 'power's clever ruses' and a faith that agency is not impossible, even though it may be malleable and subject to constraint.

We began in Chapter 1 with Pinar, and, in a sense, we have come full circle. It seems appropriate, therefore, to end with a repeat of Pinar's heartfelt appeal, quoted at the conclusion of that opening chapter:

> Through remembrance of the past and fantasies of the future, I am suggesting, we educators might write our way out of positions of 'gracious submission'. Not in one fell swoop, not without resistance (both inner and outer). But creating passages out of the present is possible. We know that. That is why we believe in education; we see how powerfully schooling crushes it, and yet, still, there *is* education, despite the schools. There is God despite the church, justice despite the government, and love despite the family. We educators must prepare for a future when the school is returned to us and we can teach, not manipulate for test scores.
>
> *(Pinar 2004: 127)*

Dissidence might never be entirely comfortable, and might not always bring about immediate material changes or happier psychic states, but it is never, by its very nature, pointless. Indeed, we might argue, as Oscar Wilde once did,[10] that it is precisely through the existence and actions of dissidence, of 'disobedience', that, historically, the most significant improvements in democracy and society have come about. If the keeping alive of alternative views and understandings – of education, of society, of humanity – is more important than ever in times of enforced consensus to the neoliberal ideal and to the kinds of human subject that neoliberalism seeks to produce, the need for resistant individuals, still enjoying and celebrating their unique sense of self, to come together in alliances of mutual support is, surely, equally pressing. Indeed, it might be seen as a requirement.[11]

NOTES

Preface

1 The meaning of 'affect' as I am using it is elaborated in some detail in Chapter 2. For now, it may be taken to refer to feelings that may be understood as both psychic and biological in nature, that lie deeply within us, that help guide our responses and decision-making, that produce what we generally refer to and recognise as emotions and that contribute to or perhaps even determine our sense of self. Unlike instinct, which is generally understood as 'hard-wired', affect is produced and developed through processes and experiences of social and symbolic becoming.

Chapter 1

1 This study, undertaken mainly at Goldsmiths University of London between 1998 and 2001, is ESRC award number R000237640.
2 This is a decision whose validity I have subsequently come to doubt. Findings that are drawn from large-scale qualitative studies, which themselves are bound to elicit a great deal of detailed, highly complex data, must always make use of and extrapolate from some data while shelving others; they have to. Furthermore, we may like to reassure ourselves that our choices have been 'grounded' in the data – effectively, that our data has 'spoken to us' – even though we might acknowledge in our more reflective moments that this cannot possibly be true and that there will always be other influences, rooted, sometimes invisibly, in our own biographies, determining our choices as to what to draw on and therefore what to neglect. All we can do, all that we always strive to do, is our best: our best to minimise the impact on our analysis of our pre-existing theories, prejudices and ideologies; our best to be as objective as it is possible for any social analyst to be.
3 Of course, there might well be some other reason, too – a reason that speaks as much about the researchers and about the theory of discourse within which they had operated as about the data itself.
4 By functionally compliant I mean compliant in practice rather than (as in 'actually compliant') in terms of persuasion. This is, at least for many teachers and students, a forced compliance that does not necessarily imply a genuine compliance or acceptance of a policy or an ideology or a system to which one may feel opposed. In similar vein, the

notion of the resistant teacher does not imply actual (functional) resistance (i.e. not doing what one is told, or doing something different from what one is told) but rather a resistant *orientation* in which an oppositional view is retained even though one's actual practice may be one of forced compliance. Individual functional compliance is thus not dissimilar to notions of institutional 'orientation change' described by Ball (1997) after McLaughlin (1991), while 'actual' compliance is more akin to 'colonisation change' (ibid.).

5 For a pithy attack on psychoanalysis, see Gilles Deleuze's brief essay 'Five Propositions on Psychoanalysis' (Deleuze 2004b: 274–280). Deleuze objects, not just to psychoanalysis as practised in the clinic, but to the way it insinuates itself into understandings and analyses of human behaviour in the wider social world, including in schools. Taking as his starting-point the notion of the unconscious as produced rather than as naturally occurring or as a left-over 'appendage' of consciousness, Deleuze argues that the unconscious is constructed not so much through familial relations, as classical psychoanalysis might have it, but rather through our relations with and within the wider social, cultural and economic circumstances within which we grow and develop. Psychoanalysis not only limits and misleads in relation to our understandings of the roots and causes of specific psychotic states; it also, more generally, acts as an inhibitor to genuine conversations and exchanges of ideas, in spite of its self-stated identification as the talking cure. One particular problem for Deleuze concerns the power-relations embedded within psychoanalytic theory and practice, wherein nothing the analysand says is to be taken at face value but is always subjected to interpretation by the all-knowing analyst. This particular objection to psychoanalysis is accompanied by Deleuze's parallel concerns regarding Marxism: that is to say, its tendency to depend, and to expect others to depend, on 'sacred texts' to guide thinking and support interpretations and understandings, rather than referencing directly 'the situation as it is' (ibid.: 276). The view I am taking is that it is perfectly acceptable to agree with some of Deleuze's criticisms of psychoanalysis as it is often conceived and practised without rejecting the notion that elements of psychoanalytic theory, when applied to understandings of everyday experiences and situations, can be beneficial. When Deleuze argues that instead of psychoanalysis, with its emphasis on expert, carefully guarded interpretation and its obsession with the impact of the individual's family life, 'one should … start with the real individual statements, give people the conditions, for the production of their individual statements, in order to discover the real collective arrangements that produce them' (ibid.: 275), he is very close to the kinds of psychoanalytically informed reflexivity for which I am arguing.

6 Similarly, it would be misleading to think that our past can, in anything like its entirety, be accessed for revisitation and analysis. Gibbs (2001: np), in a discussion of memory, notes that 'emotional memory … makes up the bulk of memory: it is memory encoded in our very being rather than articulated in language' – a characteristic which suggests that it is not retrievable for discussion and presentation. Gibbs continues:

> Memory here is not something deriving from a particular point in the past, but something that has been repeatedly confirmed – it is the past which has snowballed … into an attitude, an affective complex that may be contained, organised and given manageable form by a series of ideas which will also serve to explain and justify it.

Gibbs seems to suggest that affect, to which we will return in the next chapter, *constrains* us and that our attitudes, perhaps our beliefs and at some level our ideologies, although they might be consciously rationalised in words, may, at heart, have nothing to do with rationality at all. Such a view immediately raises the question: can an individual's affective world be accessed, modified, perhaps, by the individual? Or are we doomed, from a certain point in our development, to 'be who we are, and think what we think'? I would suggest that even asking such a question of ourselves marks an important (reflexive) move away from acceptance (of who we think we are, of the essential rightness of what we do, and of how we respond to people and events) toward the possibility of a happier, more productive relationship with ourselves and with others.

7 In this book I have tended to use 'fear' and 'anxiety' to denote different manifestations of what is essentially the same affective response. Fear is identified as something that is experienced in sharp, heightened ways, in relatively short bursts, perhaps producing physical symptoms such as shaking, sweating or a feeling of despair, often in response to the same 'object' as anxiety. (While we may say 'I have a fear of spiders', that fear is, generally and except in cases of extreme phobia, only experienced as fear when there is an immediate or potential threat of our encountering a spider.) Anxiety, however, is understood here as a more ongoing, underlying, less dramatic response that can be more debilitating and produce its own (more durable) symptoms, such as depression or ongoing psychosomatic stomach problems and headaches. In other words, I approach both anxiety and fear as responses to 'an object' and the possible negative consequences of its being encountered in the future. It is clear that some of the participants in my studies may have had generally more 'anxious profiles' than others and be more likely to worry about things and perhaps take a more pessimistic view of life, but this is not dwelt on in any depth in this book. Of greater concern is the way in which affect is made use of in educational policy to control and manipulate teachers and their students, calling upon them not just to implement often unpopular policies in practice but to become the active bearers of those policies.

8 Like so many other bottom-up developments, the notion of 'becoming' is all too open to discursive hijacking in the official recontextualising field (Bernstein 2000) of public policy. The point about becoming is that we decide as individuals – and/or as consensual groups – on the direction, nature and pace of our development, rejecting on our own terms the comfort of stagnation. Thinking that we can always do, be, think better, however, is a far cry from thinking – or being made to think, or having others be made to think – that we are simply not, and never can be, 'good enough'. Recent policy, certainly in England, has tended to adopt precisely this latter stance, replacing notions of becoming by strapping teachers (and students) to what Keck (2012: 160) calls the 'wheel of betterment' with its accompanying 'supposition of eternal deficiency'. The ubiquitous existence and impact of guilt experienced and expressed by so many teachers and not a few young learners in my studies is in no small part a consequence of this discursive hijacking. Just as 'consumption' – and its encouragement and naturalisation – might be seen to enter 'into the psychic lives of people … tapping into the level of unconscious desires' (Bocock 1993: 116–117), so 'debt' ('owing something to society', 'always falling short', 'never being quite good enough', 'requiring improvement') seemed never far from many teachers' thoughts, and indeed infested the centralised school inspections through which their adequacy and 'performance' were being judged. While becoming has no end goal (other than that of continuing to become) and eschews perfection, betterment, as configured in public education policy, insists on perfection – at the same time as rendering its achievement impossible through continuous redefinition.

9 Notions of 'outside' and 'inside' are used for convenience here. In reflexivity, as in accounts of affect and its workings, there are no clear boundaries between the 'inner' and the 'outer' worlds.

10 I have been challenged in the past for using 'we' and 'us' when referring to teachers – on the basis that I am no longer a teacher (at least, in the formal, paid sense) and indeed have not been a *school* teacher for many years. It still feels very natural, however, for me to do this, leading me to conclude that 'teacher' remains one of my strongest and most cherished identities. I hope readers will understand my continued use of the first person plural in this book and perhaps forgive me if they feel they need to.

11 For a preview of this debate, which will be returned to in Chapter 8, see Amy Allen's fascinating summary (Allen 2008) of the discussions between Judith Butler, Seyla Benhabib and Nancy Fraser regarding the possibility of ever developing genuine

self-understanding, given that 'who we are', our sense of self, is constructed by and within power relations that we can never, so to speak, step outside of – so that what we may take to be self-understanding may be merely a (re)conceptualisation of self according to dominant discourses which we may be unaware we have internalised.

Chapter 2

1 'Mental' manifestations of emotionality such as feelings of happiness, self-justification, anger, hatred, love and fear may be accompanied by – or 'substituted by' (when emotions are repressed) – physical manifestations such as shaking, sweating, stomach aches, nausea, and raised energy levels. During each of the studies on which this book is based, both kinds of manifestation were abundantly evident in both teachers and students, sometimes chronic in their experience, more often synchronic with and 'attached to' specific events, such as being observed by an Ofsted inspector or feeling a strong sense of achievement in a specific teaching or learning experience.

2 If this sounds as though affect is being presented as a negative force – an unfortunate fact of our individual and collective live, perhaps – it is not meant to. While it is true that affect can work against our better interests, it is the interactions and interrelationships between affect and intelligence that mark us out as humans. Affect may render us susceptible to manipulation. It might also induce in us momentary or enduring negative feelings in relation to our lives and to those about us. But it also enables us to experience the social and natural worlds in unique and special ways, to be moved by music, art and nature; to sympathise – and empathise – with our fellow human beings; to experience joy and sorrow, love and sensitivity and commitment beyond the simple diktats of our instinctual drives.

3 It also (Shouse 2005) had chronological/develop-mental primacy.

4 As with teachers' names, I am using a pseudonym here.

5 It is not just teachers, of course, who find themselves subjected to this linguistic/ideological/affective bombardment. In her detailed account of student experience and understanding of metalearning in a UK primary school classroom, Paraskevi writes of young children regularly using such expressions as 'extend your learning', 'achieve your targets', 'consequences', 'the method', 'reflect on', 'focussed', 'uplevelling', 'challenge(d)' and (most worryingly of all, perhaps) 'self-regulate'. Significantly in Paraskevi's study, the excitement of 'getting to the next level' and 'achieving your target', and the ability to define 'good learning', seemed to be more important to many students than learning itself – so that motivation to achieve a target or a level, and the great pleasure to be achieved therefrom, became more important than learning itself or than any consideration of how learning might be useful in the future. In essence, it did not seem to matter if it was ever going to be of use; for it was not the usefulness of learning that was at stake for these children, it was being praised at school and/or at home for being able to demonstrate that it had taken place – even if, post-praise, it was immediately forgotten. The failure to measure up to expectations, to achieve the happiness it would bring, could result in misery and stress – so that when one student got 'stuck on a challenge' (a by no means unique occurrence), she observed: 'I can't concentrate enough, all the sounds around me are getting louder and louder and I can't concentrate' (Paraskevi 2016: 157).

6 A similar appeal to a mythic Golden Past can be traced in the appeal to the United States electorate by Donald Trump in the 2016 presidential election. Trump's repeated references to 'Making America Great Again' quickly became a mantra among large numbers of his supporters; however, there was never any discussion about what 'great' actually meant or what aspects of America's history might be selected as examples of its hitherto greatness. These were, to use Chomsky's expression (Chomsky 1999), among Trump's propaganda's 'black holes'. To have attempted to offer such elaborations would, of course, have betrayed the reality – that greatness is a bestowed quality, not an intrinsic one – thereby completely undermining the fantasy.

7 Just as words become saturated with positivity in policy rhetoric and media coverage, so others become saturated with negativity. An example of a word/idea/concept that has become negatively saturated in recent times in England is 'socialism'. Despite the fact that socialism has much in common with the ideals of Christianity and most other world religions, the word itself has been rendered 'dirty', to such an extent that we may find ourselves (self-)consciously avoiding using it. Polarities can, of course change, and what was once charged with positivity may one day find itself negatively charged – and vice versa. When Milton was writing *Paradise Lost*, for example, ambition was considered a sin – an affront to God's authority and power. Nowadays, in the entrepreneurial times we inhabit, it is more likely to be considered a virtue. Sometimes, words and the ideas and ideologies they carry with them may be forcibly expatriated, which may render them all the more – or some might argue all the less – difficult to re-saturate. Žižek identifies one such word as 'capitalism', the system it signifies being successfully 'naturalised' by the simple expedient of removing its term of reference from the conversation of polite society: 'No one, with the exception of a few allegedly archaic Marxists, refers to capitalism any longer. The term was simply struck from the vocabulary of politicians, trade unionists, writers and journalists – even of social scientists!' (Žižek no date). Of course, the fact that a term is 'struck from the vocabulary' of many key players in public policy does not mean that we should all follow suit or be too afraid to continue to keep it alive. In a passage that has clear links with a subject to be raised later on, concerning the capacity of language both to enthral and to liberate, Mark Fisher, taking the example of 'neoliberalism', urges us to recognise the critical empowerment that can be achieved precisely by refusing to allow a term to naturalise itself into the surroundings in this way. The 'increased use of the term neoliberalism since 2000', for example, is described by Fisher as 'a symptom of the weakening of the power of neoliberalism. The more it is named, the less its doctrines can pose as post-political' (Fisher and Gilbert 2016: 125).

8 See also McNally (2011: 2) on what he calls the 'invisibility' of 'the capitalist grotesque' – of

> the ways in which monstrosity becomes normalised and naturalised via its colonisation of the essential fabric of every-day life beginning with the very texture of corporeal experience in the modern world, of 'capitalist monstrosity's' 'elusive everydayness, its apparently seamless integration into the banal and mundane rhythms of quotidian existence'
>
> *(McNally 2011: 2)*

McNally's appeal to the physical, in references to (for example) the 'texture of corporeal existence', gives notice that discourse is not some kind of disembodied symbolic phenomenon that appeals only to the intellect, but that, through its hold on affect, it manipulates us physically as well as psychically. In what might be seen as a criticism of discursive analysis of the kind I am suggesting (depending, of course, on our understanding of what discourse is), McNally has urged us, very lucidly and persuasively, to approach the idea of discursive power with extreme caution. In an extended critique of post-modern, post-structuralist political and social analysis, he challenges the validity of modes of psychoanalysis, particularly as developed and promoted by Jacques Lacan and his followers, for an over-emphasis on language at the cost of remembering and understanding how social control and stratification rely principally upon – and indeed precipitate – differentiated control of the human body. McNally argues in *Bodies of Meaning* (McNally 2001) that, in what he calls the 'new idealism' of much psychoanalytically informed commentary and analysis, even feelings – themselves sites of struggle, resistance and control – are abstracted from the physical world to be consigned *to* that 'other world' of language and discourse – the Lacanian 'Big Other'. The problem for McNally is that this perceived (over-)emphasis on language and discourse in post-modern, post-structuralist thinking acts as a kind of revisionist, counter-revolutionary smokescreen in which the body itself – so important in Marx's accounts of the repressive and partial workings of Capitalism – almost ceases to exist as anything worthy of our attention, effectively deflecting our analysis and any corresponding counter-hegemonic strategy to a virtual battleground of ideas. For McNally (2001: 2): 'The extra-discursive body, the body that exceeds language and discourse, is the "other" of the new idealism, the entity it seeks to efface in order to bestow absolute sovereignty on language'. In this recontextualisation of critical analysis to the 'empire of the sign', '[e]ven desire is commonly abstracted from the body, reduced to a metaphysical drive to overcome ontological "lack", our incompleteness as beings' (ibid.). Whatever we may make of McNally's critique, including his analysis of Lacanian theory, the account of discursive power suggested in my own argument is one which, I hope, avoids falling into the trap he suggests. It certainly does not deny the ways in which bodies are differentially controlled within capitalist societies, but rather views discourse as an essential element and tactic in ensuring (as far as is able) subjective acceptance of or compliance with such control.

9 For a lucid account of the nature of – and relationship between – discourse and ideology in the field of public education, see Althusser (2014) – and, for a gentle objection to aspects of Althusser's theory, Eagleton 1991: 150–155.

Chapter 3

1 Foucault's notion of 'governmentality' relates to the strategies undertaken by central government in an attempt to (re)produce a citizenry/subjectivities best suited to – and most likely therefore to be accepting of and to bear out in practice – its own ideologies and pre-determined policies and ideologies. In terms of process, and of an obvious linkage between governmentality and the kinds of experience I will be considering in relation to resistant teachers, it is defined as the 'encounter between the technologies of domination of others and those of the self' (Foucault 2000a: 225). As suggested earlier, discourse plays a key role in this practice. Foucault's own definition, retrospectively explained, is as follows:

> 'Governmentality' does not only refer to political structures or to the management of states; rather, it designated the way in which the conduct of individuals or of groups might be directed: the government of children, of souls, of communities, of families, of the sick. It did not only cover the legitimately constituted forms of political or economic subjection, but also modes of action, more or less considered and calculated, which were destined to act upon the possibilities of action of other people. To govern in this sense, is to structure the possible field of action of others.
>
> *(Foucault 1983: 221)*

2 For an elaborated introduction of the idea of biopolitics, see Foucault 2010. A shorter account is usefully provided by Slavoj Žižek, who writes:

> Today's predominant mode of politics is *post-political bio-politics* – an awesome example of theoretical jargon which, however, can easily be unpacked: 'post-political' is a politics which claims to leave behind old ideological struggles and, instead, focus on expert management and administration, while 'bio-politics' designates the regulation of the security and welfare of human lives as its primary goal. It is clear how these two dimensions overlap: once one renounces big ideological causes, what remains is only the efficient administration of life … *almost* only that. That is to say, with the depoliticised, socially objective, expert administration and coordination of interests at the zero level of politics, the only way to introduce passion into this field, to actively mobilise people, is through fear, a

basic constituent of today's subjectivity. For this reason, bio-politics is ultimately a politics of fear, it focuses on defence from potential victimisation or harassment.
(Žižek 2009: 34)

Elsewhere, writing of the continuing, infinite and eternal nature of (imagined and politically constructed) *threat*, Massumi talks of fantasies of 'non-existent entities' that 'come from the future to fill our present with menace', such that:

> Even if a clear and present danger materializes in the present, it is still not over. There is always the nagging potential of the next after being even worse, and of a still worse next again after that. The uncertainty of the potential next is never consumed in any given event. There is always a remainder of uncertainty, an unconsummated surplus of danger. … The future of threat is forever.
>
> *(Massumi 2010: 52)*

3 Letwin's words call to mind those of John Holt, many years ago: 'Fear is the inseparable companion of coercion, and its inescapable consequence' (Holt 1964: 175). Holt was writing about the fear experienced by young students, and the coercion imposed on them by schooling; however, the dependency on spreading fear for the successful exercise of high levels of social control applies equally in relation to teachers and central government, and is particularly relevant in relation to the voiced experiences of many teachers in my own studies. Pertinently, Letwin's comments drew from Mark Serwotka, General Secretary of the Public and Commercial Services Union (PCSU), the response: 'Public sector workers are already working in fear – fear of cuts to their job, pension, living standards and of privatisation' (ibid.).

4 'Additional Inspectors' were inspectors recruited by private companies contracted to supply inspection services to Ofsted in order to help cope with the rising number of inspectors required (partly) by an increased level of inspection.

5 It is important to note that, while this book is mainly about teachers and the ways in which they work and experience life in school, it also, inevitably, touches on the lives of young students, insofar as they are the recipients, the beneficiaries and perhaps, at times, the victims of the views and practices of the adults charged with their education. Unlike the young people described half a century ago by John Holt (1964: 170), whose minds 'froze' through an inability to express or 'even acknowledge the fear, shame, rage, and hatred that school and their teachers had aroused in them', it was rare for the young learners I came into contact with to express any fear of their teachers *per se*. Many of them did, however, express fears regarding the future consequences of academic failure, or of what might happen if their parents should receive negative reports of their behaviour. In the students I have had contact with, both the fear and the coercion of teachers appeared to have been replaced by fear and coercion in relation to the wider system – that is, to curriculum and assessment. Not unexpectedly, given the imminence and constant reminders of very high-stakes public examinations, students in Secondary Two seemed much more concerned about academic success itself than students in Primary One, and rather less concerned about what their teachers – or indeed what their peers outside of their established friendship groups – thought of them. A striking feature at Primary One was how much more these younger students feared the absence or loss of *love*, and how painful this could be. The impact on students' self-esteem and capacity to perform in the classroom of psychological bullying that took place in the playground, the fallings in and fallings out between children, and the tears and fights that inevitably followed, was painfully obvious. But equally evident in some children was the desire for love and respect from the teacher – so strong in some as to render the achievement and maintenance of such love, and the fear of its absence, a more pressing matter than the potential benefits of academic success in its own right or fear of the negative material consequences of academic failure. (For an example of this, see Moore 2013.)

6 John has been completing a part-time Masters degree in Education, in which Foucault's work currently features prominently. Knowing from previous conversations about my own interest in Foucault, we have had conversations previously about the panopticon metaphor and self-policing.

7 Not all teachers were afraid to approach members of their senior leadership team, and not all senior leaders were unapproachable and unsympathetic – though some teachers may not have been convinced of this. One of the senior leaders at Secondary Two who did not take part in the study itself (in the sense of not being interviewed) told me, when she heard more about the topic of my research, how she had 'lost count' of the number of teachers who had come to her office in floods of tears during the two-and-a-bit years she had been in post. Whether these tears were brought about by longstanding issues (perhaps to do with workload, which was a common source of upset at Secondary Two) or by one-off confrontations, I was not able to find out.

8 Of course, not all teachers 'love' their students (or indeed their work) in the same way, nor is it always love that inspires a teacher to take up the profession. I have frequently encountered teachers who survive very happily on a different set of rewards – whose satisfaction is derived more simply and straightforwardly from a job well done and, perhaps, to return to the notion of symbolic identification, a feeling of existential justification.

9 This is an allusion to a character from George Orwell's *Animal Farm*. Benjamin the donkey is characterised by his cynical stoicism and his somewhat pessimistic outlook on life, doubting whether things will ever be any different than they currently are.

Chapter 4

1 Mark manages and trains the school's fledgling (boys only) football team, organising fixtures with other schools in the neighbourhood, and puts on mixed football training sessions after school on Wednesdays and Fridays. I have found him somewhat aloof and detached. He tends to 'perform' in the staff room rather than engaging with colleagues, dropping in at break times to pick up an instant coffee, rarely staying longer than it takes to make it. He has his own mug with 'Top Mark' printed on the side and resents anyone moving it from its assigned position on the draining board, let alone using it or washing it up. His attitude with the students seems similar. Despite spending hours with the football team, he displays no obvious affection for them or for any of the other children I see him with, and indeed he tells me that he has no particular affection for his students generally, though he has 'taken a bit of a shine' to two boys who remind him of himself when he was a child. He doesn't much care about what the children think of him, as long as they do as they are told and show him 'due respect'. It all seems to be business with Mark, and I can't help wondering what it is about him that makes him so distant and so unflappable – whether it's a conscious decision, in the manner of a strategy, or whether this is just who Mark is. One thing I have noticed about him is that he appears to take pleasure in giving instructions. There is a confidence in the way he does so that clearly brooks no argument. He calls me 'the prof' or occasionally 'the theory man'. I get the impression he thinks I have never experienced life as a schoolteacher. When I tell him I taught for 18 years in inner-city schools, he softens toward me a bit – but still calls me 'the prof' and 'the theory man'.

2 I wonder, too, though this must be for another time, if it might be fruitful, picking up on Deleuze and Guattari's aim of elaborating 'the relationship between psychic and economic life in capitalist societies' (Bogue 1989: 104), to trace and talk about the experience and effects of an 'immanent debt which permeates [all] economic (and hence social) relations, creating in private individuals an infinite, internalized debt' (ibid.).

3 This idea has come from Bion and Britton, the latter of whom describes psychological processes that occur in early infancy but that may well find their echoes and repetitions in later life:

If the [ensuing and inevitable] frustration [of no longer having what one desires] cannot be tolerated, the negative realization (that is, the absence of something) is perceived as the presence of something bad – 'a bad thing' – with the notion that it can be got rid of; hence the phantasy that a state of deprivation can be eliminated by abolishing things.

(Britton 1992: 40)

Chapter 5

1 I have taken Archie's pseudonym from the 'star' of a highly popular radio programme of the 1950s – 'Educating Archie' – that I used to listen to with my parents during Sunday lunchtimes. Given the full name of Archie Andrews, Archie was, in fact, a ventriloquist's dummy (itself a curiosity for a radio programme!), physically manipulated and voiced by Peter Brough, who also acted as a kind of parent or guardian in the storylines, being at once master, owner, creator and carer. This being a comedy, however, it was Archie who narratively manipulated Brough in each episode, repeatedly outwitting him with an almost instinctive ease that included an endless stream of put-downs and one-liners. Despite a long-suffering Brough's tireless attempts to get Archie to tow the adult line, Archie proved himself again and again to be far too sharp for either Brough or any of the other adults in the stories, managing to do exactly what he wanted and very successfully avoiding their combined attempts to 'educate' him. This Archie had in common with the Archie of Primary One something we might call 'naughtiness', each in their own way actively disrupting adult systems created and sustained *by* adults – including the institution of education. However, they are also completely unlike each other. Archie Andrews engaged with the adults about him, taking them on in – and simultaneously subverting – their own terms. His was a naughtiness that his mainly adult audience could laugh about, and even admire – perhaps secretly wishing that they could be more like Archie, or perhaps that they could have been more like him when they were at school. In short, they could identify with Archie, laughing with him for his wit, as well as laughing *at* Brough for his relative stupidity. Nobody minded if the adults ended up teaching Archie nothing, for it was made plain that they had nothing of any value to teach him anyway; he already had all the intelligence and nous he needed to succeed in life. Unlike this fictitious Archie, the Archie of Primary One, has to make do with living in the real world: one in which naughtiness is seldom smiled upon, and in which the possible causes of naughtiness are only half-heartedly addressed to the extent that systems allow them to be. While we were invited to accept and applaud the deliberately subversive naughtiness of Archie Andrews and other fictional scamps (such as Dennis the Menace), the naughtiness of Primary One's Archie, which also often presented itself as subversive, was clearly born of a troubled mind rather than of a particularly rebellious one.

2 For fuller accounts of current identifications of and policies on students with special needs in English schools (an area in which criteria and policies remain somewhat shifting), see Association of School and College Leaders (ACSL) 2015 and Department for Education/Department of Health (DfE/DoH) 2015.

3 One way of making sense of Archie's behaviour and the ensuing response to it is as an echo of the Lacanian notion (Lacan 1977, 1979) of 'eruptions of the Real' into the Symbolic Order (including its localised crystallisation in the school and classroom), and of the subsequent and ongoing 'suturing over' of the tear or wound in the Symbolic Order that such an eruption causes. For the most part, Archie's apparently odd behaviour can be explained away fairly easily by his teachers within the language and understandings of the (wider and local) Symbolic Order: that is to say, in terms of (mis)behaviour, choice and inclusion. His behaviour might be odd, but it is only so odd as to be constructed as a relatively minor deviation from – or subversion of – standard(ised) behaviours and practices. When Archie accuses his teachers of being 'stinky', its unexpectedness, its perceived uniqueness, have the effect of producing something akin to

horror. ('This sort of thing just doesn't happen! It can't happen!') This makes such accommodations more difficult, resulting in more extreme action being taken to effect the necessary suturing – that is, to restore normality: in this case, that of the removal of the perpetrator, and, by implication, of the act, from the normality and routine of the classroom until a way is found of re-siting the deviant act within the Symbolic Order so that it no longer draws attention to itself as a stark reminder that the symbolic order has been breached. That way necessitates Archie having to do something else that he has never done before: produce a written apology, the writing of which itself is imbued with additional symbolic significance.

4 Susan's observation has echoes of that of another of her colleagues at Primary One, Ruth, who told me in interview:

> You have to cut corners. Not necessarily the academic ones. The academic results are too important for the school as a whole. And it's not *just* a time problem; it's something about creative energy that gets sapped out of people. There isn't the space for *imagination* – to bring a more imaginative approach to these day-to-day behaviour issues.

5 The idea that children – often very young children – choose their behaviour, including individual actions, represents a transfer of an aspect of neoliberal policy and ideology from the adult to the juvenile world. As with the adult world, it assumes and confers an overriding rationality on the individual subject, that may take little or no account of personal material or psychic circumstances. Rules is rules, and must be applied equally and fairly within another (subverted) neoliberal discourse of equity. There is no excuse for deviant behaviour, for 'choosing' to flout the rules, any more than there is for not going out and finding paid employment.

6 UK academies are publically funded, (semi-)independent schools. They don't have to follow the National Curriculum and can set their own term times – as well as revised conditions of service and pay levels for staff. Funding comes direct from central government rather than from local councils, with greater power given to the Secretary of State for Education. They are run by 'academy trusts', which employ the staff. A school converting to an academy receives a cash boost, which is obviously an attraction in the eyes of many headteachers and school governors. Heads sometimes receive salaries well above their equivalents in non-academies (Local Authority schools) too, and may exercise more control than other headteachers over such things as the length and structure of the school day. Initially introduced with a view of helping raise the quality of education in deprived areas, academisation has increased rapidly over the last decade, with moves afoot at the time of writing to force all schools to eventually become academies regardless of their student intake, Ofsted grades or geographical location.

7 'Other things' included, inter alia, marking, break duties, line management, lesson preparation, PTA involvement and following up on behaviour issues including meetings with individual parents.

8 The 'other kind of Head', the 'modern Head' described by Martin is 'the Executive Managerial Head, who hardly ever feels the need to leave her office and deliberately distances herself from the rest of the staff and the students'.

Chapter 6

1 This particular emphasis on the individual is very different from, and in constant tension with, the emphasis on the individual that has been discussed in previous chapters with reference to reflexivity and to the importance of recognising, understanding and embracing difference.

2 We might say that neoliberalism is an ideology that seeks to assuage and disguise an inevitable tension between a dominant national and global economic system and

ideology of free-market capitalism and a dominant national and global political system and ideology of democracy. The tension arises from the fact that profit and loss, plenty and lack, unequal and hierarchical pay structures, and the exploitation of labour are fundamental requirements of a free-market capitalist system. What might happen – what threat might ensue to capitalism and/or to democracy – if significant numbers of those who do not benefit sufficiently from the system were to rise up against it – or, at least, against its greater excesses? Neoliberalism seeks to avoid such a refusal in a number of ways, the most pertinent one here being the spread and manipulation of hegemony and discourse, in which people buy into beliefs in such things as personal responsibility, freedom and choice. ('It's up to us as individuals to take advantage of the many opportunities that the economic system places before us, and it's our fault if we don't'.) Other neoliberal strategies include re-configuring electors as, fundamentally, consumer-citizens, so that this becomes a core identity in which the citizen devotes time and energy to buying (and, these days, very often to selling) within a local, national or global marketplace, rather than debating, critiquing and challenging the way in which the market operates.

3 See, again, Althusser (2014) and the role of the school/public education as a central 'Ideological State Apparatus' (ISA).

4 Although Elliott talks of student 'responsibility', this is not the same kind of responsibility as that of the performativity discourse. It is to be understood not simplistically in terms of decontextualised 'choices', but instead involves the development of much more nuanced understandings of behaviour on the part of both teachers and students – alongside a more collaborative approach to academic/creative/expressive learning (with Elliott, the emphasis is always on the learning rather than on the 'product'), and to social relationships and interaction. It challenges the only-I-matter version of competition and individualisation, even as it encourages individuals to take more responsibility for their actions, including, very importantly, 'responsibility *for each others' well-being*'. Performativity, by contrast, informed by the wider discourse and politics of neoliberalism, emphasises an individualism in which freedom to choose is lauded only as long as the choice is accepted and validated within neoliberalism itself and within the systems it creates and sustains. This kind of individualism is tied to forms of responsibility related to obeisance to arbitrary social norms and regulations, rather than to celebrating and encouraging difference and social critique. The neoliberal subject is thus (ironically, perhaps) also a compliant, obedient, conforming subject.

5 For an introduction to Nietzsche's writing about public education, readers are directed to *Anti-Education* (Reitter and Wellmon 2015) – a translated collection of five original lectures entitled, collectively, 'On the Future of Our Educational Institutions'. The first of these lectures (Nietzsche 1872) is also accessible online. Nietzsche's thoughts on public education can – and have been – drawn on for support by both right-wing and left-wing thinkers. The following snippet from the 'First Lecture' might help readers make up their minds as to whether or not they wish to read the lectures themselves. In this lecture, Nietzsche talks of how, 'all too often' the state tried to exploit young people for its own purposes – 'luring civil servants it can make use of as early as possible and then securing their unconditional obedience with exaggeratedly strenuous exams' (Nietzsche 1872, in Reitter and Wellmon 2016: 13).

6 So-called 'residuals', given their reliance on statistics, measurement and comparison as well as on the ways (in spite of their focus on student exam performance) they are apparently being used in some schools by way of judging teacher competence, may be seen as another of performativity's delinquent offspring. With various historical roots in quantitative research, in science and mathematics and in the world of business, residuals are used in the analysis of GCSE examination results, though adopted in some institutions simply to denote the difference between a student's predicted exam grades and their actual exam grades. For an analysis of residuals and their uses, see Patrick MacNeil's summary on the 'schoolzone' website (MacNeil nd: np).

7 As the case of Rosetta suggests, there is considerable blurring between the two categories of imaginary and symbolic identification. Imaginary identification concerns how
we wish others to see and feel about us, but also relates to how we feel about ourselves,
with the proviso that to an extent the latter is dependent on the former, and vice versa.
Though Rosetta is unconcerned about whether or not she is loved by others (by any
other), having a job can make her feel better about herself and earn her a degree, if not
of popularity, then at least of respect.

Chapter 7

1 By 'contingency', I refer to the different social groupings with which any subject might
identify, and how our willingness and capacity to 'speak the truth' (about our opinions
and feelings) might change accordingly. Thus, within an institution like a school we
might be drawn, for the various reasons outlined in this chapter, toward practical acceptance of dominant views and philosophies that we might not wholeheartedly support,
perhaps simply remaining silent as regards such difference. Outside the institution,
however, we might feel more comfortable about expressing our views and philosophies,
perhaps keeping quieter about or seeking some justification for our apparent 'selling
out' within the institutional setting. John, for example, like his friend James, felt himself
having to make compromises within Secondary Two in order not to be considered a
'misfit' or become an 'outcast'; however, he was able to continue to express his more
genuinely held views and philosophy outside the school setting among friends more
sympathetic to his 'truths' (and also, within the school setting, somewhat secretively
with James).
2 John is referring to observations I made about contingency and idiosyncrasy in teaching
in an earlier book, *The Good Teacher* (2004), which he had read during the course of his
Masters degree course.
3 See Bernstein 2000: 44.
4 Actually, there were two days: one when only senior and middle leaders came in to carry
out their analysis and a second, the day after, when most staff came in along with several
students. My account refers to the second day.
5 'Value added' relates to a calculation whereby a school's examination results are con-
textualised according to the school's intake – recognising the problems of comparing
the results of a school with, for example, large numbers of developing bilingual students
or students from financially poor home backgrounds with schools with large numbers
of what might be termed socially and economically privileged students. Once the value-added calculation has been made, it can raise a school's position in national and local
'league tables', offering a truer reflection of the school's and its students' performance
through baseline referencing. Whether prospective parents pay much attention to such
re-calculations of results is, of course, another matter.
6 In fact, I did find three teachers out of those I interviewed formally (and the many more
I talked to informally) who felt that SATs and league tables had helped to raise academic
standards and also, in the case of two of these respondents, had impacted positively on
their own practice – as one respondent put it, making 'me feel and act more like a professional' and 'generally push me into taking a more rigorous and inclusive approach'.
I have no evidence that these proportions of negative-positive views and experiences
would be repeated nationally, and have not as yet analysed in sufficient detail the possible
reasons for these differing views and experiences.
7 Figures have been modified in order to preserve anonymity, but the scale of the improvement has been maintained.
8 As Raymond Williams argued many years ago, of a system and an ideology that have
changed all too little in the intervening years, in which people are sold the idea of a
'ladder of opportunity': '[T]he ladder is a perfect symbol of the bourgeois idea of society,
because, while undoubtedly it offers the opportunity to climb, it is a device which

can only be used individually: you go up the ladder alone' (Williams 1958: 331). That the ladder cannot accommodate everyone (though it has the potential to accommodate anyone) is replaced by a concealing, 'sweetening' lie that serves to promote competition between individual subjects, to fragment society, to maintain a hierarchical, socio-economic status quo, and to represent an 'alternative to solidarity' (ibid.) as it weakens what we might hope to be a comprehensive principle of 'common betterment'.

9 The term 'love' as I am using it here refers, as elsewhere in the text, to a responsive feeling residing in and produced by the individual experiencing it. The feeling 'being loved' is understood as internally produced (despite any corresponding, independently produced feelings in the other) but mis-recognised as being received. The experience and belief in the 'receipt of love' may thus, as Harris (1989) implies in his study of the emotional development of young children, be illusory – though nevertheless very powerful.

10 For students taking examinations, there are also necessary investments of desire to set alongside and to support and enable the successful outcome of investments of interest. A feature of the Results Day visit was that students seemed ecstatic about having achieved good grades *per se* rather than in relation to any future prospects their results might offer. These investments of interest were also evident but tended to be expressed and accounted for, if at all, in a more rational, less exuberant register. The students appeared not to question the 'naturalised' exam system. Nor did the teachers – at least at this extended moment in time.

Chapter 8

1 By propaganda I refer to the deliberate, widespread dissemination by powerful and influential groups – often, national governments – of a specific view of reality that is 'sold' to other, larger but less empowered groups not as opinion but as fact, with a view to encouraging sufficient numbers in those large groups to subscribe to a particular world-view and to actively support the powerful groups and their beliefs and ideologies. (For an interesting account of propaganda as deployed in so-called democracies, and of propaganda's 'engineering of consent', see Chomsky's critique [1999: 53–55] of Edward Bernays's works on propaganda: *Propaganda* [1928] and *The Engineering of Consent* [1958].) We might say that propaganda encourages us – even impels us – to accept illusions as realities. Neoliberal propaganda has proved very successful in this regard in persuading people that we are all, either individually or as a family or in other localised social units, exclusively responsible for our own actions (see also Littler [2016] for a very lucid account of how this operates). We are then susceptible to persuasion that (for example) when young men carry knives and join gangs it has nothing to do with their socio-economic background or the enduringly racist society in which they find themselves living – certainly nothing at all to do with neoliberalism – and if we dare to suggest otherwise we can be a guaranteed a hostile, accusatory reception. Sufficient numbers might also be persuaded that a bipartite education system of grammar and non-grammar schools should be re-introduced on the same grounds of social equity, access and choice on which it was previously abandoned, or that poverty is a naturally occurring phenomenon rather than an effect of weakly regulated free-market capitalism, from which it is within the individual's capacity, should they choose to do so, to escape with minimal assistance from the State.

2 This offers one road to comfort, potentially leading to personal growth. There are other roads, which do not seek to 'resist' or 'refuse', such as those described earlier in terms of virtuous pragmatism and the pursuit of normalcy.

3 There is an argument here, perhaps, for resurrecting what now seems like a very old idea of 'relative autonomy', but transposed to the psychic domain.

4 Schools are different from universities, of course, and the experiences of some of the teachers in my study and the young women referenced by Brumberg and Allen are not by any means identical. However, Brumberg's account raises issues that are very relevant

to the current discussion. As will already be evident, a feature of life in the schools I have visited, which may have come as a surprise to some but that will be all too familiar to others, is that although there are close friendships between and among many teachers it is difficult to locate a secure culture of collegiality. This is fostered, I think, not only by discourses, ideologies and perceptions of competition but also by the way in which learning, especially in secondary schools, is broken down into discrete subject disciplines. If the system militates in this way against collaboration within schools, it seems even less likely that there will be a culture of collaboration between schools. It is true that two of the teachers I came to know quite well in Secondary Two (Margo and Abigail), and one in Primary One (Delores), did put in many extra hours working on the production of shared teaching materials (in the case of Margo and Abigail) and on primary-secondary liaison work (Delores). However, an education system that compels schools to compete against one another for students, anxious to 'perform better' and so move higher up published league tables, does not foster let alone facilitate the development of such a culture.

5 For quotations from the 1972 (French language) edition of *Psychoanalysis and Transversality* (*Psychanalyse et Transversalité*), I have followed the translations used by Ronald Bogue in *Deleuze and Guattari* (1989).

6 It has been suggested to me that the recent emergence in England and elsewhere of so-called school 'clusters' might be an example of – or provide opportunities for – the kind of group and the kinds of group activity that I am suggesting. Clusters are groups of schools, usually in the same immediate geographical location, who work together for reasons that may combine the financial (for example, economies of scale regarding administrative costs), the practical (for instance, in relation to primary-secondary transfer and national curriculum coverage) and the pedagogical (for example, sharing experience and 'good practice' in order to improve the quality of teaching and learning). Many of these clusters in England are managed and organised by 'trusts', and participating schools tend to be academies, so that although each member-school might be given (at least rhetorically) a degree of freedom and independence in going about its business, there will also be a requirement to buy into the trust's 'core values' – which may or may not chime with those of the schools' classroom teachers. Even where clusters are developed as the result on local initiatives, led by groups of headteachers in non-academy schools, there is also likely to be a need to keep a constant eye on how the cluster as a whole and its individual components are being perceived – and judged – by the external authority of public policy, central government, and government's various forms of governance. While clusters – especially those that are based on these local initiatives – might well provide opportunities and affordances for the kinds of discussion I am arguing for, it seems highly unlikely that group reflexivity will be high on participant schools' agendas, not least because of the amount of time and energy that headteachers are likely to find themselves devoting to the daily maintenance of the cluster and to those financial, practical and strictly pedagogical issues (i.e. focussing on 'good *practice*') referenced above.

7 Since Guattari wrote about group subjects, much in national and global society has changed. In particular, we have witnessed the astonishing growth of digital technologies, including developments in social media platforms and their widespread use, principally though not exclusively by younger people, to forge groups, to promote causes and to establish and mobilise a variety of social and political movements – affording, at least for the time being, opportunities for creating and discovering spaces that may be directly unreached and unreachable by traditional discourses that are still promulgated largely via earlier technologies or by already colonised areas of the new ones. While there is no direct evidence to support the claim, there is a widespread view that the mobilisation of the young vote – and the sharing of political opinion – via social media in the last UK General Election played a significant role in turning a projected Conservative landslide into a hung parliament, with the opposition Labour Party performing well above its predicted share of the vote in opinion polls and by media pundits. As I have acknowledged elsewhere (Moore 2015) social media can become a home for a diversity of groups

and for the exchange of a variety of ideas – some of which we might approve of and qualify as 'good', some of which we might disapprove of and qualify as 'bad'. One of the main characteristics of group subjects is that they define their own terms of reference and nominate their own issues. This is not to say that we cannot oppose other groups and their views, their ideologies and their practices (indeed, there is a strong element of opposition at the heart of any group subject), but we can only assume (shared) responsibility for those to which we have accessed membership.

8 One such group, lucidly analysed by Bailey (2015), is the global 'Teach First' movement, which, Bailey suggests, sets itself up as pioneering and groundbreaking while actually endorsing a fundamentally unchanging system and set of power relations. This particular example also demonstrates the role of affect in the deliberately constructed faux group subject, in this case through its repeated mantra that 'no child should suffer educationally because of their socio-economic background': an apparently laudable mission, which rather overlooks the fact – one of propaganda's 'black holes' (Chomsky, op. cit.) – that inequalities in relation to social background are themselves social constructs that we are encouraged to understand as natural social phenomena.

9 This may be seen as a battle within the UK's own version of America's 'History War' (Schiro 2013) – a 'war' conducted around the principal question regarding 'whether it is more important to teach knowledge of the past or to build strategies for critically analyzing and reconstructing society in the future' (ibid.: 1).

10 'Disobedience, in the eyes of anyone who has read history, is man's original virtue. It is through disobedience that progress has been made, through disobedience and rebellion' (Wilde 1948: 13–14).

11 However difficult the realisation of that requirement might be, it is only likely to be made more difficult by the repression or avoidance of feelings and by validating a belief that in taking an oppositional stance we are somehow exiling ourselves to the spurned fringes of society and social discourse. As Foucault has very wisely observed, in what might be seen as a celebration of the positive potential of affect when it is embraced as an energising force that can help us avoid being sucked in by the gravitational pull of dominant discourses: 'Do not think that one has to be sad in order to be militant, even though the thing one is fighting is abominable. It is the connection of desire to reality (and not its retreat into the forms of representation) that possesses revolutionary force' (Foucault 2013: xiii).

REFERENCES

Ahmed S. (2004) *The Cultural Politics of Emotion*. Edinburgh: Edinburgh University Press.

Ahmed S. (2010a) 'Happy Objects' in Gregg M. and Seigworth G.J. (eds), *The Affect Theory Reader*. Durham, NC: Duke University Press, pp. 29–51.

Ahmed S. (2010b) *The Promise of Happiness*. Durham, NC: Duke University Press.

Aitkenhead D. (2012) 'Ditch Austerity: Kickstart the Economy NOW!' interview with Paul Kruger, *The Guardian*, Monday 4th June 2012, pp. 7–8.

Allen A. (2008) *The Politics of Our Selves: Power, Autonomy, and Gender in Contemporary Critical Theory*. New York: Columbia University Press.

Althusser L. (2014) *On the Reproduction of Capitalism: Ideology and Ideological State Apparatuses* (originally published 1971; G.M. Goshgarian, trans.). London and New York: Verso.

Anderson A. (2006) *The Way We Argue Now: A Study in the Cultures of Theory*. Princeton, NJ: Princeton University Press.

Anderson R. (ed.) (1992) *Clinical Lectures on Klein and Bion*. London and New York: Routledge.

Apple M. (2006) *Educating the Right Way: Markets, Standards, God and Inequality* (2nd edition). New York and Abingdon: Routledge.

Association of School and College Leaders (ASCL) (2015) 'ASCL Guidance Paper: Summary of the Special Educational Needs (SEN) Code of Practice 2015: https://www.ascl.org.uk/download.E808B657-D080-4DES-A3445A3F5751A309.html (last accessed 2/7/2017).

Atkinson D. (2017) 'Disobedience'. Unpublished paper: Department of Educational Studies/Centre for the Arts and Learning, Goldsmiths University of London.

Bailey P.L.J. (2015) 'A Critical Ontology of Policy and Power'. Unpublished PhD thesis, University College London, Institute of Education.

Ball S.J. (1997) 'Policy Sociology and Critical Social Research: A Personal Review of Recent Education Policy and Policy Research'. *British Educational Research Journal* 23(3): 257–274.

Ball S.J. (2003) 'The Teacher's Soul and the Terrors of Performativity'. *Journal of Education Policy* 18(2): 215–228.

Ball S.J. (2008) *The Education Debate*. Bristol: Policy Press.

Ball S.J. (2017) *Foucault as Educator*. Heidelberg: Springer.

Ball S. J., Maguire M. and Braun A. (2012) *How Schools Do Policy: Policy Enactments in Secondary Schools*. London and New York: Routledge.

Berlant L. (2011) *Cruel Optimism* Durham NC: Duke University Press.

Bernays E. (1928) *Propaganda*. New York: Routledge.

Bernays E. (ed) (1955) *The Engineering of Consent*. Oklahoma: University of Oklahoma Press.

Bernstein B. (2000) *Pedagogy, Symbolic Control and Identity: Theory, Research, Critique*. Oxford: Rowman and Littlefield.

Bibby T. (2010) *Education – An 'Impossible Profession'? Psychoanalytic Explorations of Learning and Classrooms*. London: Routledge.

Bibby T., Moore A., Clarke S. and Haddon A. (2005–2007) 'Children's Learner-Identities in Mathematics at Key Stage 2'. ESRC-funded research study, Institute of Education University of London.

Billig M. (1997) 'The Dialogic Unconscious: Psychoanalysis, Discursive Psychology and the Nature of Repression'. *British Journal of Social Psychology* 36: 139–159.

Blacker D. (1998) 'Intellectuals at Work and in Power: Toward a Foucaultian Research Ethic' in Popkewitz T.S. and Brennan M. (eds), *Foucault's Challenge: Discourse, Knowledge and Power in Education*. New York: Teachers College Press.

Bocock R. (1993) *Consumption*. London and New York: Routledge.

Bogue R. (1989) *Deleuze and Guattari*. London and New York: Routledge.

Böler M. (1999) *Feeling Power: Emotions and Education*. New York and London: Routledge.

Bott Spillius E. (1992) 'Clinical Experiences of Projective Identification' in Anderson R. (ed.), *Clinical Lectures on Klein and Bion*. London and New York: Routledge, pp. 59–73.

Bourdieu P. (1977) *Outline of a Theory of Practice*. Cambridge: Cambridge University Press.

Brenman Pick I. (1992) 'The Emergence of Early Object Relations in the Psychoanalytic Setting' in Anderson R. (ed.), *Clinical Lectures on Klein and Bion* London and New York, pp. 24–33.

Brik O. (1964) *Two Essays on Poetic Language*. Ann Arbor, MI: University of Michigan.

Britton R. (1992) 'The Oedipus Situation and the Depressive Position' in Anderson R. (ed.), *Clinical Lectures on Klein and Bion*. London and New York: Routledge, pp. 34–45.

Britzman D. (1991) *Practice Makes Practice*. Albany: SUNY.

Britzman D. and Pitt A. (1996) 'Pedagogy and Transference: Casting the Past of Learning into the Presence of Teaching'. *Theory into Practice* 35(2): 118–123.

Brumberg J.J. (1997) *The Body Project: An Intimate History of American Girls*. New York: Vintage.

Chomsky N. (1999) *Profit Over People: Neoliberalism and Global Order*. New York: Seven Stories Press.

Coffield F. and Williamson B. (2011) *From Exam Factories to Communities of Discovery*. London: Institute of Education University of London.

Collier S.J. (2009) 'Topologies of Power. Foucault's Analysis of Political Government Beyond "Governmentality"'. *Theory, Culture and Society* 26(6): 78–108.

Davies W. (2014) *The Limits of Neoliberalism: Autonomy, Sovereignty and the Logic of Competition*. London: Sage.

Deleuze G. (2004a) 'On Capitalism and Desire' in Deleuze G. (D. Lapoujade, ed.; M. Taormina, trans.), *Desert Islands and Other Texts*. Los Angeles, CA, and London: Semiotext(e), pp. 262–273.

Deleuze G. (2004b) 'Five Propositions on Psychoanalysis' in Deleuze G. (D. Lapoujade, ed.; M. Taormina, trans.), *Desert Islands and Other Texts*. Los Angeles, CA, and London: Semiotext(e), pp. 274–280.

Deleuze G. and Guattari F. (2013) *Anti-Oedipus: Capitalism and Schizophrenia* (R. Hurley, M. Seem and H.R. Lane, trans.). Viking Press: New York.

Department for Education/Department of Health (DfE/DoH) (2015) 'Special Educational Needs and Disability Code of Practice 0 to 25 Years: Statutory Guidance, January 2015'. DfE: London.

Devine N. and Irwin R. (2005) 'Autonomy, Agency and Education: He tangata, he tangata, he tangata'. *Philosophy and Theory* 37(3): 317–331.

Eagleton T. (1991) *Ideology: An Introduction.* London: Verso.

Elliott J. (2000) 'Revising the National Curriculum: A Comment on the Secretary of State's Proposals'. *Education Policy* 15(2): 247–255.

Evans R.J. (2013) 'Myth-busting' in The *Guardian Review*, 13 July 2013, pp. 2–4.

Evetts J. (2009) 'New Professionalism and New Public Management: Changes, Continuities and Consequences'. *Comparative Sociology* 8(2): 247–266.

Falzon C. (2013) 'Making History' in Falzon C., O'Leary T. and Sawicki J. (eds), *A Companion to Foucault.* Chichester: Blackwell, pp. 282–298.

Feldman M. (1992) 'Splitting and Projective Identification' in Anderson R. (ed.), *Clinical Lectures on Klein and Bion.* London and New York: Routledge, pp. 74–88.

Fisher M. (2009) *Capitalist Realism.* Winchester: Zero Books.

Fisher M. and Gilbert J. (2016) 'Capitalist Realism and Neoliberal Hegemony: A Dialogue' in Gilbert J. (ed.), *Neoliberal Culture.* Chadwell Heath: Lawrence and Wishart, pp. 124–141.

Foucault M. (1977) *Discipline and Punish.* London: Allen Lane.

Foucault M. (1983) 'The Subject and Power' in Dreyfus H.L. and Rabinow P. (eds), *The Foucault Effect: Studies in Governmentality.* Chicago: University of Chicago Press, pp. 87–104.

Foucault M. (1985) *The Use of Pleasure: The History of Sexuality vol. 2.* New York: Pantheon Books.

Foucault M. (1988) *Politics, Philosophy, Culture: Interviews and Other Writings, 1977–1984* (L.D. Kritzman, ed.; A. Sheridan A. and others, trans.). New York and London: Routledge.

Foucault M. (1990) *The Care of the Self: The History of Sexuality vol 3.* Harmondsworth: Penguin.

Foucault M. (1992) *The Archaeology of Knowledge.* London: Routledge.

Foucault M (1994) *Dits et Écrits (Tome 3: 1976–1979).* Paris: Gallimard.

Foucault M. (1997) 'What Is Critique?' (L. Hochroth, trans.) in Lotringer S. and Hochroth L. (eds), *The Politics of Truth.* New York: Semiotext(e).

Foucault (2000a) 'Technologies of the Self' in Rabinow P. (ed), *Michel Foucault: Ethics. Essential Works of Foucault 1954–1984 Volume 1.* London: Penguin Books pp. 223–251.

Foucault M. (2000b) 'The Ethics of the Concern for Self as a Practice of Freedom' in Rabinow P. (ed), *Michel Foucault: Ethics. Essential Works of Foucault 1954–1984 Volume 1.* London: Penguin Books pp. 281–302.

Foucault M. (2000c) 'On the Genealogy of Ethics: An Overview of Work in Progress' in Rabinow P. (ed), *Michel Foucault: Ethics. Essential Works of Foucault 1954–1984 Volume 1.* London: Penguin Books pp. 253–280.

Foucault M. (2006) *Psychiatric Power: Lectures at the Collège de France 1973–1974* (G. Burchell, trans.). Basingstoke: Palgrave Macmillan.

Foucault M. (2010) *The Birth of Biopolitics: Lectures at the Collège de France, 1978–1979* (G. Burchell, trans.). Basingstoke: Palgrave Macmillan.

Foucault M. (2013) 'Introduction' in Deleuze G. and Guattari F. *Anti-Oedipus* (R. Hurley, M. Seem and H.R. Lane, trans.). London: Bloomsbury, pp. xi–xiv.

Foucault M. and Rabinow P. (1991) *The Foucault Reader*. Harmondsworth: Penguin Books.

Freud A. (1931) *Introduction to Psycho-Analysis for Teachers: Four Lectures* (B. Low, trans.). London: George Allen and Unwin Ltd.

Freud S. (1930) 'Civilisation and Its Discontents' in Strachey J. (ed.), *The Standard Edition of the Complete Psychological Works of Sigmund Freud (vol. XVII 1920–22)*. London: Vintage, pp. 65–143.

Freud S. (1968) 'Introductory Lectures on Psycho-Analysis, Part Three' in *Standard Edition, vol. 17* (J. Strachey, trans.). London: Hogarth Press.

Gibbs A. (2001) 'Contagious Feelings: Pauline Hanson and the Epidemiology of Affect' *Australian Humanities Review 24*, www.australianhumanitiesreview.org.

Gilbert J. (2016) 'What Kind of Thing Is "Neoliberalism"?' in Gilbert J. (ed.), *Neoliberal Culture*. Chadwell Heath: Lawrence and Wishart, pp. 10–32.

Gregg M. and Seigworth G.J. (eds) (2010) *The Affect Theory Reader*. Durham, NC: Duke University Press.

Guattari F. (1972) *Psychanalyse et transversalité*. Paris: Maspéro.

Guattari F. (2015) *Psychoanalysis and Transversality* (A. Hodges, trans.). South Pasadena, CA: Semiotext(e).

Halpin D., Moore A., Edwards G., George R. and Jones C. (1998–2001) 'Educational Identities and the Consumption of Tradition'. ESRC Award R000237640.

Hanson M. (2017) 'Ofsted Has Caught on – 30 Years Too Late', *The Guardian Review* 27th June 2017, p. 13.

Hargreaves E. (2015) '"I Think It Helps When You're Not Scared": Fear and Learning in the Primary Classroom'. *Pedagogy, Culture and Society* 23(4): 617–638.

Harris, P.L. (1989) *Children and Emotion: The Development of Psychological Understanding*. London: Blackwell.

Harvey D. (2007) *Neoliberalism as Creative Destruction* The Annals of the American Academy of Political and Social Science 2007 610: 21 Sage www.sagepublications.com.

Holliday A. (2011) *Intercultural Communication and Ideology*. London: Verso.

Holt J. (1964) *How Children Fail*. Harmondsworth: Penguin.

Hook D. (2006) '"Pre-Discursive" Racism'. *Journal of Community and Applied Social Psychology* 16(3): 207–232.

Keck C. (2012) 'Radical Reflexivity: Assessing the Value of Psycho-Spiritual Practices as a Medium for the Professional Development of Teachers''. Unpublished PhD thesis, Institute of Education, University of London.

Klein N. (2008) *The Shock Doctrine: The Rise of Disaster Capitalism*. London: Penguin.

Kristeva J. (1984) *Revolution in Poetic Language* (M. Waller, trans.). New York: Columbia University Press.

Lacan J. (1977) *Ecrits*. London: Tavistock.

Lacan J. (1979) *The Four Fundamental Concepts of Psycho-Analysis*. London: Penguin.

Lasch C. (1978) *The Culture of Narcissism: American Life in an Age of Diminishing Expectations*. New York: Norton.

Lazzarato M. (1996) 'Immaterial Labour' in Hardt M. and Virno P. (eds), *Radical Thought in Italy: A Potential Politics*. Minneapolis: University of Minnesota Press, pp. 133–147.

Littler J. (2016) 'Meritocracy as Plutocracy: The Marketising of "Equality" under Neoliberalism' in Gilbert J. (ed.), *Neoliberal Culture* Chadwell Heath: Lawrence and Wishart, pp. 73–100.

Lukacher N. (1986) *Primal Scenes: Literature, Philosophy, Psychoanalysis*. Ithaca, NY: Cornell University Press.

MacNeil P. (nd) 'Residuals in Value-added GCSE Result Assessments' Schoolzone Educational Intelligence www.schoolzone.co.uk/resources/articles/Residules.asp (last accessed 11/07/2017).

Massumi B. (2013) 'Notes on the Translation and Acknowledgements' in Deleuze G. and Guattari F., *A Thousand Plateaus*. London: Bloomsbury, pp. xv–xviii.

Massumi B. (2010) 'The Future Birth of the Affective Fact: The Political Ontology of Threat' in Gregg M. and Seigworth G.J. (eds), *The Affect Theory Reader*. Durham, NC: Duke University Press, pp. 52–70.

McChesney R.W. (1999) 'Introduction' in Chomsky N. (1999) *Profit Over People: Neoliberalism and Global Order*. New York: Seven Stories Press, pp. 7–16.

McLaughlin R. (1991) 'Can the Information Systems for the NHS Internal Market Work?' *Public Policy and Management* (Autumn 1991): 37–41.

McNally D. (2001) *Bodies of Meaning: Studies on Language, Labor and Liberation*. Albany, NY: SUNY.

McNally D. (2011) *Monsters of the Market: Zombies, Vampires and Global Capitalism*. Leiden and Boston: BRILL.

Moore A. (2004) *The Good Teacher: Dominant Discourses in Teaching and Teacher Education* London: Routledge.

Moore A. (2006) 'Recognising Desire: A Psychosocial Approach to Understanding Education Policy Implementation and Effect'. *Oxford Review of Education* 32(4): 487–503.

Moore A. (2012a) 'The Role of Affect in the Adoption and Implementation of Resisted Policies in Public School Settings'. Paper presented at the annual AARE conference, University of Sydney, December 2012.

Moore A. (2012b) *Teaching and Learning: Pedagogy, Curriculum and Culture* (2nd edition). London: Routledge.

Moore A. (2013) 'Love and Fear in the Classroom: How "Validating Affect" Might Help Us Understand Young Students and Improve Their Experiences of School Life and Learning' in O'Loughlin M. (ed.), *The Uses of Psychoanalysis in Working with Children's Emotional Lives*. Plymouth UK: Jason Aronson, pp. 285–304.

Moore A. (2015) *Understanding the School Curriculum: Theory, Politics and Principles*. London: Routledge.

Moore A. and Ash A. (2001) 'Key Factors in the Promotion and Obstruction of Reflective Practice in Beginning Teachers' University of London funded research study, Institute of Education, University of London.

Moore A. and Ash A. (2003) 'Reflective Practice in Beginning Teachers: Helps, Hindrances and the Role of the Critical Other'. Education-line, BEI www.leeds.ac.uk/educol/documents/00002531.htm.

Moore A. and Clarke M. (2016) '"Cruel Optimism": Teacher Attachment to Professionalism in an Era of Performativity'. *Journal of Education Policy* 31(5): 666–677.

Mulkay M. (1988) *On Humour*. Cambridge: Cambridge University Press.

Nietzsche F. (1872) 'On the Future of Our Educational Institutions: First Lecture'. http://la.texas.edu/users/hcleaver/330T/350kPEENietzscheFutureTableCut.pdf (last accessed 26/06/2017).

Observer newspaper (2011) 'Public Sector Workers Need "Discipline and Fear", Says Oliver Letwin', *The Guardian*, www.theguardian.com/politics/2011/jul/30/public-sector-jobs-oliver-letwin (last accessed 10/06/16).

O'Shaughnessy E. (1992) 'Psychosis: Not Thinking in a Bizarre World' In Anderson R. (ed.), *Clinical Lectures on Klein and Bion*. London and New York: Routledge, pp. 89–101.

Osler A. and Starkey H. (2005) *Changing Citizenship: Democracy and Inclusion in Education.* London: Open University Press.

Ozga J. (2000) *Policy Research in Educational Settings.* Maidenhead: Open University Press.

Paraskevi M. (2016) 'Metalearning: A Contribution to Theory and Empirical Investigation of Year 4 Pupils' Reflections on Their Classroom Learning'. Unpublished PhD thesis, Institute of Education, University of London.

Perryman J. (2009) 'Inspection and the Fabrication of Professional and Performative Processes'. *Journal of Education Policy* 24(5): 611–631.

Pignatelli F. (2002) 'Mapping the Terrain of Foucauldian Ethics: A Response to the Surveillance of Schooling'. *Studies in Philosophy and Education* 21(1): 157–180.

Pinar W. (2004) *What Is Curriculum Theory?* Mahwah, NJ: Lawrence Erlbaum Associates.

Pitts-Taylor V. (2010) 'The Plastic Brain: Neoliberalism and the Neuronal Self'. *Health* 14(6): 635–652.

Posch P. (1994) 'Changes in the Culture of Teaching and Learning'. *Educational Action Research* 2(2): 153–161.

Reid J. (2013) 'Interrogating the Neoliberal Biopolitics of the Sustainable Development-Resilience Nexus'. *International Political Sociology* 7(4): 353–367.

Reitter P. and Wellmon W. (eds), D. Searls (trans.) (2015) *Anti-Education: On the Future of Our Educational Institutions.* New York: New York Review Books.

Rose, N. (1989) *Governing the Soul: The Shaping of the Private Self.* London: Free Association Press.

Rose N. (2001) 'The Politics of Life Itself'. *Theory, Culture and Society* 18(6): 1–30.

Rose N. (2006) *The Politics of Life Itself: Biomedicine, Power and Subjectivity in the Twenty-first Century.* Princeton, NJ, and Oxford: Princeton University Press.

Ruti M. (2009) *A World of Fragile Things: Psychoanalysis and the Art of Living.* Albany, NY: SUNY Press.

Sacks O. (1984) *A Leg to Stand On.* New York: Touchstone.

Sameshima P. (2008) 'Letters to a New Teacher: A Curriculum of Embodied Aesthetic Awareness'. *Teacher Education Quarterly* 35(2): 29–44.

Schiro M.S. (2013) *Curriculum Theory: Conflicting Visions and Enduring Concerns.* Los Angeles, CA: Sage.

Seigworth G.J. and Gregg M. (2010) 'An Inventory of Shimmers' in Gregg M. and Seigworth G.J. (eds), *The Affect Theory Reader.* Durham NC: Duke University Press, pp. 1–25.

Shouse E. (2005) 'Feeling, Emotion, Affect'. *M/C Journal* 8(6), http://journal.media-culture.org.au/0512/03-shouse.php (last accessed 7/9/2016).

Singh P., Heimans S. and Glasswell K. (2014) 'Policy Enactment, Context and Performativity: Ontological Politics and Researching Australian National Partnership Policies'. *Journal of Education Policy* 29(6): 826–844.

Smyth J., McInerney P., Hattam R. and Lawson M. (1999) *Critical Reflection on Teaching and Learning: Teachers' Learning Project, Investigation Series.* Flinders Institute for the Study of Teaching/Dept of Education, Training and Employment South Australia.

Starr M. (1929) *Lies and Hate in Education.* London: Hogarth Press.

Stengers I. (2008) 'Experimenting with Refrains: Subjectivity and the Challenge of Escaping Modern Dualism'. *Subjectivity* 22: 38–59.

Tomkins S.J. (2008) *Affect, Imagery, Consciousness: The Complete Edition.* New York: Springer Publishing Co.

Tseng, Chun-Ting (2013) 'A Discourse Analysis of Teacher Professionalism in England since the 1980s'. Unpublished PhD thesis, Institute of Education, University of London.

Veyne P. (2008) *Foucault: Sa pensée, sa personne.* Paris: Albin Michel.

Veyne P. (2010) *Foucault: His Thought, His Character*. Cambridge: Polity Press.

Wilde, O. (1948) *The Soul of Man Under Socialism*. London: Porcupine Press.

Wilkins C., Busher H., Kakos M., Mohamed C. and Smith J. (2012) 'Crossing Borders: New Teachers Co-constructing Professional Identity in Performative Times'. *Professional Development in Education* 38(1): 65–77.

Willetts D. (2012) 'Preparing Britain for the Future: Education and Skills Conference' GovKnow [events@govknow-mail-com], sent 17 Jan 2012.

Williams R. (1958) *Culture and Society 1780–1950*. London: Hogarth Press.

Worsnip A. (2012) 'Against Pragmatism: The Vapid Philosophy of Modern Politics', *Prospect Magazine*, www.prospectmagazine.co.uk/politics/against-pragmatism-blair-cameron-clegg.

Zembylas M. (2003) 'Interrogating "Teacher Identity": Emotion, Resistance, and Self-Formation'. *Educational Theory* 53(1): 107–127.

Žižek, S. (1989) *The Sublime Object of Ideology* London: Verso.

Žižek S. (2009) *Violence: Six Sideways Reflections* London: Profile Books.

Žižek, S. (no date) 'Censorship Today: Violence, or Ecology as a New Opium for The Masses, Part 1', www.lacan.com/zizecology1.htm (last accessed 21/10/2016).

INDEX